LET ME BE FRANK

BY FRANK BRUNO WITH NICK OWENS

Mirror Books

Published by Mirror Books,
an imprint of Trinity Mirror plc,
1 Canada Square, London E14 5AP, England

www.mirrorbooks.com
twitter.com/themirrorbooks

Mirror Books 2017

ISBN 978-1-907324-71-0

First hardback edition

Some names and identifying details have been changed.

Printed and bound in Great Britain by CPI Group (UK) Ltd, Croydon, CR0 4YY

Every effort has been made to fulfil requirements with regard to reproducing
copyright material. The author and publisher will be glad to rectify any omissions
at the earliest opportunity.

Cover: Barry Marsden for Mirrorpix

I dedicate this book to my late Mum and Dad, the two people that made me who I am today... and for that I thank you. My brother Michael, for protecting me when I was younger (even though I never knew until much later) and continuing into adult life. I miss you all dearly.

I would like to thank all the people who have helped my journey through my boxing career, there are too many to name but they know who they are. Most importantly, Terry Lawless, George Francis and Harry Carpenter must never be forgotten and will always have a special place in my heart... and not forgetting my good old friend Jimmy Tibbs.

Carmen, my PA, who has supported me and helped me to accept the past, the present and shown me a different path to my future.

Dave Davies, my agent, who has been through some difficult times with me but has stood by me and continues to keep my ducking and diving striving!

Thank you Nick, for writing this book and helping me along this journey and piecing my life together for me, this chapter can now be closed and I will only look forward.

My children, what can I say... I'm back and for good, thank you for supporting me through thick & thin, I love you.

The British Public and, in fact, those all over the world – that have supported me, from my early professional days to even now over 20 years later still buying tickets for events, sending nice letters and leaving lovely messages and support on my social media. 365 days a year my fans remind me how blessed I have been throughout my life to be held in their valued opinion.

Finally, I should also say a big thank you to God. He knows why...

FROM NICK

First of all I'd like to say thank you to Frank for putting up with me over the last year. Your bravery in speaking so openly about your illness shows what a warrior you are both inside and outside the ring. I'm proud to be able to call you a friend. Respect, "Boss".

To Dave Davies and Carmen, this book simply would not have been possible without you. Frank now has the best team around him. Thank you.

To those who agreed to be interviewed for the book but can't be named, thanks. You know who you are. To Fran Goodman for her brilliant job in editing this book. And to Jo Sollis and Fergus McKenna at Mirror Books for their encouragement.

Heartfelt thanks to my parents for all their support.

And finally to my wife Gemma and daughters Emily and Francesca, thanks for everything: I love you loads.

I'd like to dedicate my work on this book to anyone suffering from a mental health problem in silence. I hope you find the strength to get the help you need to recover, in the way that Frank has.

CONTENTS

INTRODUCTION

I thought long and hard about what to call this book. Day after day, as I sweated my guts out in the gym, I would think about the perfect title. In the end the answer was staring right back at me in the mirror: *Let Me Be Frank.*

You see, from the troubled teenager who dreamed of one day becoming the greatest boxer on the planet to the man who stood in the centre of the ring at Wembley a world champion, all I have ever wanted is to be true to myself.

But since I retired, one thing has come between me and being the man I want to be: my mind. Five years ago it saw me locked up against my will and pumped full of so many drugs and tablets I didn't have the strength to stand. Forget the pain of being on the end of a knockout punch. When I am in the grip of my bipolar disorder and the drugs start to mess with my brain I am paralysed for days. But I will always get back up. It is the only way I know.

I've been sectioned three times now and it strips me of who I am. It makes me paranoid and forces me to watch everything I say and everything I do. But telling this story of my recovery and of how I am learning to stand tall again has been a form of therapy.

What I am going to reveal in this book might surprise you. It may even shock you. After all, you probably think you know me. I'm Frank Bruno: boxer, national treasure, pantomime character – the guy as famous for his rumbling laugh as his right hook. The man who can't walk into a room without cracking a joke and making everyone smile.

'Know what I mean?'

But the truth is, I'm actually happiest when I'm alone. So these days I keep my head down, mind my own business and stay healthy. I turn up at events, smile for photos, shake everyone's hands. I'm very happy to do that and I've been told I'm damn good at it, too. The British public have helped me earn a living since I retired from boxing. But my biggest smile comes when I walk through my own front door and I feel I'm back in my own skin.

So that's how I plan to live the rest of my life. I have always been a bit of a loner, most boxers are. When the bell sounds and you move to the centre of that canvas you are on your own.

During my days in the ring I had the best cornerman in the business in George Francis. George, God rest his soul, had my back and if he ever saw me taking a beating he'd throw in the towel. Thank God it didn't happen too much, but when you are on the ropes, out on your feet and unable to defend yourself, that towel is the difference between life and death.

And too many people are silently fighting mental health problems without anyone in their corner. That has to end. Which is another reason I had to write this book: to try to give others a little bit of hope and to tell you about the campaign I'm supporting to bring about change.

By speaking out I hope to show everyone that there is no shame in asking for help if they need it. Mental health problems can affect anyone: your mum, dad, brother, sister, son or daughter. It doesn't matter who you are. Celebrities, sports stars, millionaire businessmen, judges, dustmen – I've met them all along the way and listened to how mental ill health can ruin lives. It almost destroyed mine.

Even Prince Harry has recently been brave enough to admit he suffered for years and years after his mum died. If a member of the Royal Family can open up about how they feel, then anyone should be able to speak out. Sadly though, many are still too ashamed.

This book is as open and honest as I've ever been in my life and I hope you enjoy reading it. It's not been easy, because there were large parts of the last five years I can't remember. The drugs the doctors insisted I took often turned the lights out on my world. Also, when you are in the grip of mental illness you withdraw from what's going on around you.

I've been clear in this book that I do not believe medication works for me. When I am on tablets for my illness it feels as if the world is shutting down around me.

When I come off them I feel alive. And I feel far more able to cope. I know that will become a talking point. I want to be clear from the start that I am talking about MY experiences and mine alone. I know many people rely on medication to control their mental health conditions and I would encourage those people to carry on doing what works for them.

But the reality for me is that my hardest days came when I was on meds. Getting off them let me win back control of my life.

So, working with my ghost writer Nick, telling my story has been a bit like putting together a jigsaw. I have had to construct the broken pieces of my mind to build a picture of what my life has been like. I am also going to tell you about some of the patients I met along the way. I'm not using their names but absolutely everyone I met in hospital left an impression and what many of them said to me inspires the campaigning work I am doing now.

It's not been easy to write down how I feel. I am a private man. But it has helped me put my problems where they belong: in the past.

There have been a lot of ups and downs since my last memoir, Fighting Back, was published back in 2005. At my lowest point I have had to come to terms with the fact someone very close to me stole hundreds of thousands of pounds from me while I lay helpless in a psychiatric unit. I've been attacked in the street. I've been locked up and left feeling like a caged animal in a zoo – trapped in a nightmare I feared would never end.

But the nightmare did end. I've come through my illness. I've managed to rebuild the relationship with my family and I've embarked on a whole new fight to help people with conditions like mine.

And that hasn't been easy. There have been shocks and challenges that left me reeling. I lost my mum not that long ago. She was my best friend, an absolute tower of strength. She supported me through the darkest days of my illness and she suffered appalling racist abuse during my boxing career. I have never spoken about that before: now I feel it is time.

The death of my brother Michael to cancer has also been so painful. He was a hero to me because no one believed in me more than Michael. I've also lost two of the people who had the biggest impact on my career – my inspiration Muhammad Ali and BBC commentator Harry Carpenter.

Then there was the disgust I felt on finding out that Jimmy Savile, a man I'd joined in a lot of charity work, was a predatory paedophile. When I think about all the times we spent together my blood runs cold.

I also had to come to terms with the fact that at 55 my boxing career is over. Recent newspaper reports have claimed I will be returning to the ring. I won't. So chill out everyone: I will *not* be doing a George Foreman.

That doesn't mean to say my relationship with the sport is over. I was looking back over my fight records the other day and I realised it is 35 years since I stepped into the ring for my first professional bout. So it's been great to revisit some of the highlights of my career. There were many.

I am still fanatical about boxing. My son Franklin Jr and I were ringside to watch Tony Bellew beat David Haye against all the odds. What a fight, and what a great reminder of how British boxing is alive and well. Then, a couple of weeks later, I was privileged to see Anthony Joshua beat Wladimir Klitschko in one of the biggest fights in British boxing history. He is a great champion.

I worry deeply about what the future holds for today's fighters and I am concerned about the way some fighters struggle after retirement. When the music stops and the show is over, life can be very difficult. I look at Tyson Fury and Ricky Hatton, and the problems they have had, and I see myself. Boxers, just like anyone else, should never be afraid to ask for help.

As for me, as I write this, I feel good. I accept I will probably have my condition for life. But, as I will explain, I am now in control of it. That's because I've learned to spot the signs of my illness and if it returns I am no longer afraid to ask for help.

I will be going toe-to-toe with it until the end of my days. But I am up for the fight. Like that teenage boy who dared to dream of boxing stardom, I am not afraid any more. Like the champion I grew to be, I know, in the end, I will be victorious. Just as long as one thing is allowed to happen:

that people Let Me Be Frank.

I've been as open and honest as I can be as I take you through a story I never, ever want to have to tell again.

It is the story of the toughest fight of my life.

So, let's get started....

God bless,
Frank Bruno

PROLOGUE
13 April 2012

I was dancing when my world fell apart. Jigging around the kitchen at home with the iPod on, headphones in, my music up full blast.

So I didn't even hear the knock. But when the track ended, the bang of a fist on the front door boomed through my house like a sledgehammer smashing concrete. Not another door-to-door salesman, I thought.

"I'm not interested in double glazing," I shouted over the music as I went to open the door. But the six police officers standing there were not smiling.

"Frank Bruno?" one of them asked, as if they didn't know.

My first thought was someone had died. My next was that the neighbours would think some terrible crime had happened in my house. Then I looked past them all to a woman in a suit standing in the middle of my driveway, clutching a handful of papers. Then I saw the ambulance beyond her and I knew it was here to take me away.

"Frank, you need to come with us," she said firmly. "Now."

I froze. It had been nine years since I was first sectioned, forcibly detained in a mental health unit, but back then I knew in my heart that I needed help. My retirement from boxing had sent me on a dangerous spiral of self-destruction. This time it was different. I wasn't ready to be locked up again, no way.

"Who is it, Frank?" shouted my girlfriend, Nina, who was washing up in the kitchen.

"Don't worry, darling," I yelled back. "It's fine."

But it wasn't and I knew it. My mind started to race. Who had called the doctors? And why? So many questions. But I didn't have answers.

1

And I didn't have time. I felt bewildered, scared and angry. Suddenly I was in a corner, so I tried to defend myself.

"I don't need to go anywhere," I said, firmly, stepping back into the hall.

"Come on, Frank," said one of the coppers. "You need to come with us."

"There's nothing wrong with me," I pleaded.

"Come on, Frank," said another.

"I want to stay here," I kept insisting, really aware now of how pathetic my voice was starting to sound.

By now the woman with the papers had moved centre stage and she was waving them under my nose.

"COME ON, FRANK..."

A bead of sweat dripped from my forehead but words – well, they were beginning to fail me. My eyes were fixed on the woman firing a load of questions at me. I could see her mouth moving but the sounds didn't make any sense. Her voice felt like punches raining down. I tried my best to answer but it was no good. I was in a state of shock.

I could hear Nina's footsteps approaching so I pulled the door tightly shut. Then one of the coppers started laughing.

"Please don't laugh at me," I said to the officer. "If you laugh, they'll take me away."

Then I realised it was too late to plead with them – the decision had already been made. As I walked towards the back of the ambulance, a huge wave of nausea swept across me. I felt 10 times as scared as I'd been nine years ago.

I bent over and tried to be sick. But, like my words, nothing came out. As I stood back up I felt as if I was having an out-of-body experience. My legs had turned to jelly. Suddenly it was like I was standing on the side-lines, watching the whole scene unfold. "Not again, Frank," my head was telling me. "You won't get out this time, you know."

As they loaded me into the ambulance, with Nina waiting anxiously outside, I felt beaten up. She'd pleaded to come with me, but I'd told her no. I knew this was a battle I had to fight on my own.

Five minutes earlier I'd been dancing. Suddenly I barely had the strength to stand.

I crawled on to the stretcher and started to shake. Someone threw a blanket over me. I pulled it over my head, petrified a photographer or even someone walking past would take a picture of me and flog it to the papers. As they closed the ambulance door I saw a crowd of my neighbours gathered at the bottom of the drive. I shut my eyes so I didn't have to see their faces. They were still tightly shut when a voice said they were taking me to a hospital in Basildon, Essex.

I was actually relieved. That was an hour from my home and by the time I got there this balls-up would surely be sorted out. One of my kids would get on the phone and tell them it was all a mistake. My agent would get wind of the aggro and get me home.

It quickly became clear that wasn't going to happen. The ambulance doors opened and as I was ushered inside the hospital I realised I was now Patient Frank. The hospital door slammed behind me, the lock to the psychiatric ward clicked, then everything went dark. And I truly believed that this time I would *never* get out.

Chapter 1

THE ULTIMATE BETRAYAL

I shouldn't be writing this.

Sorry if you feel a bit mugged off with me saying that after you've kindly dipped into your pocket to buy this book. But as I sit here today, the one thought racing through my mind is that everything I am about to share with you should never have happened.

When I released my life story, *Fighting Back*, I thought I had nothing left to say. I believed I'd written about every drop of blood, sweat and tears shed on the journey that took me from a tearaway kid packed off to a special boarding school to mend his ways to the man who became WBC Heavyweight Champion of the World.

I wrote down all the highs and lows. And I ended it on the toughest moment of my life – the day I got locked up in hospital in 2003 and was described as "BONKERS BRUNO" on the front page of *The Sun*. Overnight my world changed. Suddenly Frank Bruno, sporting hero, was now Frank Bruno, the man with a mental health problem.

"What happened scared the wits out of me," I wrote all those years ago. "I can't imagine going back to hospital. I am not sure what I would do if I broke down again..."

But I was forced to find out. My illness, once again, pushed me to the brink of self-destruction. Truth be told, I wasn't prepared back then to talk about how I felt about my illness. Now I am. Now I finally feel ready to let my guard down.

I have learned facing up to my past is the only way to deal with whatever the future might throw at me. And today, the future looks bright. I am able to deal with it. Yeah, today feels really, really good.

Most days do now, particularly when I am sitting in the spot I love best of all. I can look at the sea through the window. I can see the waves, I can see the tide is coming in and that the sun is about to set above the water. It's beautiful, calm and peaceful: just like my mind.

I am sitting in my caravan by the way. Yes, my caravan. I shouldn't call it that – I always get a big ticking-off from my agent when I call it that. If I ever talk about it using the c-word he will remind me: "Frank, no, no, no. It's a mobile home, for goodness sake."

Always make me laugh. I wind him right up when he says that, put on my posh man's voice and say: "Oh, oh, terribly sorry ol' chap, you are right. Let me say that again, I am ringing from the ol' mobile home."

But it IS a caravan. A bloody big one, too – I paid nearly £50,000 for it, so not small potatoes. It's big enough for me to get lost in whenever I need to. It's on the Isle of Sheppey in Kent and I come here a lot, usually two or three times a month. I stay for a few days and once or twice I've even put my world title belt on the mantelpiece while I chill out a bit. It's no biggie.

I like talking to the people who own the other caravans. They thought it was a bit odd at first, Frank Bruno popping over for a cuppa. But now it's normal. My old mate Frankie, who has a place here, always cooks me a lovely steak and chips when I come down. And when we sit and talk afterwards there's nowhere else I'd rather be.

There are not many places in the world I haven't been. I have stayed in some of the most luxurious hotel suites you could imagine. I have lived in a mansion. I still own a big house. I have got a Bentley with my FB number plate parked outside. There is enough money in the bank to not have to worry about working again and to be able to look after my family.

But I have learned all that counts for diddly squat if I don't have peace of mind.

Of course, when the papers found out I had dipped into the Bank of Frank to buy a caravan on the Isle of Sheppey, they had a bloody field day.

I saw what people were saying and I imagined what they were thinking. Frank's gone mad. Frank's gone bloody bonkers again. But I am not mad. And I am not bonkers.

I do, however, according to the doctors, have something called bipolar affective disorder.

Bipolar. It is a word I am going to use a hell of a lot in this book. And that's why I want to tell you a little bit more about it.

My boxing history is out there for everyone to see: 40 wins from 45 contests, 38 by KO. I am very proud of my record. The fights are part of my life. Part of my story. But so too, I now accept, is my battle with mental illness. And my recovery to where I am sitting today, in this caravan, has been as tough as any of my fights.

Being heavyweight champion of the world taught me a lot, but it made me realise one thing above all. And that is that everything you fight for, everything you dream of, everything you build up, can be snatched away in the blink of an eye. Let your guard slip, then boom, from nowhere, you are out.

It happened to me on March 16, 1996, in Las Vegas when Mike Tyson knocked me down and turned out the lights on my boxing career. And then it happened to my happiness, my health and even my liberty, too.

When I was first diagnosed with bipolar in 1998, two years after retiring, I struggled to even pronounce it. Even today I get it wrong now and then.

"I have bi-polo," I will say and sometimes people will laugh.

But there is absolutely nothing funny about mental illness. I know my condition inside out now, better than any opponent I ever faced in the ring. It has become a part of me and yeah, I accept, I will probably have it for the rest of my life. Some days I am not so sure it is bipolar – the doctors say it is – but, as I have found out many times, the doctors are not always right.

I know I suffer terribly at times with anxiety and stress and when I am in the grip of a battle with my illness the world is a tough place to be in. People always ask me: "OK, Frank, tell me, how does it make you feel?"

I always sigh. I am not being difficult, the truth is it's hard to find the words to describe how it affects my life. I will try. When my illness takes hold the world swings from high to low. I can see the change coming but I can't stop it. It is impossible. The illness is like a force of nature. A hay-maker of a right hook that rocks me from side to side.

Have you ever been caught outside in a horrendous storm with nowhere to take shelter and you start panicking that the strength of the wind might knock you off your feet? So you run as quickly as you can to get inside and find a bit of shelter. When my bipolar strikes it feels as if that wind is constantly pushing me back.

When I am on a high, I open my eyes in the morning and I feel like I can climb a mountain. Nothing is beyond my reach. I look in the bathroom mirror, splash my face with water and the person staring back is young Frank – that teenage kid who was full of dreams and who had all the guts to see it through to become the best fighter in the world.

But when I am low and in the grip of this illness, well, then God help me. There will be a heavy feeling in my chest, a bit like how you feel when someone close to you dies. I will feel acutely alone, withdrawn, angry and on edge. Being able to even walk from the bed to the bathroom mirror feels like a bit of a mission. Sometimes I will barely recognise the person staring back. Some days I will not even get that far, my head stays firmly on the pillow and my duvet protects me from that wind and rain. My world is covered by a fog. Little of what is going on around me will matter. Light or dark. Day or night. Summer or winter. The world I see will be the same shade of grey. I do talk to people but I don't always take in what they say. I will walk down the street and notice almost nothing. The thoughts in my head are too much of a distraction. What are they? Fears, anxiety, a bit of paranoia now and then. Often about nothing in particular. But enough to make my legs heavy and my heart sink on low days.

Only those people who have ever suffered from bipolar or depression will understand how it really feels when these lows strike. Often, when they do, I will come here, to the caravan, and look out of the window and wonder when the fog will lift.

Other days I will go to the gym. And I will run. Run for my life. But the illness will always be waiting to catch me up. That's the hardest thing I find in dealing with my condition: not knowing when it will hit or how long it will stick around.

Boxing was straightforward. Hard, yes, but not hugely complicated. I trained. I prepared. I stepped in the ring. When I saw a punch coming I moved, quickly, or I defended myself. Then, bang, I made sure I knocked out my opponent before he had the chance to reload. I always aimed to get out of there as quickly as I could to pick up the cheque. Most times it worked. (We won't talk about the five times it didn't just yet, if you don't mind.)

My bipolar though comes from nowhere, it appears from the shadows, and it is impossible to defend yourself from a punch you can't see. I face it and I fight it. But even on those occasions I beat the crap out of it, I know deep down it may come back. And I know that there may be a day, any day, that I can't knock it out.

That's what happened in 2003 when I was sectioned the first time. It came after the most distressing period of my life. My marriage had broken down and my world had collapsed. My wife Laura and my three kids, Nicola, Rachel and Franklin, moved out in 2000 and suddenly there I was, all alone. And I didn't like it one bit. I was trying, and failing very badly, to cope with retirement from the ring.

Then in 2002 my former trainer George Francis took his own life. That was the final blow. *George.* When I think about him now I wish I had listened. After I walked out of the press conference following my defeat to Mike Tyson, he pulled me aside and warned me that retirement would not be all sweetness and light. I felt the public adulation vanishing along with my professional success and things quickly crumbled.

Without my family around me, my career over or my cornerman no longer there to keep me on track, my mental health suffered. When they took me to Goodmayes Hospital in Romford on September 22, 2003, I was kicking and screaming.

The treatment I received rescued me from the hell I was in. When I got out six weeks later I thought I had come through the toughest battle of my life. But straight away in the days, weeks and months that followed there was a new fight. *Meds.*

I was so heavily sedated, living off lithium tablets prescribed by the doctors, that I couldn't think straight. I had no energy, I couldn't train and life became unbearable.

That was tough. But then came the news of the *ultimate betrayal* which I am still struggling to come to terms with today.

A few weeks after I got out of Goodmayes my management team were asking a lot of questions about money. My accountants were freaking out at the amount of cash flying out of my account. At the height of my illness I had been waving banknotes around like a lottery winner, but blowing cash on stuff you don't need is a common sign of bipolar disorder. What the accountants couldn't understand was why it was still carrying on. They were under the impression my time in hospital had put me back on the right path. Yet, some months, I was apparently spending tens of thousands of pounds.

The phone would ring and I'd be asked: "Frank, what's going on? What the hell are you buying?"

I didn't know what they were on about. I explained I was barely going outside the front door. I told them all I was focused on was getting better – not going shopping. I was terrified that people would not believe me and that eventually the doctors would cart me back off to hospital.

So I pleaded with my accountants to check things out. And that was when things took a sinister turn. When the bank manager started to follow the cash going out of my account it became clear where the money had gone.

I was called in for a meeting and presented with the evidence. As I looked at it my mind was racing and my heart was breaking. Someone close to me had set up a system to take money from my account month after month.

As I listened, I could hardly get my head around what they were telling me. When I was married, Laura always dealt with the money side of things. So after we got divorced I'd allowed someone else to have access to my money and help me manage things.

But it was clear they'd been taking advantage, treating the Bank of Frank as a cash register. And for them it was ringing overtime.

That wasn't the worst of it. This betrayal started when I was sick and helpless, forcibly locked up inside Goodmayes, and went on for a long time afterwards. Yes, when I was on my knees, when I needed help the most, this person who was supposed to be helping me had decided to take my money.

I can't tell you who it is. They know who they are and they know how heartbroken I am. I have made that clear to them. We no longer talk to one another and I doubt we ever will again. This person sent me a letter admitting what they did, trying to make peace. But I am not able to.

I could have called in the police and maybe I should have. But when I discovered the fraud my main priority was to get back my peace of mind – not bring more heat down on me. Even now I feel angry and upset. It still hurts like hell and is difficult to live with. Only my divorce has caused me more pain.

In all, I fear about £300,000 was taken from my bank account. A £40,000 Cartier watch which I loved also vanished after I was sectioned. I've no idea who took it, but I dearly hope to get it back one day. I have managed to get a lot of the money that was stolen from me returned but I am still owed more than £100,000 and the matter is now in the hands of my lawyers.

Telling the world what happened is not something I am doing lightly. I know there might now be a guessing game as to who the person is but I don't care. Money is not my God and, despite what happened, I am still able to live a very comfortable life. But that's not the point. What this person did was unforgivable.

I need to talk about what happened because I want people to understand how hard I have found it to trust people since I retired from boxing. And the fraud didn't just break my heart. It left me, once again, fighting for my sanity. The weeks and months afterwards sent me into such a downward spiral. I started to withdraw into my own world. I didn't feel as if I could trust anyone so I shut myself off.

I had already gone from fighting in front of 30,000 people in sold-out arenas to spending most days on my own in the lounge with no-one to talk to. When I did venture outside I noticed the way people looked at me had changed.

After I was called Bonkers on the front of *The Sun*, people would often cross the road rather than stop to say hello. It felt like being back on stage in Aladdin, my panto debut alongside Michael Barrymore.

"Look out, it's Frank…and he's behind you…"

I heard the whispers loud and clear. I clocked the funny looks. I noticed the expressions many people pulled when they saw me out and about. Sometimes I felt tempted to walk down the street wearing my champion's belt to remind the world there was more to me than a man who had lost control of his mind.

Others were far more cruel. Much later, in the autumn of 2011, eight years after I was released from Goodmayes, I was enjoying what I thought was a very normal day out shopping with my eldest daughter Nicola. We had popped to Bovingdon Market, not far from where I live in Bedfordshire, to pick up some food for dinner.

Above the noise of the market traders I heard a geezer shout – "Frank. Oi, Frank."

I felt a hand on my shoulder and turned around expecting to see a friendly face or someone asking for a selfie. Instead there was a guy standing in front of me with pure evil in his eyes.

"Here you go, have this," he sneered. Then he head-butted me full in the face.

Oblivion. Suddenly I was dazed, on the ground, totally out of it. That hadn't happened since the day Tyson knocked me down.

In a heartbeat a beautiful crisp and sunny day descended into darkness. The only thing that brought me back round was the noise of screaming from two women standing nearby. The guy had long gone.

I sat there in a state of shock. Then, suddenly, there was a moment of clarity as I saw passers-by staring at me. I was Frank Bruno, for goodness sake. I had to get up. I couldn't let people see me like this. I raced back to the car and, after what seemed like an eternity, Nicola arrived back weighed down with bags.

"Dad, where did you go? I've been looking everywhere for …."

She took in my bloodshot eyes, the mark on my head and the anger on my face.

"Dad, what's happened to you?" she screamed.

"It's nothing, Nic, just some kid trying to make a name for himself," I said. "Please, let's not make a scene."

"But Dad, your eye doesn't look right. We should get you to A&E."

"No," I insisted. "I ain't going to no hospital – I just want to go home."

But as I tried to make sense of what had happened the anger was building up inside me. I hadn't felt rage like it since my days in the ring. I just wanted to find the guy, get in his face, teach him some manners and give him a lesson he would never forget for the rest of his life. But where would it get me? A police cell probably.

Again, of course, I should have got the Old Bill involved. But I was ashamed about what had happened and I didn't want to relive it. I was a big man, a former world heavyweight champion, for goodness sake, and I had been reduced to nothing.

When I look back now I can see that way of thinking is stupid and wrong. But I was mortified by what he had done. So, in the end, the only person in authority I told was my doctor.

I was worried the head butt would cause further problems to my right eye which had already been so badly busted from boxing. I had to have an operation to put things right in the end. If I hadn't, the doctors said there was a chance I could end up losing my sight. They patched me up. But the scars ran deep. The attack was totally senseless and as I sit here I can picture the guy's face, I can see the look in his eyes as he attacked me. I still struggle to understand it. How could someone just come at me like that for no reason? I know evil and idiots like him can be found in all walks of life – but it made me even more suspicious of people than I was after the fraud.

A few months later came another incident that pushed me closer to the edge. The day it happened started, as it usually did, with me heading off at first light to train at Champneys, a health farm close to my home.

The traffic was heavy that morning so I went via a back route and as I drove down a country lane I passed a police car parked up at the side of the road. Before I knew what was going on, it was behind me with its blue light flashing and the officer was waving his hand at me to stop and get out.

As I parked up, the policeman came over and was looking up and down at my motor, a Mercedes 4x4 ML. Then he asked me to get out.

"We've had a lot of these high-profile cars stolen in this area you know, sir," he said. "Can you please get out of the car while we make a few calls?"

I couldn't believe what was going on. I expected someone to jump out of the bushes with a camcorder and tell me it was some sort of practical joke. My car had a personalised number plate and I was well known in the area, but I was being mugged off, made to feel like a criminal.

"Sir, I'm not being funny, but most people round here know me," I said.

The copper went back to his car and kept making lots of calls on his radio asking different police officers back at his HQ to run my number plate through the system.

"Why don't you sit in your vehicle while we investigate, sir?"

"I'm fine here, it's a sunny day, officer," I replied. What I wanted to scream was: "What the hell are you investigating? And why are you stopping me?"

But I kept it zipped. I was standing there for over an hour in the end before he eventually let me go on my way. He looked a bit embarrassed when he realised who I was. There was no apology until many months later when I was down the gym and bumped into one of the top cops in the area who went out of his way to say sorry.

But it was too late. The incident made me feel even more paranoid and on edge than I had been before. I started to think I was being watched and that everywhere I was going I was being monitored. I felt the world closing in on me. I was wondering: "What trick are 'they' going to try and pull on me next?"

From nowhere, after years of keeping my illness at bay, it was beginning to creep up on me. I was starting to lose control. Things were beginning to unravel and feel scrambled in my head. I was scared at how I was feeling. I thought my illness was a chapter I had closed and would never be revisited. Surely my problems were in the past?

I was wrong. My illness was still lurking in the shadows and, day by day, by the end of 2011, it started to take over. But I didn't expect what came next. It was about to strike in a way I could never have predicted.

Yeah, what happened in 2012 made my earlier stay in Goodmayes Hospital seem like a walk in the park. That was the year of the Olympics, Britain's golden summer of sporting success, not least for Anthony Joshua, who won gold in the super-heavyweight division.

But, for me, it was the year darkness descended on my world again. When I close my eyes I can still feel the fear and terror as the ambulance drove away from my home to take me back to hospital in April of that year.

In split seconds my world came crashing down, as it had that night against Tyson. And, you know what, just like that fight in Vegas in 1996, I didn't see any of it coming.

Chapter 2
TEARS, FEARS... AND PIERS

I've always loved the way the world looks first thing in the morning. When I was preparing for a fight, my favourite time to be out on the road, running, was always dawn. Seeing the sun rise in the sky above my head would drive me forward.

It would push me on. While everyone else was sleeping I was moving and dreaming. Dreaming of becoming a World Champion.

I remember at the start of March 2012 how glorious the mornings were as the first signs of spring began to show in my garden. I had no idea the shadows of my past were about to arrive at my door and bring darkness into my world all over again.

I was making plans, ducking and diving and keeping my head down. I was free, I was working and I was earning. Sure, the work was different to being a sportsman. Since I retired in 1997 I had been travelling up and down the country, talking about my career at dinners, meeting my fans and sharing stories about my days in the ring.

A wet Wednesday in Coventry for *An Evening With Frank Bruno* didn't quite have the glamour of a fight night at the MGM Grand in Las Vegas. But there was one major advantage – nobody was trying their hardest to knock my head off my shoulders. So it suited me nicely. It was great to be able to stand up in front of the punters and talk about my career. My agent always gave me a script but I preferred to shoot from the hip and crack a few jokes. I just loved being around my fans.

"Brunooo, Brunooo, Brunooo."

The chant would always boom out when I turned up at a theatre, hotel or shopping centre for an event. It felt like being back in the ring again. It made me feel alive and on my game. I was earning my corn and I was paying my bills. And it is easy to take that for granted.

I was just a kid when my dad Robert died, but one of the last things he said to me became my motto for life. "Franklin, son," he said to me. "As you get older, trust nobody but yourself."

I kept those words close to me after I retired and often it has kept me out of trouble. Life after boxing isn't easy. Many of the people who were fighting in my day are now either six foot under or banged up. And loads more are surrounded by wrong 'uns.

Boxers, particularly those who have retired, can find themselves easy targets to the wrong kind of so-called mates. Lots of retired pros have money in their pockets and time on their hands. So there will always be blokes coming along saying they are Mr Big Shot and they are more than happy to tell you how to spend it – then mug you off.

I have not always invested my dough in the right way and I have been stitched up by the odd deal here and there. And what I had discovered after coming out of Goodmayes in 2003 had only left me more paranoid about the people I trusted with my money. But I was enjoying my work in that spring of 2012.

It was a quieter life of course, but the loneliness of the past was not such a big problem, because finally there was someone new in my life. Yeah, I'd found a really lovely girl. I first met Nina at a wedding of an old buddy of mine in Glasgow and we hit it off straight away.

She was a smart lady, a businesswoman who ran her own hairdressing salon and I fancied her from the off. We made each other laugh and, more importantly, I felt I could trust her. It was my first serious relationship since my divorce from Laura in 2001.

I don't know why it took me so long. After my marriage ended I was a bit wary of getting too close to women. Well, no, I rather enjoyed the getting close bit but I didn't like the idea of them running off to the papers and leaving me with a headache.

However, I knew Nina wasn't that way. It wasn't easy though. She was living in Glasgow and I was down on my own in Bedfordshire. But we were making things work and we were happy so I was smiling properly for the first time in years. Things always seem easier in the world for me when I have a lady around.

When I split from Laura I had to do everything for myself: cook, clean, pay the bills, all the little things that couples share the workload on.

All right, all right, I know what you're thinking: do me a favour and put the violin away, welcome to the real world, Frank! But the little things in life are the ones that stress me out. And that knocks on big time with my illness and leaves me feeling manic.

For more than 20 years, when I was boxing, everything was done for me and taken care of. But when I retired that support had gone and I found it hard to cope with the simple things that you can probably do standing on your head. Ask me to run 12 miles and I'll do it. Sort out a to-do list of jobs? Forget it.

So Nina was keeping me on an even keel and having someone to stand alongside me and help me cope with life's challenges felt like a really beautiful thing.

I tried not to tell too many people about us. My daughters Nicola and Rachel and my son Franklin, who were all living with their mum, had met Nina a couple of times, but I sensed they didn't exactly all get on like a house on fire. It felt a bit awkward.

Sadly, my relationship with Laura had gone down the pan and it is fair to say we were no longer friends. It is hard for the kids when a marriage ends and the parents aren't able to remain on good terms.

But, as my relationship got more serious with Nina, it became a source of a bit of earache. My children and mates would be calling to say they were concerned about the time I was spending driving up and down to Scotland.

They wanted me to be happy and were only looking out for me. But they warned me to slow down, to not overdo things and to be aware of my condition. It was nothing new.

Ever since I was first sectioned in 2003, I have learned to accept my family and friends will be watching me to see for any changes in the way I am acting. But having so many eyes on me can leave me paranoid.

I didn't want to hear it and I was being stubborn and difficult. I was enjoying my new life with Nina and the way I saw it I could do without the stress. I did my best to block out the noise, but it was increasingly putting me on edge.

Thankfully there were other things to focus on. I'd taken on a new agent, called Dave Davies, who seemed to be opening doors for me. My previous agent, Laurie Mansfield, had been trying to sort out a big TV interview for me and we had been in talks with ITV who were interested in getting me on to talk about my life.

I have been around showbiz long enough to not take stuff too seriously. Deals are discussed all the time and then come to nothing. Showbiz is not too different from boxing that way.

You spend half your time thinking a big fight is being sorted out – only for it all to be scrapped. I am old school, so I only start worrying about business when I know the ink is dry on the contract.

But one afternoon when Nina and I were out shopping I got the call to tell me a big deal had been agreed and I was going to appear on *Piers Morgan's Life Stories* on ITV.

It would be my biggest TV interview in 10 years – a proper comeback. It was a massive coup, it would get my face back out there and I hoped it might throw up some more work. The episode on me was to be screened in mid-April 2012 and I was really excited about it.

I've always had a lot of time for Piers. I'll admit I used to be a bit wary of him. Back in the day, when I was still boxing, Piers was the main man at newspapers like the *News of the World* and the *Daily Mirror* so I knew he would stick me on his front page in a heartbeat if I didn't keep my nose clean.

I've never had a brilliant relationship with the tabloids. I like the boxing guys, the ones who know their stuff and who actually write stories about fights. Colin Hart at *The Sun* is a dear friend of mine and many of the others writing on the sport like Jeff Powell at the *Daily Mail* and Kevin Mitchell from *The Observer*, who co-wrote my life story, have been hugely supportive over the years through the highs and lows.

But it's the reporters trying to get a front-page story that bother me. It was bad enough *The Sun* calling me Bonkers after I was sectioned in 2003, making me a laughing stock in the eyes of the punters.

Then, in 2006, the papers were at it all over again when the tabloids stuck me on the front page. This time it was about my short-lived romance with a lady I had met which led to us having a beautiful daughter, Freya.

But the relationship, for many reasons, was never going to work out and we split after Freya was born. When the papers got hold of the story they tried to make out I had dumped Freya's mum and that I had started describing her to my friends as a gold-digger.

It was total baloney and in the end we had to get my lawyer Magnus Boyd involved to sort it out. The truth is I love all my kids and make sure they are provided for. I don't see Freya now but maybe in years to come when she is older that will change. I dearly hope it does.

So with what has happened in the past I have always gone out of my way to give journalists a bit of a wide berth. Piers, though, has always seemed pretty straight. I felt comfortable doing the interview with him because I knew he wasn't going to try and stitch me up.

We had a history, too. As I always remind old Piersy when I see him, it was ME who gave him his big break. I let him interview me when he was a 19-year-old cub reporter on the South London Press newspaper. He asked me what I wanted to achieve in life.

"Become world champion," I said.

I held up my end of the deal and I guess he didn't get on too badly either!

I knew the Piers interview was a big deal. It was my first major TV appearance in a decade and millions of people would be tuning in. ITV had already warned my agent it would be a warts-and-all interview.

"They'll want to know everything," Dave said to me after we'd signed on the dotted line.

How I coped with the death of my dad when I was a teenager, how it felt being knocked out by Mike Tyson to lose my belt, divorcing Laura, being sectioned.

Dark chapters of my life would be reopened and replayed. Nothing was off limits – and my battle with bipolar would be at the centre of it all. But I wasn't bothered. No. That was one of the main reasons I wanted to do it. The Piers interview presented me with the chance to go out and show people I was fit and well.

I wanted to draw a line under my past and move on. Well, that was the plan...

But as the days ticked down to the interview I started to feel more and more tense. The anxiety was similar to the emotions I felt in the run-up to a big fight. I could feel my bipolar creeping up on me.

It wasn't long until the nagging doubts crept in and negative thoughts began rolling round inside my head.

"Are you ready for this, Frank?"

"Don't let yourself get mugged off here, fella."

They were like body blows which came first thing in the morning, and they were still there last thing at night – jabbing away at my brain.

For me the only way to deal with them, the only way I have ever known to deal with stress, is to train. So I hit the gym. Training became my salvation. At first, the sessions were nothing heavy. An hour or two in the morning before getting on the road for a job or driving north to be with Nina.

It worked. The soundtrack of negativity between my ears stopped. The fog lifted.

But the peace of mind that training brings is like a drug to me when I've been having dark days. So I craved it more and more.

I didn't need it, of course. I was in brilliant physical shape. There wasn't an ounce of fat on my body. But I began to convince myself I had to look perfect for this TV comeback.

In the end I was working out for five or six hours a day then going back in the middle of the night and doing another few hours in the gym. It began to have a knock-on effect big time, and my sleep really began to suffer.

The hassle with my nearest and dearest over my new life with Nina was becoming more and more stressful, too. And I felt myself getting wound up so much quicker.

So I began to shut myself off from friends and family. The kids would leave message after message asking me to get in touch. But most of them went unanswered. The more they rang the more paranoid I got that I was no longer coping.

Living inside my own bubble became the easiest way to cope. I was keeping everything bottled up and it was obvious to everyone – except me – I was about to explode.

It wasn't long before it started to have an impact on my work. My agent was bearing the brunt of my moods – I'd become abusive over the most minor of things. I would shout and scream over stuff which really wasn't important and thought everyone had it in for me.

I'd turn up to events totally shattered, often finding it hard to make the big speech people had arrived to hear. I always got through it somehow, but there were times where I nearly fell asleep at the top table. Little wonder really, seeing as I was existing on about two hours' sleep a night.

It didn't look good. In fact, it looked terrible.

I didn't want to admit it to anyone but physically and mentally I was really starting to struggle. I could feel my illness closing in on me gradually and my world shutting down.

When I went to events and had to talk about my problems in the past it became hard to relive it. It was gruelling and would grind me down.

But I knew it was nothing compared to what I'd have to face with Piers. And when that thought flashed into my mind I just hit the gym harder and harder to make sure I looked good. I wanted to ensure my mind was sharp for the questions that were going to be coming my way.

I thought if I stayed on my toes in the gym I would be ready, mentally, for whatever Piers might throw at me. But really I was just exhausting myself on purpose so my mind would slow down. It was a deadly carousel and I could not get off.

My mum, Lynette, tried to help me. As a former nurse she could see I was overdoing it.

"Franklin," she would say to me. "Stop, rest, make sure you are eating right."

I heard her warnings but I wasn't listening to anyone. Instead I was juggling training and my work diary and it became so difficult. I was up and down the motorway and often not coming back from gigs until two or three in the morning.

Nina was around now and then but she had her own business to run in Scotland so I spent a lot of time in the house on my own. And, because I was living on my own, the normal pressures of daily life soon became overwhelming. Those days in the build-up to the interview seemed like a marathon. Life felt like a race all of the time.

Get up. Go to gym. Race home. Check post. Shit, there are a load of bills to pay. Oh no, a parking ticket to sort out. *Come on, Frank.* Right, now, go shopping. Get home. Now eat. Get a suit for the event for that evening. Clean my shoes. *Come on, Frank.* Go to the gym. Get home. Eat. Get dressed. Pack up the car. Drive up the motorway. Get to the gig. Be funny. Smile. Get out of there. Wait. OK, one more photo. An autograph? "No problem, boss." Drive home. Fall into bed. Then repeat. *Come on, Frank.*

Pretty quickly I was burning myself out. I was keeping family and friends at arm's length and I was overloading myself.

Dave kept saying I needed to take on some help and to let him get me a driver.

"Why don't you let me bring someone in?" he suggested time and time again.

"Leave off," I'd always reply. "I don't need a minder."

Plus all I could think about was how I'd been let down in the past. How could I trust someone else not to steal from me and stitch me up if I let them into my world? I just felt safer being on my own.

As the petrol in my tank got lower and lower, I turned more and more to the gym. I was snappy, I was fast, my mind was racing and I was stressed. I can see now why people were a little concerned about how I was behaving. I was saying yes to things when I wasn't listening properly. I was trying to be nice to everyone and found I could never say no to people.

"Can you come and do this charity thing, Frank?"

My answer would always be the same – "No problem, boss."

My management team were also asking a lot of questions about how much money I was spending again. Whenever it came up I'd get angry. It was like history repeating itself. How could they be sure someone wasn't stealing from me?

"They aren't, Frank," they'd insist. "That's in the past."

The truth was I was blowing quite a lot of dough – particularly on food and clothes.

But my mind was racing so much I'd go to the market and buy enough fruit and steak to last me a fortnight, and then I'd do it all over again a few days later.

My family could sense that I was on the edge. They recognised there was a problem but I didn't want to accept any help.

Of course, I should have just stopped. I should have taken a week or two and gone to a health farm to relax. If I had, things may have turned out very differently. But I couldn't stop. I'd never been as busy in my life and I wanted to continue providing a good life for my children. That meant keeping up with my speaking engagements and maintaining my public profile.

Another thing affecting me terribly was the fact my brother Michael was very ill.

Michael, who was 12 years older than me, had always been my hero. I totally idolised him and when we were kids he protected me so much. It wasn't easy being a young black boy on the streets of South London in the 1970s. When I was growing up and as word spread about my love for boxing, it felt like people were lining up to try and teach me a lesson and give me a good hiding. But Michael always had my back. He could look after himself just as well as I could. And more than once, he put a few warnings out telling people not to touch his little brother.

So when I learned he'd been diagnosed with terminal liver cancer I took it very badly. It was another thing I didn't want to stop and face up to.

If I kept on moving then I wouldn't have to think about Michael. If I kept on moving then I wouldn't have to think about being on my own all the time. If I kept on moving then I wouldn't have to think about the money that was stolen from me. If I kept on moving then I wouldn't have to think about my illness that I knew was quickly taking hold. If I kept on moving then none of it could catch me.

But, the truth was, the faster I kept moving the closer I was heading towards a breakdown. As time passed my behaviour got worse and stupid things started to come out of my mouth. I'd go to gigs and tell fans I fancied fighting again and I could hold my own with anyone. At one event I bragged Dereck Chisora wouldn't be able to cope with me.

Next thing it was all over the newspapers and eyes were on me. And when I am low I just want to be on my own. I gave a speech to students at my boxing academy, the Priory School in Orpington, Kent, in late March 2012. I was only meant to be offering some tips but all of a sudden I was making a speech hinting at a comeback.

"I train every day," I told the kids. "I train like a bastard, weights, freezing room, altitude training. I wouldn't like anyone to mess around with me because I think I'm more dangerous than when I was boxing.

"But I'm not disturbing anyone, giving it large. I'm just holding my corner but if someone was messing about with my son or my girls, I'd have to defend them. Same if you had kids."

The kids were stunned – many of them looked on at me open-mouthed. It carried on when one of the young boxers asked me about my defeat to Lennox Lewis in 1993.

"If I had to meet Lennox Lewis at a boxing show and he comes towards me, what do you want me to do? Run away like a chicken, stand at the back? You've got to defend yourself."

I was talking strange. And the next day the quotes were in the paper. The heat was on me again.

Other things happened which left me really frightened. One gig at Butlins in Minehead I messed up completely after accidentally pro-gramming the satnav in my car to a setting which avoided all motorways. In the end I arrived eight hours after setting off from my home – and about two hours late for the show.

Luckily the good old British public were staying on site so they waited for me. And at the end I got a standing ovation. But the applause couldn't drown out the noise in my head that was warning me trouble was down the line.

Word quickly spreads in the industry when stuff like that happens and there was talk about whether I should put the Piers interview on the back-burner. I knew in my heart I'd been training way too hard but there was no way I was going to tell anyone.

I wasn't pulling out. No chance. I was the former world champion – I wasn't about to run away from Piers-blinking-Morgan.

When I woke up on the morning of the interview I felt totally knackered. I was burnt out physically and mentally. But I wouldn't throw in the towel.

"Come on, Frank," I said to myself. "Let's put on a show."

I picked the brightest suit in the wardrobe – pink – and jumped in my car to head off to London.

Fair play to ITV, they know how to put together a programme and I've no complaints about the way Piers went about his business that night. He was a total professional.

Ahead of the interview, which was a pre-record, he came into my dressing room and asked if there was anything I'd rather not talk about. I told him not to be so daft.

"Relax yourself and bring it on, Piers," I said as he left.

Then they brought the cameras into my dressing room and then into Piers' room and asked us to talk to each other as if we were about to go toe-to-toe in the ring.

"He might have taken on Mike Tyson, but I want to see if he can handle Mr Morgan," Piers said with a little twinkle in his eye. I told them that I was up for a fight and urged him to throw his best punches. I knew what the producers wanted, I knew the script. I'd done panto enough times! A KO for Piers would be me breaking down in front of the country.

"BIG FRANK IN TEARS" – That would give the newspapers a headline.

As I walked from the dressing room to the studio it felt like a ring walk on fight night. The fear, the butterflies, the roar of the people waiting for me to make my entrance.

"Don't let them mug you off, Frank. Don't let them mug you off." Those dark thoughts again – they were never far away.

I looked at the audience and I could see Nicola, Rachel and Franklin. They'd grown up having to deal with my bipolar. Now they were about to hear it all over again.

How I dearly wished that part could be deleted from my life story. But it was too late for that. My mind switched to the guy who attacked me at the market. Would he be watching? I hoped he would. I'd show him. I was back. Back to my best.

Would the person who stole my cash be tuning in? I hoped so and I hoped they felt rotten when they saw me standing tall.

"3,2,1," said the producer, counting down to my entrance. "OK, Frank, that's you – good luck."

As I walked out the claps and applause from the audience gave me a massive lift. Everyone was cheering and the interview hadn't even started.

But I still felt as nervous as hell when I sat down opposite Piers.

As he started firing questions at me I felt my hands getting shaky but I told myself to chill out and try to be myself. When I got a few laughs I started to loosen up. The audience seemed to buzz off me.

Even so, the interview passed me by in a bit of a blur and later I struggled to remember what I'd said.

They played footage of my relatives talking about the impact my illness had had on them. It was the first time I'd seen many of them interviewed about it. There was my dear old mum willing me to stay well.

Next up was Michael. It was hard to look at him on the screen talking about how cut up he'd been left by my mental breakdown nine years earlier. With all the problems Michael was suffering in his own life it was painful to see him talking about mine. It was so tough to hear and I had to hold myself together as he spoke.

Then, finally, there were the kids, explaining how they felt when they came to see me in hospital. I felt tears well up in my eyes. But as I sat in that chair I clenched my fists and forced myself to stay strong.

People who watched it tell me they could see I wasn't right – but I think I did OK, given that I was struggling with an iceberg I couldn't yet see.

There was plenty I could have said that would have triggered head-lines. I could have told the world about the attack in the market, the money that had been stolen from me, the heartache of my divorce – but I chose not to. Those were the parts of my *Life Story* I couldn't face people hearing at the time.

There are things I wish I hadn't said. For instance, I sounded a bit snappy when I told Piers not to describe me as a superstar. But that's the truth. I hate people calling me that. I'm no different to any other man or woman in the street.

Then I went and started blabbing that I was seeing Nina. I had no intention of telling everyone about our relationship, but I was so happy at how that area of my life was going the words just spilled out. Part of me also hoped if I went public it would make everyone see how serious I was about Nina.

The interview ended on a high with Piers telling everyone how great I looked.

"We all just want you to stay healthy, Frank," he told me, including the audience.

"I want to make sure I never end up back in hospital, Piers," I said.

With that the audience burst into cheers and started applauding again. But even as I soaked it all up, I knew I had a big fight on my hands.

I had no idea how quickly I would lose it. Looking back, maybe I already had. As soon as the cameras stopped rolling Piers bounded over, slapped me on the back and told me how brilliantly I'd done. I'd come through our little battle without any blood on my nose. He hadn't got his tears. No headline. Job done.

Afterwards in the green room, where everyone gathers for a beer, the kids suggested a bite to eat to round off a brilliant night and suggested we go to a restaurant in Camden.

Everyone was in celebratory mood. I didn't feel much like going but I knew if I didn't there may be more questions. As we sat in the restaurant I joined in the toast to how well the interview had gone.

This was supposed to be a turning point. But where I should have felt elation, I felt emptiness. Where I should have been planning to build on the comeback, my only desire was to get home. And to get away. Quickly.

Was I running from my illness that night? Possibly. But I was absolutely certain at that point I was able to deal with it in my own way and on my terms. I knew I was involved in a fight but I was convinced it was one I could win.

As I drove home, Nina, who I was speaking to on the phone, tried to give me the confidence I needed to build on the interview and put the dark thoughts aside. But when I walked back through the front door I sank down on to the sofa and felt shattered. Nothing felt right.

The comedown after the interview had left me feeling the way I did after a fight. All the anger, all the anxiety, all the tension came out of me like the sweat used to in the ring. I grabbed a duvet which I always leave draped over the sofa in my lounge and made a bed up.

Then I reached for my phone and flicked on YouTube. Often, when I feel low, I will replay the moment where I became world champion. As I waited for the footage to load I closed my eyes.

I could picture myself at Wembley walking out in front of 30,000 fans.

I could smell the smoke from the fireworks which exploded as I made my way to the ring. I could see the look of terror on Oliver McCall's face when he eventually emerged for the fight.

I could feel the connections I made on his head in those opening rounds. I could hear Nigel Benn screaming me on in those final minutes. And I could recall the elation as the bell went in the 12th and I knew I had done it.

I tossed my mobile on to the armchair, walked into the kitchen and looked outside. The moon was shining in a perfectly clear sky. Tomorrow was looking like it was going to be another glorious day.

"Come on, Frank," I said out loud. "Let's start again in the morning."

I flicked off the lights and there was darkness. I'd got through the big interview.

But within two weeks I would discover there was only one comeback awaiting me – to a locked door and a hospital bed.

Chapter 3

LOCKED UP

I heard the shutter slide across the door to my room and the voice of a nurse outside.

"All OK, Frank?" she said softly.

But I kept my eyes firmly shut. Why open them? The darkness was the only thing protecting me from the nightmare my life had become.

I was lying in a bed in the psychiatric ward of Basildon Hospital in Essex, broken, frightened and confused. Especially confused. Questions I couldn't answer went round and round my head. Which member of my family had given the nod for this to happen? Or was it someone else? Was it all my doing? How did things ever reach this point? And where did I go from here?

That date – April 13, 2012 – will forever be stamped on my brain. It was the second time in my life I had been taken away but this was the first time I had been locked up against my will. When I was sectioned in 2003 I knew I needed help. This was so different.

The journey from my home to the door of that ward in Basildon had taken around an hour. All the way there my head had been telling me to scream and shout. But I didn't make a sound. My mind was racing.

Where were my friends? What was going on? Why was nobody stopping this?

I knew I was at rock bottom. Lying on that bed in the back of the ambulance was the most embarrassing and degrading experience of my life.

When the doors swung open and daylight burst in I was in a daze and I could no longer think logically. The ambulance man guided me to the bottom of a long staircase which led to the door of the mental health unit.

It felt like being ushered back to the corner after being saved by the bell in a fight.

In my hand was a suitcase, which Nina had packed for me. I'd only asked for my clothes, an iPod and a mobile phone. I didn't know it then but that phone would be a lifeline.

As I was walked up the stairs to the ward, I was guided inside through a maze of entrances and I heard the sound of three doors close behind me.

Clink. Clink. Clink.

Even today when I hear a door lock I am transported back to the moment I first arrived at Basildon Hospital.

Then I was hit by the smell. Stale, clinical, antiseptic. It reminded me of the TCP that mum used to dab on my knees when I fell over as a kid. It had filled the air when I was locked up in Goodmayes Hospital nine years earlier. And as I breathed it in again I felt like it was suffocating me.

There was another smell too – the stink of my own fear. Yeah, I was in a hospital. But, in my mind, I may as well have been standing in a prison.

No, in fact, it was worse than that. At least if I had been banged up I would have been able to understand it. Do the crime, do the time and all that.

But I didn't understand why I was being punished in this way. None of it made any sense.

"Hello, Frank," said a nurse who was sitting behind a desk, doing her bits and pieces, writing on some paperwork.

"You have been detained with us under Section 2 of the Mental Health Act," she said. "I need you to read this form."

She put some papers on the counter in front of me, along with a pen and returned to her work. I've no idea what the paperwork said because my eyes were fixed on the tray of tablets next to it, also destined for me.

"I'm not interested in those," I told her firmly. "I don't believe I should be in here, you know."

The nurse gave me a look that told me it was a line she'd heard a million times before. She looked mugged off. But I was the one feeling mugged off.

Nobody had explained why I had been sectioned. The woman at my front door had waved some papers at me to prove that they could take me away, but she hadn't given me the reason why. And nobody had told me who had made the decision saying I should have been taken to hospital. That thought kept niggling at me.

OK, maybe in my heart I knew why I was in this situation. But I couldn't bring myself to even think about that. There were enough dark thoughts going through my mind.

"Frank, the reasons should have been made clear to you," she said, sighing. "But you will be able to speak to someone tomorrow if you are unhappy. For now you need to take this medication and just have some rest. Things will be better after that."

The tablets were pushed across the table. I pushed them back.

I was asked to wait a few moments while my room was being sorted out and was ushered into a garden area. I gulped in the fresh air, grateful of a break from the smell of the ward. I had to stand on my tiptoes to see the real life that was going on beyond the high mesh fence.

In the distance I could see people getting on with their daily lives. They were not doing anything major but, God, how I wished I could swap places with them.

I saw men and women coming and going from the main hospital reception. Cars pulling up, buses stopping outside, vans arriving to drop off medical supplies. I watched a little boy happily running out of the double doors with his dad chasing after him.

No-one could see me where I was standing behind the high fence.

A few yards away from me was a young woman, sitting on the bench wearing her pyjamas. It was 4pm. She was crying and looked dazed and scared as two nurses helped her to her feet. All I wanted to do was run away.

I pictured myself getting out, climbing the fence and sprinting. I didn't have a clue where I would head for but anywhere, anywhere at all had to be better than this. Then a nurse arrived at my side.

"Come on, Frank," she said.

I was led to a room which was to become my new home. As I stepped inside my heart sank. It was no bigger than a police cell and had a single bed in the corner which took up most of the space. The room reminded me of the tiny dressing rooms I was given in my amateur fighting days.

Back then I would not be alone though. I'd have my trainer with me and my team. When I was down in a fight those people – my corner – would pull me back, sort me out and guide me through. Now I was on my own.

As I paced the room my trainers stuck to the lino on the floor and I noticed large patches of blue paint peeling off the walls. I put my suitcase on top of an old wooden chest of drawers and sank on to the narrow bed.

Then I realised there were no windows in the room. This truly was a cell.

I shook my head at the sheer injustice of it all. I was a former heavy-weight champion of the world, for God's sake. Now look at me. I felt like an animal in a zoo. I had been stripped of my dignity.

"It's only for a couple of days at most, Frank," said the nurse, as I sat there trying to make sense of what was going on. "When we feel satisfied that you don't pose a risk to yourself or anybody else you will be moved to a different part of the hospital."

That really got my goat.

"Who are you worried I am going to hurt? I'm not a violent man. And how long are you keeping me here for?" I asked.

The nurse just looked at me. "I'll be back later," is all she would say.

They brought me some dinner but I didn't feel much like eating and I certainly wasn't ready to see any of the other patients.

The lights went out at 10pm – but sleep didn't come easy that night. As I sunk on to the bed I could feel the plastic sheet underneath. It reminded me of the ones Mum used to put on when I was a little kid in case I wet the bed. The indignity of it all really got to me that night. All I wanted was to be back in my bedroom at home.

I lay in the dark, my mind racing, and slowly came to terms with a reality I had been putting off all day – that my family and friends had made the call to have me locked up.

And as it went round and round my head I was up on my feet, like a caged lion, pacing the room, trying to piece together the reasons.

Why? Why? Why?

Then the dark thoughts arrived to keep me company.

"Why had they betrayed me?"
"What had I done to them, to anyone?"
"How was I going to get out?"

I didn't have any answers. I closed my eyes and played back the few weeks which had followed the Piers interview. They had not been easy. The interview had been a massive strain, far more than I was even willing to admit to myself.

I knew my behaviour had been causing more and more concern to those who cared about me. I had been running on adrenaline from gruelling sessions down the gym. I couldn't slow down. I was spending quite a bit of money on things I didn't need.

My relationship with Nina was becoming more and more serious too and, as a result, I was shutting myself off from my nearest and dearest. It had become a source of friction and I was starting to get a bit snappy on the phone.

I knew the way I was behaving was causing aggro and there were days where my recollection of events were a little hazy – mainly due to the fact I was feeling so low and so tired.

Calls were going in to my management from people who had been on jobs with me who were concerned at how I was or things I was saying. I sensed that a lot of eyes were on me and it made me feel uneasy.

But did I feel my bipolar disorder was taking over my life? No. No way. As I sat on the bed I compared myself to how I felt on the first night I had arrived at Goodmayes. Back then, I knew I was completely out of control. My life had become one dangerous mess.

Yet, as I lay in that bed in Basildon, I firmly believed the best place for me was at home – not trapped in a psychiatric ward.

I felt I could deal with my problems on the outside on my own terms. But that was no longer my *right*. And *that* was the most frightening aspect of all.

I knew, for the first time ever, I was no longer in control of my own life. Doctors now called the shots. I could be in this place for months and months. I felt utterly bewildered and betrayed.

As I fell asleep that night, exhausted from the stress, that thought was still running through my mind. And it was still there the next morning when the nurse gave me an early wake-up call.

"All I want to do is ring my agent and tell him to get me out pronto," I told her.

"There will be time for that later," she said calmly. "Right now you need to leave your room for a bit."

"If I must," I said. I was dreading stepping out and seeing the other patients for the first time. I sensed trouble up ahead.

As I stood in the corridor that led to the main entrance to the ward I found it hard to stand still because I was so anxious. Then – clink. That noise again as the door opened.

I had butterflies as I stepped through and came face to face with the other patients on the psychiatric ward at Basildon.

But I had to stop kidding myself: I was involved in the same fight as them. I was Patient Frank now.

There were about 12 of us in all – men of various ages – wandering up and down the corridor in their own little worlds. But as the nurse walked me through not one of them batted an eyelid.

If I walk down the street usually I can't go 50 yards without someone beeping their horn, shouting out my name or asking for a selfie. But these were people fighting for their sanity, they were not interested in autographs or pictures.

There was this sad feeling of loneliness everywhere I looked. There were lots of nurses wandering around, keeping an eye on things. But the patients weren't talking to each other, and nobody really seemed to even exist in any way that meant anything.

It seemed to me that most of the patients were like robots, controlled by the medication being shoved down their throats.

They seemed to operate within a drug-fuelled daze. They would stare vacantly into space. Some would just stand looking out of the windows, holding books loosely in their hands or clutching letters they had been sent, but not reading them.

It was a terrible, frightening sight.

My nurse showed me round so I could get my bearings. Like me, all the patients had their own room to sleep in. Sleep seemed to play a key part of life on the ward.

Staff were able to lock patients in. If you did as you were told you could come and go from your room as you wanted but I noticed most of the patients rarely went anywhere without a nurse two yards behind them.

One of them escorted me through the canteen, a large communal area with a TV and a couple of meeting rooms for when family and friends came to see you.

That was it. This was now my home.

As I walked round I noticed the other patients had windows in their rooms.

"When will I be able to sleep in a room like that?" I asked a nurse.

"Soon," she said. "When you are feeling better."

"I am feeling fine," I told her. "I don't think I should be in here. Why won't anyone believe that?" She just gave me another one of those looks.

"Any questions?" the nurse said as we arrived back in the communal area of the ward.

"Is there somewhere I can train?" I asked. She looked genuinely shocked.

"To train. Run. Do some weights?" I said.

"There's an exercise area," she said nodding towards a door that led outside.

I walked over to take a look. The "exercise area" was a concrete basketball court surrounded by overgrown weeds and nettles. It looked like nobody had used it for years My heart sank. I knew not having a gym to go to every day was the thing I'd miss the most.

As I made my way to breakfast that first day, more of the patients from the ward were milling around. Suddenly, as I sat down to eat, everyone's eyes were on me. I was the new guy and it was clear one or two of them recognised me.

"Frank, Frank Bruno?" one fella eventually asked as I sat down.

The genie was out of the bottle. I looked up at the man standing in front of me.

"Yes, boss," I said. "And how you doing?"

"Crap," he replied. "But then, so are you, I guess."

I laughed. It was the first time since arriving that I had smiled.

He was a nice guy – warm, friendly, but clearly troubled. His speech was slow and slurred and he looked exhausted and confused. He was in his sixties and told me that he used to run a business but that things had gone badly wrong for him after it went bust.

He lost all his money, then he lost his wife, then he lost his home and then he lost his mind. I wondered how many other people in the ward had a similar life story.

"Have they told you when you can go home?" I asked him.

"This is home," he said bluntly, his eyes not showing a flicker of emotion.

It terrified me to listen. I glanced up at the clock – 9am. I went back to my room and made the call. The nurses weren't happy that I was using a phone but there was no way I was going to sit down and accept what had happened.

My agent Dave, who wasn't involved in having me sectioned, confirmed my worst fears. He had been doing his job overnight, making frantic calls on my behalf. Then he gave me the script: how it had happened.

"Frank, there's no easy way of saying this, but family and members of your management team had become concerned about how you are. From what I've heard, a lot of chatter went on behind the scenes. They called in the doctors who made the decision to have you sectioned. They believed your illness had made you a danger to yourself and to others. I know you are not going to like it, Frank, but there is nothing I can do."

He was right, I didn't like it. At that point I lost my cool and got angry.

"I shouldn't be in here," I shouted. "I don't need to be in hospital. I should be at home. Tell them. Dave, for Christ sake, you have got to get me out."

I slammed my fist down so hard on the table in my room that the suitcase in the opposite corner fell to the floor. I didn't want to end the call, I had so many questions for Dave that I felt breathless. As I struggled to get them all out I was yelling.

"How can they just knock at my door and take me away?"

"How the hell does anyone expect me to trust them again?"

"Should I just take all these drugs so I can get out of here?"

I was still screaming questions at Dave, wondering why he wouldn't answer, when I realised my phone had run out of juice.

I heard footsteps moving fast down the corridor. The nurse appeared at my door.

"OK, Frank," she said. "You need to take this."

She was holding a tray of pills. They were lithium, she explained, powerful drugs to help conditions like mine. They were the same ones I'd been put on in the past.

My heart sank. For months after leaving Goodmayes I'd followed doctor's orders to take them, but I'd managed to come off them because I hated the way they made me feel. They made me lethargic, anxious and paranoid and I suffered terrifying nightmares.

I was so relieved when I'd been able to come off the stuff. I am not saying that is right for everyone – but for me it had been vital to my first recovery.

Now I knew what was coming. I was back to square one and a whole new fight was about to start. I slumped back on the bed and turned my face to the wall.

"Frank, listen," the nurse said. "If you don't take this you are going to be in here even longer."

I felt physically sick as those words sank in. It was like being a kid again. I could almost picture my mum in the kitchen with a bottle of jollop.

"Frank, here's the spoon – now take your medicine."

The nurse was right, though. If I didn't toe the line in here this grip the doctors had over my life would only get tighter. So I reluctantly popped the pills into my mouth. Then, totally defeated, I quickly drifted off to sleep.

Hours later, when I woke up, I barely had the strength to stand. The drugs had left me feeling exhausted, and my mind was numb, like I was in a fog. I was wobbly and shaky on my feet and I had lost the ability to walk straight.

I had lost so much more than that, though. I had lost my self-esteem.

I looked at the clock and was shocked to see it was nearly 5pm. I'd been out for hours, most of the day.

As I was led back into the canteen for dinner, I sat down on my own at the end of the bench. I wasn't interested in speaking to anyone.

As I picked at my food, I looked up and a guy, probably in his forties, was standing in front of me. He seemed tense.

"You OK, boss?" I asked politely, hoping he wouldn't want to chat. "How you doing?"

He didn't answer me – but I noticed he kept his eyes firmly fixed on mine. He was stocky, tall and on his toes. Suddenly I sensed danger. This was the market all over again.

Then, before I barely knew what was happening, he'd grabbed a knife from the cutlery tray. And he was lunging towards me. Fast.

I jumped from my seat, taking my tray with me as a shield as he lurched forward with his blade. He was prodding the knife towards my chest. His eyes were wild and his mouth was wide open.

I felt my fists clench. I knew if I didn't drop the geezer his knife was going into my chest. As I prepared to land one on him, out of nowhere two nurses jumped on his back, wrestled him to the floor and held him down.

Then two more arrived. He was screaming as they dragged him away. Screaming and crying.

None of the other patients even seemed to have noticed, apart from the woman I'd seen the day before in the communal garden, who was laughing hysterically in the corner.

"Someone's in trouble now," she shouted as a group of nurses sat me back down.

"Sorry about that one, Frank," one of the nurses said. "He can be a bit excitable. Now can I get you some more dinner?"

I glowered at them. "That guy could have stabbed me," I said. "Can't you see that?"

They did their best to calm me, but I was a ball of anger and didn't want to listen. The guy could have killed me yet the nurse was shrugging it all off like it was no biggie.

I assumed things like that were part and parcel of life in the hospital. But I wasn't sticking around to find out.

I stormed back to my room and slammed the door. I knew what I had to do next.

After all, I had been doing it all my life...

Chapter 4
FREE TO GO

That knife attack changed everything. It was the moment I realised I had to fight to get out of that place. But, for once in my life, I couldn't rely on my fists.

No, now I had to use my brain. I realise a lot of people think I haven't got much going on between my lugholes. Yeah, I am dyslexic and I wasn't the best at school and I wasn't massively interested in learning my times tables or getting top marks for spelling. I was more interested in causing mischief, being with my mates and playing sport than being in class. So when I left school I struggled to write and for a long time I couldn't read all that well. But my people skills are solid and I'm smart. And I am definitely streetwise.

I always had to be.

So, in the days after that fella shoved a knife towards my gut, I was up and on my toes. I decided enough was enough: I had to take back control.

One thing that helped was speaking to the kids and to Nina. I rang them the day after the knife attack and made clear I was going to be doing all I could to get all the hell out. Nina promised she'd support me and although I could sense concern in my kids' voices nothing was going to change my mind.

The real turning point came on my third day in hospital when I asked to speak to the doctor in charge of the ward. We sat in his office, chatted for a bit and he read my paperwork. Then he came out with it.

"Well, Frank," he said, looking puzzled. "I'm not sure why you are here."

There was a long pause.

"Sorry, sir, do you mind saying that again?" I eventually asked him.

"I'm not sure why you are here," he repeated.

I had to slap myself across the chops to make sure I wasn't going doolally.

Finally. *Finally*, after more than 48 hours of telling people I didn't need to be locked up, someone was agreeing with me. It felt great.

"So I can go home then, boss, yeah?" I asked, jumping to my feet.

"Er, not quite, it doesn't work like that I'm afraid, Frank," he said. "Sit down for a minute. You've been detained here at the hospital under Section 2 of the Mental Health Act.

"That means that although there is concern for your health it is possible you could go home if you agree to take medication at home and be monitored by doctors."

"No worries, boss, let's do it," I said, jumping to my feet.

"It's not that simple, Frank," he said. "The only way you can do that is to get yourself a solicitor and ask for a tribunal hearing at the hospital."

"You what?" I shouted.

The doctor explained it was like a court case and a solicitor would need to explain why hospital was the wrong place for me to be. Then it would be up to the doctors to make a decision.

There was one problem though. I had to stay in hospital for at least seven days before they would even think about listening to anything a solicitor had to say. If I was really unlucky it could take weeks.

"Weeks!" I yelled as the doctor laid out the scenarios. "But you said there is nothing wrong with me."

I couldn't get my head round it. This guy, who was supposed to be in charge, was saying I was fine and didn't need to be in hospital. Yet no-one could unlock the door and let me go home. What was going on?

Once again I could see my liberty being taken out of my hands and it hurt like hell. Sensing my anger was growing, the doctor handed me a list of numbers for solicitors other patients had used in the past.

"He's the best," he said, pointing to a name at the top. "Ring him and arrange for him to come and see you. In the meantime, Frank, take your medication and take things easy. We're going to move you to a room with a window. Try to rest up. If you are lucky, then you won't be in here any longer than a week, but I can't make you any promises."

"Thanks, boss," I said, feeling the first flutter of hope.

Fair play to the fella, he was the first doctor I'd come across inside Basildon who seemed interested in helping me. It would have been nice if someone had explained exactly what a Section 2 was when I arrived. But nobody seemed to give a toss – that's how it came across to me at the time.

As I returned to my room, passing other patients on the way, I decided that the doctor meant well by saying I should rest, but after that meeting lying down was the last thing on my mind. I felt like I had something to focus on and something to fight for at last.

So that's what I went about doing. I contacted the solicitor he had recommended and I tried to play nice. I stopped being such a pain for the nurses, complaining about being locked up. Deep down, I knew none of it was their fault and that they were doing their job. My mum had always brought me up to show respect for people in authority. So, as much as I hated it, I decided it would be better if I just did as I was told.

From then on, while I waited for my solicitor to prepare for the tribunal, I kept my head down and I followed orders. It could only help my case.

But I was used to that, I had to do it enough when I was growing up. In fact being inside Basildon felt a lot like being a kid.

History was pretty much repeating itself...

...I burst into the world on November 16, 1961, at Hammersmith Hospital weighing in at nine pounds. I say burst in because I was a pretty lively baby, by all accounts.

Mum used to tell me that, as a baby, I would try to smash my way out of my cot. So that aggression and fire which would serve me so well in the ring was in me right from the start. Either that or I was just a little shit.

One thing is for sure, I wasn't the easiest of kids and I know I gave my mum, Lynette, and my dad, Robert, their fair share of headaches.

With two older brothers, Michael and Eddie, and three older sisters, Faye, Angela and Joan, I was always fighting to get my voice heard. I was always battling for a bit of attention. In the end I found it on the streets of

Wandsworth in South London where we all grew up.

By the age of seven I was already in with the wrong crowd, causing problems and being a nuisance. I was given free rein to roam and I made the most of it! My mum was forever getting earache from the neighbours.

Barely a week went by without my folks getting a call about me being in a fight or running riot. I was a bit of a bully on the streets, throwing my weight around and acting like a tearaway. I didn't pick on smaller kids. But if I saw lads my size trying to act like Mr Big Potatoes I would stand up to them. I was big for my age so I could look after myself. And while I struggled in lessons I got an A+ for causing trouble.

During my early days as a pupil at Swaffield Primary in Wandsworth I was in and out of the headmaster's office so often they should have given me my own desk in there. Mum was always up and down the school having to hear the latest horror story about the problems I was causing.

Eventually things came to a head on a school trip to the Houses of Parliament when I got involved in a scuffle with one of the teachers. I had been winding a girl up by trying to use her camera when the teacher came over to grab it and we ended up rolling around on the floor. It was just handbags – nothing major. But it didn't look great.

I was back in the headmaster's office again, this time with mum at my side. But this time there were no second chances.

"We're expelling you, Franklin," the head told me. "We can't have behaviour like that at Swaffield."

I was in tears. But Mum was not in the mood to feel sorry for me. Her face said it all as we went home on the bus. I knew I had let her down badly.

My dad gave me such a hiding. He used an old curtain rod instead of a cane when we'd been really bad. And I got the curtain rod good and proper that night.

I know people now would be horrified but that was just how things were back then, and what happened next was far more painful than that rod.

At the age of 12 I was packed off to Oak Hall in Sussex, a school for problem kids – like the one I had now become. They said it was a "boarding school" when I went there. But to me it felt more like a borstal and I would remain there until I was 16.

It was hard to be separated from my mum and dad. But I knew deep down I needed to go away. I would spend about three weeks at the school, and then go home for weekends.

I thought I was a bit of a bad boy until I rocked up at Oak Hall, but I soon realised I was a pussy. Some of the guys I met had big problems and issues and a lot of anger running through their veins. They wouldn't think twice about stabbing you at night or cracking a baseball bat over your nut if you annoyed them. So I was scared. It was like being in a miniature prison.

The teachers were also very strict. They had to be. There were some dangerous hombres in that place so the staff had to be firm. They ran the place like an Army barracks and I was too terrified of upsetting anyone to play up. I cried a lot in my first few weeks, I couldn't get my head around why my mum had sent me to such a horrible place.

I was bullied terribly in my first year as well. Going to bed at night I had nightmares about it and sobbed myself off to sleep.

There was one kid who was worse than all the others and he singled me out. If I was walking past him in the corridor he would punch me, if I was in the toilet and he passed by he would come in and headbutt me and hold my face to the floor.

In the dining room he would get his teaspoon, put it in his cup of hot tea and hold it against my neck. I'd be screaming at him to stop while all the other kids were just laughing. Then he'd pick his nose and wipe his fingers and bogies all over my food.

He was a couple of years older than me, this kid, he wasn't as big as I was, but he was a nasty, horrible bastard. He was part of a group of about 10 bullies at the school and they all seemed to single one guy out at a time.

I was forced to become his puppet and he used to terrorise me. He would make me go down the shops and nick cigarettes for him and his mates.

I don't know why I didn't stand up to him, but I was scared to death of the bloke and I never confronted him. At night I would lie in bed dreading what might happen the next day.

It was the bullying that pushed me towards boxing. I had already shown an interest in fighting in the months before I was packed off with my tail between my legs to Oak Hall.

Earlsfield Boxing Club in South London was the first place I put on a pair of boxing gloves. My dad had taken me there because he thought some tough love might straighten me out. One of the trainers there, a fella called Mr Levington, had heard all about my reputation as a bit of a bully boy so he wanted to see how I would cope in the ring.

I think he decided I needed to be put in my place a bit. He looked for someone big enough to spar with me but in the end he had to turn to his son Gary, who was five years older than I was.

Not just that, he was an experienced amateur boxer. That first day I got in the ring with him he gave me a hiding. Gary was a southpaw and it was a walkover. He was landing punch after punch on me just for the fun of it, and tears were streaming down my face.

But it didn't put me off. No way – I was back the next night and the night after that. I'd caught the boxing bug.

So when I arrived at Oak Hall I was rabbiting on and on to the PE teacher, John Urwin, about how much I wanted to box. He came up with a training plan for me. Mr Urwin would have me legging it round the sports field wearing a bin liner. I was sweating buckets as I ran for miles and miles. But I felt so free.

John had seen the Olympic judo star Dave Starbrook training in army boots. So he had me doing that, too. I would have to drag two large car tyres behind me as I ran in the boots. Then, when I got back in the school gym, some of the other kids would take turns to throw a medicine ball at my stomach.

The training was great – but all I really wanted to do was fight. Eventually John and the headteacher back then, Allan Lawrence, got me into the local youth club at Heathfield in Sussex when I was 13.

The guy who ran it, Mike Hannington, tried to find someone brave enough to box me. But no-one would. In the end they finally arranged for me to have a fight down at 1970s middleweight star Alan Minter's old club in Crawley.

I was so pumped up when I got down there, but when I walked through the door the kid I was supposed to be fighting took one look at the size of me and said: "Jog on."

Looking back I can't say I blame him too much. I was a young man on a mission. I was finally able to get it all out of my system when I fought a talented amateur boxer called Paul McDonald who was getting a lot of coverage in the local paper.

I had to box him at his club in Claygate, Surrey. But it didn't bother me. I'd have boxed him in a Tesco car park if I had to.

The fight didn't last long. The referee stopped it in the second round and declared me the winner.

But I have to be honest – I was scared to death of getting in the ring the first time. That fear doesn't get any less as time goes on, no matter how many more knockouts you put away in your locker. That's why you will never find me mugging off another boxer. I've got respect for anyone at any level with the bottle to step through those ropes.

That first victory meant I was off and running and I guess I have my old PE teacher John to thank for a lot of what came next.

My love for boxing was born at Oak Hall and it became like a drug. I wanted to build myself up, get myself fitter and be able to defend myself.

As soon as I stepped in the ring I loved the feel of where I was. I buzzed off the competitive nature of the sport, the excitement and the adrenaline I got from training. But more than anything I adored the discipline and the routine boxing offered. And, of course, as soon as I began to excel in the ring those bullies backed right off. Funny, hey?

I had learned an important lesson at a very early age – that boxing could help me to survive and get me through whatever challenges or dangers I might face in life.

Bullies were not the only thing I had to overcome at Oak Hall. I also had to cope with the heartache of seeing my dad slipping away.

He had left the Caribbean island of Dominica in the 1950s but he never found the dream he was looking for in London. He got a job as a warehouseman in a bakery and worked damn hard, but before he could really get his feet under the table there his health went. He had diabetes and he needed to take more and more time off work until, eventually, he became disabled.

It was a big blow to his pride. From the day I was born Dad had suffered terribly with his illness and he was weak and often bedridden when I was growing up.

I idolised him though and despite all his problems he was a wonderful father. He was strict and firm and whenever I gave my mother grief I'd be summoned to his side.

Somehow, despite being so weak, he'd find the strength to lift that curtain rod of his and bring it down on me like the headmaster's cane.

"This is for your own good, Franklin," he'd say. "Now behave for your mother."

Dad hadn't been a well man when I was packed off to Oak Hall and when I came home at weekends I noticed he was becoming more and more frail. On some occasions I had to give him his insulin injections. He had suffered a stroke too and I knew he was dying in front of my eyes so it was hard not to cry as I sat with him.

When I felt myself getting upset I'd pack up my bag and go to the boxing gym down the road. It was a way of getting away from my problems. As ever, boxing and the gym gave me an escape route.

In my fourth year down at Oak Hall, I got called in to see the headmaster. But this time I wasn't being told off.

"I am sorry to tell you your father has died, Frank," he said putting an arm around me. "You must see this as a merciful release from his suffering."

I caught the next bus home and when I walked through the door, Mum was sobbing in her armchair.

"The Good Lord has taken your father," she said to me. "He is out of pain now."

Having to leave Mum behind and go back to Oak Hall was so tough, but I had no choice. It was how the dice were rolling, and I just had to cope with it.

Not having to worry about the bullies so much made things at Oak Hall a little easier but it was still a very lively place with a lot of testosterone flying around every day. The teachers had their work cut out so they made sure we played a lot of sport. Apart from boxing, there was cross country running, football, rugby and athletics.

It got the energy out of us and it calmed us down. There was a purpose to life. You had to get up early, clean your shoes, have a shower, brush your teeth, look smart, be ready for breakfast, go to lessons, listen and work hard. Then, after lunch, you had to go and do it all over again before heading out to play sport.

Out on the field the rules were always very simple – play hard but play fair, and always aim to win. Then it would be dinner and early to bed so you would be able to do it all again the next day. That routine sorted my life out very quickly.

Discipline. Order. Exercise. It was the perfect formula for life.

...As I lay in my room at Basildon Hospital and thought about those days at Oak Hall I knew it was the formula I needed to rely on if I was going to wrestle back control of my own destiny.

Locked up in the hospital, I felt I was being bullied all over again – this time by the system. And I had to fight to get out.

The hardest thing to cope with inside Basildon was that nothing ever changed. Every day was the same. On the dot, at 8am, a nurse would appear at the door and I'd be taken for breakfast. Then I would be given some medication and told to go back to my room for rest. After lunch there would be more medication and it was back to sleep or, if I felt up to it, a bit of exercise outside.

Come the evening, if I wasn't completely out of it, there would be dinner and a bit of TV. Then yeah, you guessed it, some medication before lights out. It was the same for all the patients, as far I could tell.

People might think there was all this incredible nursing going on to help people get back on their feet and to sort out the mess their lives had become, but it wasn't like that at all. From where I was standing, I saw that people were mainly being fed drugs, and most of the time it kept them quiet.

It was a never-ending round of tablets and sleep which the hospital seemed to think was the magic cure for all of the problems everybody had. During the week when I was there, I only saw a doctor for 10 minutes at a time while he was doing his rounds. I'd be asked a few questions about how I felt, some boxes would be ticked, a form would be filled in and then the doctor would disappear.

I didn't always take my tablets. I couldn't cope with the side-effects and a lot of the time when the nurse appeared with the tray I'd pop the pill in my mouth then spit it down the toilet a few minutes later.

The medication was slowing me down and I was in a hurry – a desperate hurry to get out.

Training became my salvation. I tried to base my workouts on my early days in the ring. I was always the first up in the hospital. I'd be awake at first light to do some press-ups on the floor of my room to clear my head. I'd look out the window of my room and, standing there, I would imagine being free. That thought would spur me on and, after breakfast, I'd move outside and jog round the courtyard to work out some more.

On an average day I was doing more than 4,000 press-ups. It felt good to work up a sweat. It focused my mind and put me on a level.

A couple of times I played football with some of the other patients. It was the first time since I'd arrived I saw any of them smile.

What struck me most about the other patients I was in with, was how different their stories were.

There was one young lad, still in his teens, who had spent most of his life in care. It had led to him getting involved with drink and drugs and he'd suffered a really bad breakdown. He told me the idea of leaving was more frightening than staying. I couldn't believe what I was hearing.

It made me wonder how many others were trapped in the system like this.

Another patient, I discovered, was a paedophile who had done a long stretch years before. He'd kept his nose clean since leaving prison but then he started acting weird and dodgy. So he was sectioned.

Another patient told me how he'd tried to climb the walls a couple of times in an attempt to escape the place. Like the guy who had tried to attack me with a knife – there were people in the hospital who were clearly a danger to themselves and to others.

The hardest times were at night. As I lay in the dark in my room I would often hear the cries and screams of other patients. One cry would often set off another – like dogs in the night – and I'd pull the pillow over my head so I didn't have to listen.

Sometimes you'd hear banging on the door, then the sound of footsteps as the nurses went off to calm the person down. When I couldn't sleep I'd flick on the light and read the Bible. I prayed to God for the strength to get through it and to come out the other side.

And as each day passed I began to feel stronger. The rest, if nothing else, was helping.

People coming to visit also gave me a huge boost.

Nina was first. Poor Nina. She'd had to watch as they took me away in the back of the ambulance. She'd wanted to come with me but I'd told her not to. I told her this was a fight I had to deal with on my own. I wanted her to focus on her own life, her own business and to do what she needed to do.

I was so embarrassed that she had to see me like this. Part of me worried she wouldn't want to see me again, let alone come to visit me in hospital but as we held hands in the meeting room I realised she was on my side.

Nina got upset and said she was doing all she could to help. I told her about the doctor who'd said he didn't know why I was there and my plans for the tribunal but I could tell she wasn't getting her hopes up.

My children came to see me too – Nicola, who was 29 then, Rachel, 25, and Franklin, 17. That wasn't an easy visit. I love my children dearly and would do anything for them but part of me just didn't want to see them that day. I felt so angry and betrayed that they hadn't tried to stop me being sectioned, but I knew I had to try to listen and understand their reasons.

We sat together in the family room and the kids were in tears. They explained why they had been worried about me and how everyone felt they had no choice but to get the doctors involved. I put my side across firmly and made it clear I was taking steps to try and get out.

There was a look of horror on their faces. This wasn't part of the script. I wasn't supposed to be doing this, but I told them I had to get out. It was all I was focusing on.

After my family had gone home Dave called. News had leaked out to the newspapers about the fact I was in hospital again and he had been receiving calls from everyone. Apparently the papers knew I was there a few hours after I arrived at Basildon Hospital. I wasn't surprised. With all the police cars that had turned up at my house it was a miracle the press hadn't already broken the story.

Dave and I discussed what to do.

"We could say nothing, Frank," Dave suggested. "The press are less aggressive these days. They might just back off."

But I was worried that reporters would end up camping outside my home and banging at the doors of my family and friends. They'd been through that before and I didn't want them all to have to suffer it again – especially Michael with his devastating diagnosis, and my mum who was not getting any younger.

So Dave decided to release a short statement saying I was suffering from exhaustion and had gone into hospital to get better. My lawyers also wrote to all the newspaper editors asking them to give me and my family space. I didn't want any more headlines like last time. All I could do was hope they might listen.

Then, on top of everything else, Dave told me ITV were thinking of not running the interview I'd filmed with Piers due to my illness.

That was the last thing I wanted. I'd got myself into such a state for it. Now there was a chance they were not even going to show the damn thing?! Everything had just turned into a mess. But I didn't have too much time to dwell.

The day after the newspapers ran with the story about me being back in hospital I had the first visit from my solicitor. And he told me the news I had been waiting for – the hospital had agreed to a tribunal.

The date had been set for April 20 which was seven days on from the day I'd been sectioned. The night before the hearing I could barely sleep. I knew within 24 hours I could be a free man again. In the end it would come down to the decision of a bloke in a suit.

On the morning of the hearing I stood there in my crappy room wishing I had a suit to wear myself. I shuffled over to my suitcase and pulled out a clean track-suit. It would have to do.

"You ready, Frank?" said a nurse at the door. I had no idea.

"Come on then," she said, "I'll take you over."

We walked down the corridor and towards the main door that led to the exit. It felt like a ring walk. The butterflies, the nerves, the tension, all of it.

Then there was normality and the sound of real life as we stepped inside a lift in the hospital's main reception.

After a week of being shut away, I soaked it up: people talking, the busy to-and-fro of patients and staff going about their bits and pieces. As we went up the floors, doctors and nurses got in and were saying hello and wishing me well. I was Frank the celebrity again, not the patient.

How long would that last for? I had no idea. The guys ahead of me did though, the ones I could see sitting around a long table in a boardroom as the lift doors opened on my floor. It was judgment time.

I was ready for it though. I was focused, determined and up for the fight. This was what I had been training for in the unit. I wasn't about to let some guy in a suit beat me up.

My solicitor was in my corner. He explained I was unhappy about the fact I had been sectioned. He told them he didn't believe I was a risk to myself or to others on the outside. I was happy, he explained, to go home and take my medication.

They didn't ask me to speak. That peed me off. There was so much I wanted to say. I wanted to ask them who they thought they were – mugging me off and taking me away to hospital but I kept it zipped. I knew where it would get me. In even deeper bother.

The guys in suits seemed to be taking a lot of notes. I wondered where they would go. In a filing cabinet marked "Frank Bruno", I suppose.

That wound me up too. What right did these people have to mark me off as another piece of paper in their fancy offices?

But I knew I had to keep my mouth shut. Eventually they told me to wait outside and I was left pacing outside the room with my solicitor. It felt like the times I'd had to stand in the ring at the end of a fight waiting to see if the referee would lift my arm in the air or my opponent's. As if time was standing still.

I started to feel sick. The thought of staying in that hospital, being locked up in that room, the tablets. Then...

"Frank, come in."

I walked nervously back to my seat.

"All things considered, we agree," said one of the suits. "We believe you should be able to return home, Mr Bruno."

I clenched my fist under the table. Seven days after arriving I was able to go.

"Thanks, sir," I said to my solicitor. "You have given me my life back."

Walking back to my room and collecting my stuff was the best feeling but I wasn't in the mood to hang around and milk it. I chucked my clothes into my case, said my goodbyes to a couple of the patients and I made sure I shook hands with all the nurses.

Then I headed for the exit. It had only been a week since I arrived, but it felt like a lifetime. Nina was waiting for me in the car park and I had never been so relieved to see anyone in my life.

I fell into the passenger seat of her little Volkswagen Polo, wrapped my arms around her and pulled her close. As I did, I spotted an ambulance arriving at the door of the unit. Out came a guy, two nurses either side, struggling to keep him calm.

My heart sank for him. Hospital was his home now but at least I could get back to mine.

I had never been so happy to put my key in the front door as I was that day. As I stepped into my hall I felt good. I knew I had to start again. But I was ready to.

I looked into the garden and saw the pile of grass cuttings which I hadn't had time to pick up on the day I was sectioned. That would need sorting.

A half-drunk cup of coffee was on the side too, a green skin floating around on the top. I chucked the mug in the bin.

I checked up and down the road to make sure there were no press or paparazzi knocking about. When I was released from Goodmayes there were pictures of me arriving home all over the papers. That was the last thing I wanted. But the coast seemed to be clear today. Maybe people were going to leave me alone after all.

The first person I phoned was my mum. I couldn't bring myself to ring her while I was in hospital but I wanted her to know I was out and I was OK.

"I am glad, Franklin," she said. "But you need to rest up now, take things easy, watch what you eat and stay strong."

Mum always had the right words. It may have been years since she had stopped working as a nurse, but she never stopped caring about me.

Then I rang Michael. It was great to hear his voice and we arranged to try and meet up soon. I told him how much I loved him.

Eventually I sank into the sofa and flicked on the television, determined to try and put the last few days behind me and move on. As I flicked through the channels suddenly, there I was, centre stage, in my pink suit.

My Piers Morgan interview was on ITV. They'd screened it after all. My life was playing out in front of me on the day that I was given the green light to leave hospital.

A few hours earlier I was locked up – now I was sitting at home watching myself on the telly. You couldn't make it up, could you?

The camera cut to the kids, there they were, in tears in the audience. Then came the cheers, the applause and the credits. Right at the end, they played a little message as a voiceover said: *"Following the interview we are sad to say Frank has not been well but everyone wishes him better."*

I turned off the TV screen, threw the remote control across the room and held my head in my hands. Nina placed her hand on my shoulder and kissed the top of my head. But it wasn't helping this time.

"That's it then, is it, Frank?" the voice inside my head was saying. *"That's how your life story ends."*

I put my hands over my ears. I was desperate for the dark thoughts to fade away but they weren't going anywhere.

"That's how it all finishes, is it, Frank? Locked up. Again."

I raced out of the lounge, slammed the door behind me and stormed into the dining room. Nina stayed in the lounge, realising I needed some space.

I dragged the two large boxes from the corner of the room and started raking through photos, old newspapers and books on the floor. I came across a scrapbook of my boxing pictures from those early days at Oak Hall. The young man staring back at me on the first page had a look of determination on his face.

Then, as I closed my eyes, the dark thoughts stopped and I allowed my mind to travel back. This is where it had all started. But where and how had I gone wrong?

Chapter 5
I'M GOING TO BE WORLD CHAMPION

As I sat in the dining room at Oak Hall, I listened to what was being said in disbelief. I was 16, there were only a few months of term left and my friends were discussing what they planned to do after leaving school.

Some were openly saying they were going to get involved in crime: sell drugs, rob banks, put a crew together and make some money. Others were boasting of the dodgy deals they already had in place and which were happening on the streets back home where they lived. Eventually my ears couldn't handle any more of it.

"How can you live your life like that?" I snapped. "How can you be happy to spend your days in and out of prison running from the Old Bill?"

"Why would you mug yourself off like that? Where's your self-respect? You have got to have a vision, for God's sake."

The room went silent. Some of them looked at me as if I was nuts.

"OK, Mr Big Shot," one guy asked me. "What are you going to do?"

I didn't hesitate. "I am going to make some money," I replied. "And I am going to become heavyweight champion of the world."

They fell about laughing. I didn't care. I was deadly serious. I would show them: I would have the last laugh.

One person who wasn't smiling when I told her my plan to become a boxer was my mum.

"Why don't you look at training as a doctor or a lawyer, Franklin?" she said desperately. "Anything is possible if you put your mind to it. Please, son, *anything* but boxing." I didn't have anything like the right exam results for that and, in her heart, my mum knew I wasn't cut out for jobs like that. But she was still gutted. Any parent would be, I guess. "Mum," I used to plead with her. "I'm clumsy at football, always fouling. I'm crap at rugby, can't get my head around the rules. I like athletics, but they say I am too heavy boned. I'm pretty good with my fists though." "God help you, Franklin," she'd say, shaking her head from side to side. Mum was worried sick about me getting hurt but my answer to that was always the same.

"Mum, if I don't get hurt in boxing, I might get hurt in life," I'd say. "Boxing is what I do best."

There was plenty of temptation to go in a different direction. Some of my mates back in South London were setting off on the same dark journey as a lot of the Oak Hall lads.

They were getting involved in all sorts of dodgy deals on the street, but it wasn't for me. There were times I quite liked the idea of being a hustler but I was a paranoid kind of kid. My mother taught me good manners and discipline and she always made one thing crystal clear: if I brought the police to our front door that would be the end of me, so I never did.

I wouldn't be able to sleep at night if I was involved in any funny business. I was too much of a pussycat. I may not have had the balls to rob a bank but I did have the balls to get in a boxing ring and slug it out. So that is where I concentrated my mind.

I was not a naturally aggressive lad. But I quickly learned all someone had to do was provoke me and I would react.

Outside the ring, right from the start, I decided I wanted to be a character too, even though I was naturally pretty shy. I liked to have a laugh, and I could get on with anyone. Boxing was a serious sport but I liked to have fun as well and to make people smile.

I was combining boxing with lots of different jobs: a bit of metalwork, a stint in a bingo hall and shifts behind the counter at the Lonsdale sports shop in central London. I was an errand boy, basically.

"Do this, Frank. Do that, Frank. Pick that up, Frank. Collect this. Make the tea. There's a good boy, Frank."

I wanted to earn respect and I knew boxing was where I could get it.

I had left school at 16 a very strong, determined and focused young man and from the moment I joined the Sir Philip Game Amateur Boxing Club in Croydon I felt at home.

It was there, under the guidance of Freddy Rix, a brilliant trainer, I learned the art of boxing and the skills I needed to achieve my dream.

It was tough to find people willing to fight me at first. Even as a teenager I was big, weighing around 15 stone and knocking on for six foot three. So they stuck much older guys in with me. But, despite them having a few years on me, I sailed through the first couple of fights without any problems at all. Easy.

Then I came up against an Irish international called Joe Christie. God, it was a rude awakening – he knocked me to and fro across the ring like I was on a yo-yo. By the end of the fight I thought I was flying easyJet.

But that defeat taught me more than any victory did in my career. It made me see I had a lot to learn and when I got back to the gym I was more determined. My next couple of fights went well, I knocked the guys over like skittles and I could feel my power coming along. I was putting together good basic combinations, but I knew I still had a hell of a lot to take on board.

My fights were being stopped really quickly so I was left with a nagging doubt about whether my chin would cope if someone else gave me the kind of treatment Christie had dished out. I needed to be stretched and to take some punches. And I needed to know if I would cope.

It was around this time I first heard about George Francis who was a big noise in the fight game as one of the top pro-trainers. Amateurs were not meant to train with professionals but I was desperate to get into a proper gymnasium.

George had gyms in three North London pubs: The Butcher's Arms, The Load of Hay and The Wellington. His gruelling runs on Hampstead Heath and early morning swims in the icy waters of Highgate Men's Pond were the stuff of boxing legend.

So when I wandered into the Highgate Gym in 1978 I was a bit in awe of the man. George smiled and guided me to the ring. I went three rounds with one of his fighters. Then, as I stepped out and through the ropes, he barked: "Oi, where are you going, Bruno? You finish when I say."

Three rounds later and I was exhausted. But George got me on the floor doing exercises, then he had me on the bag to check out my power and the speed ball to see how good my reflexes were. I must have done pretty well because he invited me back. I was delighted.

George was training John Conteh at the time who went on to become a real hero of mine. What I loved about John was that he wasn't just a great fighter, he was a real character too. He had a way about him, he was a bloody handsome devil and when he wasn't knocking people out he liked to charm the ladies and make people laugh.

The sessions I had with George really improved me as a boxer. I was still fighting for Sir Philip Game but I knew, eventually, I would end up with George. It was just meant to be. From the start there was a bond between us. What he taught me during those workouts in the gym gave me the confidence I needed to take on Joe Christie again. I was ready to get my revenge.

This time I had to box Joe in his backyard by travelling to the Stardust nightclub near Dublin. I was bricking it going over there and had a lot of nerves as I made my way to the ring, but the fight went well. I'd learned from my mistakes and I was able to take Joe out. I left the Stardust with so much more confidence.

Beating Joe was a real turning point in my amateur career and I was starting to create a lot of noise. Managers and promoters were coming down to check out this new kid called Frank Bruno and I was more than happy to listen to what they had to say.

The person I clicked with more than anyone was a fella called Terry Lawless. I liked his style straight off. I could see he genuinely cared about the boxers he was managing and, as well as offering me advice on boxing, he wanted to offer me advice on life too.

In those early days I was trying to combine working and training and although I was not afraid to graft I knew it was boxing that would really earn me some serious money.

As word spread about me, I wasn't afraid to get my amateur opponents out of the way nice and early in my fights. I looked on the power God gave me in my fists as a gift. So when I stepped in the ring I didn't want to mess around. I wanted to get out of there as quickly as possible.

In the end I won 20 out of 21 amateur fights. The highlight came at the end of 1980 at Wembley Arena when I won the ABA Heavyweight Championship by beating Rudi Pika. I had to be at my very best to out-point Rudi that night. I felt under a lot of stress because people were already trying to offer me all sorts of sweeteners and telling me how much dough I could make when I won and turned pro.

I didn't want to get ahead of myself and tried my best to focus on the fight. I did just enough in the first two rounds, but towards the end of the second I felt a terrible pain in my left hand. I'd broken my knuckle. I was in such pain and so exhausted when the bell went for the third that I could barely throw a punch. Thankfully, Rudi was in the same boat, so I was able to hold on and win the fight.

At 18, I was the youngest ever ABA Heavyweight Champion. I was really proud to have left my name in the history books, particularly when you look at the other outstanding boxers who had landed the title before me. Jack Gardner, Joe Erskine and Brian London had all won it. Oh, and some fella called Henry Cooper also won two titles in the heavyweight division.

If there had been a lot of noise about me before the Rudi fight it was starting to become deafening. A lot of boxing writers were speculating I was a champ in the making.

My brother Michael certainly thought so. On the wall of our kitchen he wrote his prediction: *"Frank Bruno Heavyweight Champion of The World 1986."*

"Blimey, Mike, no pressure then," I said.

But I was dreaming big. I had a bit of money in my pocket for the first time and was even able to buy a proper motor – a Ford Granada Ghia X. I'd always wanted one. It had a great 2.8 litre engine and my mates thought I was the bee's knees.

I was making a name for myself locally, too. I was often being asked to attend charity events in the area where I lived and I was always pleased to help.

One event almost ended in disaster though! I'd been asked to go along to the Cricketers Pub in Hornchurch, Essex, where the regulars had been collecting money for the local hospital. It was all in this massive jar which I was supposed to open on to a sheet as the photographers clicked away. As I tipped it up it just exploded in my hands. My career would have been over if the glass had gone through an artery!

There was lot of natter towards the end of my amateur career about me going off to the Olympics. People often ask me if I regret not going down the same route Anthony Joshua and Audley Harrison did by boxing for Great Britain.

But at that time there was a brilliant Cuban fighter called Teófilo Stevenson who was smashing all Olympic heavyweight contenders around the ring.

Stevenson was the latest off the production line of amazing Cuban amateurs and I turned to Terry Lawless for advice. He warned me to steer clear and said it was too much of a risk against the Cuban fighters and that it would be better for me to move straight into the pro scene. It was good advice. Don't get me wrong, I would love to have a gold medal in my top drawer because there's no prouder Brit than me, but it was the right decision to turn pro in the way I did.

When I did make the move to professional, it was Terry I picked to guide my career. There was no one else that could come close. Under the guidance of him and my then trainer, Jimmy Tibbs, I had the perfect team around me.

I was very close to Terry. Without my dad around, he was a very big influence on my life and when he started to manage me I was able to stop working and fully focus on boxing. Even though I was only just starting out, Terry was always quick to tell me to look to the future.

"Boxing won't last for ever, Frank," he would often say. "Make sure you always have another trick up your sleeve. Your brain can make you as much money as your fists."

They were wise words that I took on board. Mind you, my career was almost over before it begun. When Terry sorted out the paperwork I needed to turn pro we all assumed it would be straightforward – until I had the medical and was diagnosed with a rare form of short-sightedness.

The condition is a weakness of the eye retina which I was warned would only get worse if not sorted out. So I was relieved when David McLeod, the top guy at Moorfields Eye Hospital, said there was a way round it. Problem was, he said, there were only two people in the world who could do the op. In the end I had to travel to Bogota in Colombia where a brilliant professor called José Ignacio Barraquer sorted me out.

The trip wasn't plain sailing though. While I was in Bogota, I got invited to a barbecue and being young, bored and a bit homesick I went along. As soon as I got there I could tell some of the guests were wise guys and hustlers and when word spread around the party about who I was and where I was from I suddenly became the centre of attention.

By the end of the night they'd asked me to take a little package back to London with me – which was actually a very large amount of cocaine for some of their "contacts" there. There was no way that was going to happen so I got out of there before the drugs cartel smashed both my eyes in!

The operation was a success. Doctors being in control of my destiny was already becoming a theme in my life. But now I was all set to focus on making my name as a pro. I won my first 21 professional fights by either KO or stoppage.

Some of them were a bit too easy and I took some stick. I was criticised at times by the fans, by the journalists and by the promoters, but I could only beat the person in front of me and when I stepped into the ring I was programmed to fight one way. I had to take the opposition out. I'm not the sort to keep a fight dragging on. Boxing is not a game to mess about in. You could get a cut, you could get an injury, so my aim was to always try and turn the other guy's lights out as fast as I could.

But I didn't have things all my own way. In October 1983 I had to come through a brutal fight with the American Floyd "Jumbo" Cummings at the Royal Albert Hall. God, what a night that was. It was my first Joe Christie fight all over again.

Cummings was nicknamed Jumbo because he had the build of a bull elephant. He was a man mountain and a mean guy too. When he was 17 he'd been sentenced to 50 years in jail along with three others for shooting a grocer dead during a robbery in Mississippi where he grew up.

Rather like myself, it seemed Jumbo had needed to go away to get his life back on track. He discovered boxing in prison and was eventually released after serving 12 years of his sentence. I'm not sure why he got out so early but he's gone back to prison twice more for robbery since.

When he arrived in London that autumn night in 1983 he was in his prime, pumped up and with his mind focused on one thing – ending all the hype that surrounded my first unbeaten 18 fights. Thinking about it now I can still feel the punch he landed on me in the first round.

I'd spent the opening part of the contest keeping him on the end of my jab. He was trying to box inside and land big shots with his right to my head, but I saw them coming and was able to block them off.

Then, as the first round drew to a close, Jumbo hit me with a clubbing over the top right which caught me clean on the jaw. The elephant had landed.

I'd gone. I may as well have been in Mississippi. The only thing that saved me was the bell – and as it sounded I fell into the arms of the referee Mike Jacobs.

My corner somehow sorted me out in those 30 seconds, and, after a brutal second round, where he had me on the run again, I was able to wrestle back control of the fight.

Eventually, after I knocked him down in the seventh, the referee stopped the fight.

I'd come through my biggest test. Just. It tested my character, it tested my balls. My willpower and my determination were there for all to see. But as I sat on the edge of the ring afterwards I was shattered.

The last thing I felt like doing was giving a TV interview. The BBC usually sent Des Lynam to speak to me. But on this occasion there was a new face, an older guy who was smiling and holding the microphone. He reminded me of one of my teachers at Oak Hall. But when I looked again I could see it was Harry Carpenter.

"That was some punch, Frank," he said. "You did well to recover from it."

"What punch was that, 'Arry?" I shot back, and he smiled.

I liked Harry straight away. You could tell he was a kind, decent and knowledgeable guy. I'd seen him around the boxing scene before that night but I didn't dare go up and talk to him. I was in awe. I had grown up listening to his commentary, so to me Harry was a dude.

But, as we sat there mulling over the fight, all those nerves floated away and I properly loosened up. There were half a dozen "know what I means" which, of course, would go on to become my catchphrase. I'm not sure why that is. I never set out for it to happen that way. It just did. It is simply the way I talk.

From that day on Harry and I became something of a double act but it didn't bother us. Harry was an intelligent guy and we both knew it was good for business. In our interviews he'd play up a little bit and ask me questions which he knew I could be a bit cheeky with.

In a way Harry became as big a part of Team Bruno in those years as my trainers. We spent a lot of time together off camera and he gave me good advice. Not just about boxing, but about living my life the right way outside the ring, and I listened. He became a father figure to me and when Laura and I got married Harry was one of our guests.

After our little chat at the end of the Jumbo fight the newspapers quickly picked up on the Frank and 'Arry story. I couldn't walk down the street without people shouting "Know what I mean, 'Arry?" But that was OK.

Harry was one of many who thought the game was up for me seven months later when James "Bonecrusher" Smith knocked me out at Wembley Arena, giving me my first taste of defeat as a pro. I've never watched the fight back. I've never wanted to, but I can still picture the 10th round. I was miles ahead in the fight, I had been battering him up for the first eight rounds.

What I didn't realise was that Bonecrusher was tiring me out. Then he dropped his bomb and there was no way back.

I was young, I didn't know the tricks, I didn't know how to hold, how to duck and dive or to go down on one knee and take a break. I was too eager to stand there and fight rather than box clever.

"Dear oh dear," Harry said into his microphone as I was helped back to the corner wobbling all over the shop. "Where does this leave the Frank Bruno story?"

When you lose a fight like that, you lose your dignity, you lose your confidence and it can be hard. But the defeat also gave me a huge amount of inspiration. I got back in the gym, practised my jab, practised my power, practised my timing and improved my style.

So when I stepped into the ring with Tim Witherspoon in 1986 for a world title shot I felt ready to lift the belt. I knew the country was willing me on and I felt it was going to be my moment. I sensed my time had arrived. Michael had predicted 1986 and I was going to do my best to make it happen.

There was a lot of talk ahead of the fight about how out of shape Tim was but I didn't listen to any of that. I knew that at his best Tim was a very, very good fighter. He was a dangerous guy. People didn't give him enough credit at the time he was champion and they still don't.

I was far more nervous boxing Tim than I had been in either of my two fights that would come later against Mike Tyson.

The Witherspoon fight was the toughest I ever had, physically and mentally it took me to places I had never been. We slugged it out for 11 rounds and it was a war. By the end I looked like ET gone wrong.

The best man won that night – no question. After the fight I rang Tim to congratulate him but, privately, I was devastated. I wanted to win the World Title so badly that I would do anything to make it happen.

I wouldn't give up. A lot of people were telling me to – but I didn't listen. Others were saying I could do it and that I had to keep going. They were the voices I listened to.

I remember one message I had, from Seb Coe, really moved me. He'd been ringside at the fight and heard me being interviewed and apologising to the country for letting them down.

"You have no need to apologise," Seb said to me. "You performed with pride and courage."

I had so many other people telling me to keep going so I focused on making sure I rested up and came back stronger. It was in the weeks after my defeat to Tim that George became my trainer. Jimmy Tibbs had crossed over to our rival Frank Warren's camp so Terry and I decided George was the perfect man to get things back on track.

"This is the end of the gentle giant," George announced at a press conference in 1987 as I prepared for a tricky comeback fight against former WBA Champion Greg Page.

With George at my side I managed to push forward, winning my next five fights, before I came up against Mike Tyson for the first time.

At that point in 1989 there was a big noise around Tyson. Everyone seemed to be talking about him but he was nothing new to me. I'd first come across Mike when I was 20 and Terry had taken me to the US on a tour of different states in 1981.

We went to places like Arizona, California and Chicago. I sparred with

Mike Weaver at Larry Holmes' camp and we then moved on to spar in the Catskill Gym in New York where Tyson was being guided by the brilliant Cus D'Amato.

Mike was only 16 but he was some fighter even then so I couldn't wait for us to get in the ring for real one day. Little did I know we'd have to wait eight years to get it on.

The whole country seemed to be talking about the fight when I headed out to Vegas and as I walked to the ring that night on February 25, 1989, I felt like I had the nation behind me. I'd waited 16 months for the fight.

Then, 11 seconds after the first bell reality hit – along with an absolute bomb from Tyson which he landed on my temple. I took the count and somehow got back to my feet. The Bonecrusher Smith defeat was at the front of my mind: "Be smart, Frank," I was telling myself. "Stay in this fight."

But as I moved back into the centre of the ring the fighter in me came out and I was attacking Tyson. Within seconds I had given him the shock of his career. He was all over the place when I landed with my left, it was probably the best punch I had ever thrown in my life.

As Mike wobbled the crowd went wild and I moved forward. Suddenly my dream was in sight and I could feel the country urging me on. Harry was too. "Get in there, Frank," he yelled into his microphone from his seat at ringside.

But often it is when you hurt somebody that they are at their most dangerous. As all great champions do, Mike found a way to stay in the fight, and 15 minutes later it was over – my dream had been shattered once again. Unlike in my previous two defeats, though, I had proved the doubters wrong.

For the first time ever, Tyson had been rocked to his boots. After the fight people were saying "maybe Bruno is the real deal after all".

Everyone was talking about Harry too. He took a bit of flak for his commentary but it was no biggie. Harry is just a passionate guy and was only saying what he felt. And there was no doubt we were now sport's biggest double act since Torvill and bloody Dean!

As a result, offers started to arrive from all different angles for me to do adverts and TV work. I was up for a new challenge at this point and before I had time to fart I was on the telly advertising HP Sauce and Kleenex tissues.

Two years running I did panto, first playing the Genie in Aladdin with Michael Barrymore at the Dominion Theatre in London. The punters seemed to like me and I ended up doing lots more stage and TV work alongside some great comics like Les Dawson and Lenny Henry. More about all that later.

At that time I got a lot of stick about the work I was doing from the media and other boxers, but I didn't care. I was doing exactly what Terry had advised me from the start – keeping my options open.

I knew that boxing was not going to be there all the time and that I had to think long term. I needed to make sure I could duck and dive and earn a crust. The British public seemed to like me and I wasn't about to turn up my nose at popular entertainment.

Boxing was still my number one priority and becoming a world champion was still the thing that got me up each morning.

Recovering mentally from the Tyson defeat wasn't my only challenge though. Once again my destiny was back in the hands of the doctors when I underwent a medical ahead of my comeback fight against John Emmen in 1991.

Professor McLeod dropped the bombshell that I had a tear in my right retina. The newspapers got hold of the story and everyone was saying it was all over for me.

Even after the operation went successfully the big cheeses at the Boxing Board of Control made me go and sit in a tribunal to decide if I could carry on boxing. For three hours they fired questions at me.

My solicitor Henri Brandman did the talking and, by the end, I was bricking it, but they gave me the thumbs up to fight. If they hadn't I would never have gone on to become a world champion.

My next chance to do that came against Lennox Lewis in 1993. Ahead of the fight there was a lot of trash talk which I always tried to avoid. He was mugging me off saying I should stick to dressing up in girls clothing and mocking me for the time I had spent in panto.

And then there was all the talk of me being an Uncle Tom. I blew my top and said I wanted to call in the lawyers. Things calmed down in the end and Lennox later withdrew the insult, but for the first time ahead of one of my fights I had a really bad feeling. I was pumped up and raging before the contest.

I'd wanted it to be at Wembley but for some reason we had to fight at Cardiff Arms Park. We eventually stepped into the ring at 1am, so the American viewers could watch us fight, but I had never felt as ready in my life. I wanted to ram the trash that had come out of Lennox's mouth back down his throat.

The first three rounds went like a dream. I felt like I was getting stronger with each passing minute and hurting Lennox. By the sixth I could hear in his breathing that he was tiring – the title seemed to be within my reach.

In the following round I was finishing him off, he was against the ropes and all the punches I threw were landing. One more haymaker and it would be all over.

But the outcome of a fight can change in a heartbeat and as we tangled we were pulled apart by the referee and Lennox landed with a left. It was a sensational punch. I knew that straight away. I was all over the place. Punches were coming at me from all directions and just 20 seconds later the towel was in. It was all over. Again.

That defeat was the hardest of all to take. In the days after so many people were telling me to retire. Laura, the kids, my mum; they all wanted me to walk away.

"Frank, it's over..." they were saying. "It's time to go home."

But I had to stand and fight. I had to keep going. It was my destiny to be a champion.

When the night finally arrived in September 1995 I knew it was probably my last chance. I was nearly 34 and there were a lot of other hungry fighters out there.

I sensed that most people believed Oliver McCall would beat me at Wembley. After all, he'd knocked Lennox out within a round. A lot of so-called experts had said that had been a lucky punch but McCall won fair and square.

He was a dangerous opponent. I knew all about him though. He was my sparring partner when I was training for the fight against Tyson and

I liked Oliver.

That's why I was so shocked at what came next. In the press conference ahead of fight night he threatened vengeance for what my friend Nigel Benn had done to Gerald McClellan in London six weeks earlier. The American had been counted out and then collapsed and fell into a coma that left him in a wheelchair.

It was an awful thing to say. The Benn vs McClellan fight had shocked the country and the entire boxing world.

After all the talk about retiring and needing to quit, it put my family on edge in the run-up to the fight but I blocked it all out. I focused purely on keeping my head down at my training camp in Leicestershire.

I wasn't going to blow my chance. There would be no mistakes this time. I knew from my time sparring with McCall that he wouldn't be able to live with my jab so I worked on that and on my discipline. To become a champion I needed to box clever. I had to make sure my heart didn't overrule my head this time.

As I stepped into the ring that night I had 30,000 fans in my corner and I needed every one of them, especially when I sat on my stool at the end of the first round with my right eye a total mess.

McCall had caught me with his glove and badly damaged my eyeball. I didn't know it then but my retina had become detached. Again!

Thankfully I was the only one who could feel the pain and there was no blood. I was not pulling out. If I had to win the fight with one eye I would. That's how badly I needed it, that's how badly I wanted it.

Nine minutes in and I knew I was well ahead in the fight but I hadn't properly hurt McCall. That all changed in round four when I landed a perfect overhand left which saw McCall reeling.

I wanted to pile in. Finish the job. But I held back. I kept my discipline. I didn't want to blow myself out. I told myself to keep using my jab, to keep boxing and to hold my nerve.

By the tenth round I knew I just had to survive to be champion. Yeah, just survive – I was so far ahead that McCall knew only a knockout would do. He was throwing everything at me, and my right eye was hurting like hell and blinking like a headlight with a dodgy bulb.

Round 11 felt like it lasted for ever. It was his strongest round and

George was screaming at me not to throw it away. Nigel Benn was on his feet seemingly feeling every punch that landed from McCall. After what he had said about McClellan perhaps this fight was personal for Nigel, too: nobody was willing me on more.

The crowd lifted me so much as I returned to my corner at the end of the 11th.

"Three minutes," screamed George.

Three minutes and I'd be on top of the mountain. Three minutes until I delivered on my promise in the dining room at Oak Hall. Three minutes until my destiny arrived.

We touched gloves. McCall had to knock me out to win. Somehow he seemed to be even stronger. How was that possible? Everything seemed to happen in slow motion as the punches rained in from all angles.

The atmosphere inside Wembley was electric – the shouting from my fans was deafening. But I kept focused. I held on. I could hear him gasping for breath. There was still time for more one onslaught, one more attack. But nothing was going to stop me that night. Nothing could hold me back.

When the bell rang there was pandemonium. Everyone was jumping on top of me.

I'd done it. I'd finally done it. The tears rolling down my cheeks were ones of happiness and of relief. Now, when I think back on it, I know nobody can take that moment at Wembley away from me.

A lot of people said later that I should have walked away at that point and quit while I was on top. It was tempting to go out on a high there and then, but to get the fight with McCall I had to promise my first defence to Mike Tyson.

I wasn't about to go back on my pledge. Champions don't go around acting like that. I was good to my word. Plus, the truth is, I wanted one final big payday for my family.

I wanted to be well-rewarded if the Tyson bout proved to be my final fight.

Of course, in the end, that's just how it turned out. Mike Tyson ended my career in less than 10 minutes on March 16, 1996.

I've never watched the fight back. Why would I? I don't stop to look at car crashes. As I got out of the ring that night in Las Vegas it was the end. The defeat to Tyson had left my right eye a mess. I had suffered a detached retina and there was no way the doctors were going to let me back in the ring again.

So I was forced to announce my retirement from the sport on my return to London. The fact injury had led to me having to call it a day eventually drove me to the point of despair. But as I sat down at the press conference that day I was trying to stay upbeat.

"I am going to be happy," I said to the media. "I am going to get a suntan here and there, use my Black & Decker here and there, just chill out with my family."

As I sat and said goodbye my mind flashed back to that day in Oak Hall when I had vowed to become a champion. I'd done it. *I'd had the last laugh.*

There was just one more goodbye to say – to George. He'd been there at the start and he was there at the end. Now he was putting his arms around me and whispering in my ear.

"Take care, Frank," he said, pulling me in tight. "And remember – the fight starts now, fella, it starts now."

"What you on about?" I said. "It's all over now, George. It's all over."

George just fixed me with a stare. He'd been trying to warn me about the battle ahead, but as I kissed him on the top of his head and made my way home I wasn't interested.

After all I was Frank Bruno. And nothing life could throw at me next was going to knock me down. At least that's what I thought then.

Chapter 6
RUNNING FROM MY LIFE

When you have been sectioned, most days back in the outside world start the same: feeling thankful that you are waking up in your own bed. Thankful that you are free. Thankful that you are able to walk down the stairs without the hand of a nurse on your shoulder.

That's why, from the day I got out of Goodmayes Hospital, my favourite time of day was always first light when I could stand in my own kitchen, drink a cup of tea and look out the window. But, coming home from Basildon was a little different.

That first morning back home I was so edgy the ticking of the clock in my hall woke me up. Nina had stayed over, but I still felt acutely alone. I pulled the duvet tightly up to my chin and stared at the ceiling.

Inside Basildon Hospital I had prayed night after night to be able to lie in my own bed again. Now, less than 12 hours after being released, I felt as if the world was closing in on me. I was out – but it felt like the clock was ticking on how long my freedom would last.

As I lay in my bed I couldn't help thinking how freedom was not supposed to feel like this. Then the mobile phone on my bedside table started going bananas about the Piers interview from the night before.

A text from Dave said that four million people had watched it. "It's a blinding number, Frank, much more than ITV had expected," he wrote, with his agent's hat on. "We've had more than 1,500 emails this morning already."

But when I flicked on Twitter I could see it wasn't all positive. All anyone was talking about was the fact I was ill again. I'd been on the box for nearly an hour talking about my life yet the chatter was mostly about the few seconds at the end of the credits.

My condition was plastered all over the papers too. There were so many headlines:

"BIG FRANK BACK IN HOSPITAL"

"WILL FRANK EVER FIND HAPPINESS?"

"SAD NEW LOW FOR FRANK"

My heart sank as I looked at them. I glanced at the scrapbook that told the story of my career, which I'd fallen asleep reading. It was clear that my being sectioned was going to be the new chapter.

"Damn it," I muttered under my breath.

These were the kind of newspaper stories I hoped I'd left in the past when I was sectioned in 2003. But it wasn't my only problem. The newspapers, my fans, the general public, all the people talking on Twitter didn't have a clue I'd been released from Basildon.

Dave had kept the decision of the tribunal private so only my nearest and dearest knew I was back home. As far as the man on the street who'd seen the papers was concerned, I was on the floor again.

Everything I had said to Piers about staying on the straight and narrow, everything I had said about staying out of hospital, everything I had said about moving forward was in tatters. Comeback? Forget it. I was back to square one.

I glanced out my bedroom window and could see a huddle of what looked like newspaper reporters gathered at the end of my drive. How did they always seem to know what was going on before everyone else? I pulled the curtains and sank back down on to the bed.

As soon as I stepped out the front door and news broke I was home the talk would start. I knew what people were going to say: they would be dissing me for checking out of hospital after a week. They would say I was running away from my troubles. Everybody's eyes would be on me. It didn't feel nice. No, that first morning back home my head just didn't feel right and rather than being ready to start again I was full of anger.

The medication the doctors had sent me home with – strong doses of lithium – was leaving me feeling anxious too. The doctors said that this was one of the side-effects and, my God, they were right. I was on edge, paranoid and highly suspicious.

But it wasn't just the drugs making me feel like that. I was angry and frustrated by the fact I was no longer fully in control of my own life. The agreement my solicitors had made with the medics at Basildon was I'd allow doctors to come and see me regularly at home to make sure I was taking my medication. The moment I stopped playing ball they could haul me back in.

So I knew the stakes were high – and the doctors were holding all the cards.

Despite all that, I was still taking risks, because I couldn't bear being told what to do by those guys.

Sometimes, in those days after my release, when the doctors turned up I'd hide upstairs and refuse to open the door. Other times when they arrived I'd grab my car keys and pretend I was on the way out.

I was making as many excuses as I could to not have to see them. I simply didn't like letting them into my territory, even though I knew I was playing a dangerous game.

I also knew my illness was not only taking hold, it was getting worse. I didn't dare admit to anyone what was going inside my head or how bad I was feeling. I was terrified that if I did, I'd be taken back to hospital. It was a vicious circle.

The only person I told was Nina, but she already knew how badly I was struggling. The way I was feeling was written all over my face. OK, there weren't any cuts and bruises but I still looked beaten up.

"Your eyes don't look right, Frank, what's on your mind?" Nina would say to me again and again during those first couple of days back home.

"The same thing, Nina," I told her, holding my head in my hands. "I don't know who the hell I can bloody trust any more. It's all such a mess."

Nina encouraged me to get out, to get some fresh air and to get moving but I didn't want to leave the house. I may have been out, I may have been free, but I was determined to stay hidden. Life felt much easier living in the shadows and being invisible.

But that's no way to live and it took its toll. Before long being stuck inside my own four walls started to become unbearable.

After a few days Nina had to go back to Scotland to look after her business so I was on my own and that just made things worse. Whenever a car pulled up at the gates I'd be looking at the CCTV cameras to make sure it wasn't an ambulance. If the doorbell rang I'd jump out of my skin. I was forever thinking: "Here we go again."

I'd walk slowly to the door and always look through the spy hole before letting anyone in. I was convinced everyone arriving was a copper with a doctor in tow. I felt under attack.

I phoned my kids pretty soon after getting out of hospital. They already knew I was out. I guess the doctors must have told them. They were surprised, maybe a bit angry, and definitely concerned. That really put me on edge. My feelings of paranoia were going through the roof.

The kids thought I had left hospital way too soon but I didn't want to discuss it. When the subject came up I tried to close it down. I made it clear I wanted to get on with things and not look back, but really I knew the threat of being put back in hospital was never far away.

I tried to make plans. I phoned my agent to see if any work had come in. But he told me it was too soon for that. He advised me I needed to rest up, to take my medication and just get myself better.

"That is all that matters now, Frank," he insisted.

But the lithium they were giving me, the "magic" stuff that was supposed to be making everything OK again, wasn't helping.

It was only making me feel more paranoid and more anxious as the days went by. It was slowing turning me into a zombie. A lot of the time I couldn't even speak properly. I'd be slurring my words and dribbling down my chin. I rarely went out. I went nowhere near the gym because, for the first time in years and years, I didn't feel like I had any energy to train. The tank was totally empty.

I was also worried that if I went to the gym I wouldn't be able to make myself stop and I'd end up caning it like the days leading up to the Piers Morgan interview. So I stayed away and spent long periods hiding away at home instead. When friends and family begged me to get some more help I shrugged it off and insisted I was fine.

"I'm not mad," I'd say. "It's everyone else giving me a hard time."

The truth was I was struggling with the tablets the doctors were making me take. It took me four or five days to pluck up the courage to go outside the front door for the first time, and even then I only forced myself to because I needed some milk.

It was the middle of spring but I put a bobble hat on and pulled it down over my ears: I didn't want anyone to see me like I was. I felt sick to the stomach as I pulled out the drive in my car. I'd worked out the nearest place I could go for groceries was the petrol station.

As I pulled into the garage there were cars everywhere. It was the last thing I needed. I put my handbrake on and waited until a parking space became free by the entrance then I quickly parked up and dashed inside.

The line of people queueing at the checkout sent my heart racing.

"That's Frank Bruno, isn't it?" I heard someone whisper.

Normally I'd have turned round for a chat, but I wasn't interested. I nearly jumped out my skin when someone tapped me on the shoulder.

"Frank, how are you doing, mate," a guy said. "How you feeling?"

I recognised the geezer straight off. He was an old boy who I'd always talk to when I popped in to fill up the car. But I wasn't in the mood for talking today.

"Not too bad, thank you very much," I lied, walking away.

Then there was another couple of fellas waiting for a word.

"Any chance of a photo, Frank?"

"Not today, guys, if you don't mind," I told them.

I just wanted to get home. The world was becoming increasingly dark, meaningless and lonely. And as the days went by, the clock – the countdown to my next loss of liberty, seemed to be ticking faster and faster.

The next crisis wasn't long coming. I remember so clearly the moment I knew I had to get away.

I had been back home for six days and I was having a shave in the bathroom. I looked in the mirror and as I leaned in I was thinking: "That ain't me, that ain't me all."

The man staring back looked about 100 years old. I was shocked by what I had become. My brain was working but not much else was. I knew I had to do something and I needed to be anywhere but at home.

I threw the razor in the sink, raced back to my bedroom, grabbed a suitcase from the top of the wardrobe, threw my clothes inside and packed up the car.

It was my idea to go to Scotland. I needed to get away from the bad vibes and the phone calls. I felt as if my family were on my case and that I was being judged all the time. They were only showing concern but I'd convinced myself everyone just wanted me back in hospital.

I knew it would not go down well with them but I had to get away. Nina drove down and helped me gather up my stuff. When I rang my GP to tell him about my plan I could tell he wasn't that happy.

He said he would make the team in charge of my care aware and he insisted I made sure I left contact details so they could get hold of me whenever they needed me. I felt like a child. I knew if I started to play up I would be in all sorts of bother, but all that mattered was getting away. As we pulled out the drive I felt so relieved. I hoped I was leaving my troubles behind me.

I thought going to Glasgow to see Nina would be a chance to start again. I could take a break and regroup and find a way forward through the fog. As we drove north, Nina and I talked about what had happened in hospital and how things were now going to get better.

"I am going to take less work on, be kinder to myself, take my medicine, rest and regroup – and then I will come back stronger," I said to Nina.

By the time we pulled up at her place I felt as if the weight of the world had lifted off my shoulders at last. Nina had a nice little place in a tower block in the Gorbals area of Glasgow.

The area was rough and ready – but I felt at home. I'd grown up on tough streets after all. The neighbours seemed a bit surprised when I parked up the red Bentley and took out my suitcase though. I saw them looking through the windows, but to me it was no biggie. I was where I wanted to be.

It wasn't long before I was bombarded with phone calls from family and friends frantic with worry about how I was and what I was doing. That put me on edge again. Why wouldn't people give me some space?

In the end I lied and said I was somewhere I wasn't and that I was staying with some friends because I just wanted to be on my own for a bit. It wasn't the smartest thing I've ever done but I needed to get away from all the negative vibes. It was my way of shutting myself off from any more grief or stress. I didn't handle things well, I can see that now, but at the time it was the only way I could cope with the way my illness was making me feel.

For the first couple of days things were great in Scotland and I started to feel a lot better.

Nina would go off to work at her hair salon in the day and I would just rest up in the flat, watching films and trying to get myself back together. I'd go for walks and was finally able to enjoy being free again.

I tried my best with the medication but I couldn't cope with it. The tablets were knocking me out, making me feel drowsy, frustrated and slow. I'd always been so driven, so active. Now I was becoming everything I hated to be. So in the end I stopped taking them and decided I was just going to get out a bit more and do my own thing.

I had started to miss training so I made myself go over to my old mate Alex Morrison's gym in the East End of Glasgow. I rang ahead and he said he would be delighted to see me. It was nothing heavy at first, just some weights and a bit of running.

His fighter Ricky Burns was getting ready for a world lightweight title fight and it was nice to be around boxing again for a bit.

But the phone calls from home were never far away and they were becoming more and more regular. I felt as if I was being monitored all the time – and the questions never seemed to stop.

"Dad, where are you? What are you doing? When are you coming back?"

"Why have you got the phone on loudspeaker?" I'd snap back. "Tell me who else is listening?"

In my mind I could picture them all standing in the lounge, with a doctor, writing down notes. Yeah, I was being paranoid, but I couldn't help how I felt in my head.

All everybody wanted, as far as I could see it at that time, was me back in hospital. The hands on the clock in my head seemed to be ticking like crazy – how long had I got before I ended up there again?

Then things just started getting out of control.

One morning, when I didn't feel like going to the gym, I decided to do some press-ups on Nina's balcony. It was a beautiful day, I had my top off and my shorts on enjoying a bit of sun on my back.

Nina had this big tree trunk on the balcony which she had taken from a cottage she owned and she used it as a little seat. So I started to bench press it over my head.

A few seconds later I saw a couple of paparazzi clicking away on their cameras down in the car park. Shit! They were here already. Where had they come from – and who had told them I was here?

I went inside and slumped on to the bed. I was being followed by the press again. Why wouldn't people just leave me alone?

Then, sure enough, a couple of hours later my agent rang. The papers had been on saying they had pictures of me looking like Tarzan, holding a tree trunk over my head and walking around a housing estate in Scotland with my top off.

They were apparently saying I'd been paying the kids on the estate to guard my Bentley while I was in town. It was a load of rubbish – but why let a little white lie get in the way of a good story?

Just days after persuading doctors I should be allowed out of hospital I knew how it would look: *Mad old Frank wandering around Scotland like a lunatic.*

When the story appeared in the paper the next day, albeit with a kinder headline, my phone was ringing non-stop.

"You need to come home," my family and friends were telling me. "We're worried about you. What's going on?"

A lot of people were leaving comments on social media saying the real reason I had gone to Scotland was because I knew the laws were different and that I knew I couldn't be sectioned up there. That wasn't true. I just wanted to have the break that I should have had before the Piers interview and I simply wanted to be with my girlfriend for a bit. But aggro was starting to come at me from all angles.

There were calls from the doctors back in Bedfordshire too. They were worried, especially when I admitted I wasn't taking my medication every day.

"Some days I do," I told them. "But it's spacing me out." They insisted I go and see a doctor straight away so Nina arranged for an appointment with her GP, but I was just sent off with a load more lithium and sleeping pills. It seemed to me that all anyone wanted to do was drug me up and slow me down. They were determined to press pause on my world, while all I wanted was to get on and live.

I couldn't see how people were trying to help me. In the end the calls and the stress just became a burden so, when the phone rang, I just ignored it. I felt as if my every move was being monitored. It was horrible.

Taking my medication on and off really started to mess with my head too. My body didn't know if it was coming or going half the time. Less than a week after arriving in Glasgow it started to have a bad impact on the way I was behaving.

I had some terrible rows with my agent on the phone. I told him I was thinking of moving up to Scotland for good and letting Nina run the business side of things.

"Frank, you are not thinking straight," he'd say. "I'm worried about you."

I was doing some odd things too that were totally out of character. For instance, I was driving around in the Bentley with the windows down and music up full blast, waving at people as I drove past. It was totally out of character. I prefer to keep my head down when I am out and about in the car. I even treated myself to a cigar one afternoon and smoked it out the window as I went for a drive out to the countryside. I don't know why I did it. Looking back now I can see I wasn't myself. And it wasn't long before everyone else started to see it too.

The papers picked up on where I was straight off and were writing stories saying I was getting out of control and that someone needed to help me. I was bringing heat down on myself.

Then things got a hell of a lot worse. One afternoon, to get away from all the pressure, Nina and I went out for the day to Loch Lomond, a stunning spot in a national park.

As we were returning home a police car was suddenly alongside us and a copper was demanding we pull over. I parked up the car and looked in my wing mirror to see this young PC talking into his radio. Tears welled up in Nina's eyes. My mind flashed back to the morning near my home when the policeman thought I had stolen the Merc I was driving.

"What the hell is going on now?" I said to Nina before I got out of the car and walked over to the officers.

He seemed to be talking for ages into his radio before he looked up.

"Frank, we've had a call from someone back home," the officer eventually said.

"There's been some concerns expressed for your safety. You need to go to the nearest police station. Right now."

I couldn't believe what I was hearing.

"Who has called? What's happening here?" I asked. "Why can't people just leave me alone?"

"Frank, we are only doing our job," he said. "Why don't you follow me in?"

On the way to the police station Nina got a call from her son on her mobile. Unable to find me at her flat, the Old Bill had turned up at his place in Glasgow, like they were on some sort of drugs raid, to try and speak to me.

"We've got to get this sorted, Nina," I muttered. "We can't keep living looking over our shoulders like this all the time."

I felt as if the world was quickly closing in. When we got to the police station I was scared as I walked in, worried they were not going to let me go.

The sergeant came over and led Nina and I into a little interview room and closed the door. I glanced up at the wall. There was a wanted poster for a guy they were hunting over a shooting in the city. Underneath was a picture of a teenage kid who had been missing for weeks.

What was I doing here? I was an adult. I hadn't hurt anyone. Why couldn't people stop sticking their noses into my business?

"Frank, there have been some concerns about you," the sergeant said. "We have had some phone calls and I need to make sure you are OK."

The police officer explained how calls had gone into the doctors back home from my family and a member of my management team. They were worried I was going to do something stupid. So the police had been called and the message had gone out to officers in Glasgow to find me straight away.

As I listened the anger was bubbling up inside. Why should I have to live my life like this? As I sat there I was getting more and more irate and I had to tell myself to hold it all together.

"Listen," I eventually said. "I don't know how many times I have said this now to everyone but I will say it again and I will say it slowly. *I. Feel. Fine.*

"I am not finding my medication very easy to cope with but – look, I just want to go home. Please. I don't want to cause anyone any grief or headaches."

The policeman stared at me for a bit and then excused himself and left the room.

"I'm not getting out of here, am I, Nina?" I said to her as we waited. She put her hand on mine and looked to the floor.

Then, as I stood up, the policeman came back in with a load of paperwork.

"OK, Mr Bruno, I am happy to let you go," he said. "You seem OK to me and I have passed that message on."

He looked a bit embarrassed by the whole thing – but that didn't stop him and about seven of his police colleagues asking to have their photo taken with me.

I was still reeling from what had happened and they were asking me to pose nicely and say cheese.

Twenty minutes earlier I thought they were about to section me. Now I was being asked to smile for the camera. I agreed. What else could I do?

As we walked out of that police station I'd come to realise that I had to go home. I couldn't ignore the ticking of that clock in my head. I couldn't keep running. Things couldn't carry on as they were so Nina and I travelled back to my place in Bedfordshire the following day.

I stood in the hall, taking it all in. Everything looked just the same, and so were the problems I'd tried to pack away into my suitcase.

Ignoring the familiar sinking feeling, I got changed and started getting ready to head off to a charity event I had promised to attend in Gravesend, Kent. I was going to be guest of honour, starting a running race at an athletics track where they wanted me to shake hands with the local mayor.

I told Nina that I had to call in on the kids on the way home to see my son Franklin for his birthday. She warned me to stay away, that it wouldn't be a good idea, but I wasn't listening. I can be stubborn and I wasn't in the mood to be told what to do.

So I went round to see my kids later that day and we had a row. I was upset, emotional and all the anger that had been building up in me over the past few weeks came out.

I was still shaking with anger when I got home. Nina gave me a look that said I should have listened to her, but it was too late for that. So I went into my spare room, put my music on loud and closed my eyes.

When the doorbell rang three hours later I knew who would be standing on the porch.

I knew it would be the Old Bill. And I knew my world was about to collapse again.

I let the police sergeant in. He said he was from down the road in Dunstable and he seemed to me like a reasonable guy. We sat down in the kitchen and I made a cup of tea for him and the copper with him.

With a pained expression on his face, he said: "Frank, we are here because there has been a concern raised about you and we have been asked to wait here while you are assessed by the doctors."

I heard the words but they washed over me. I started to get angry.

"What's going on?" I asked. "What the fuck have I done? I'm just trying to get on with my life."

"Frank, it's nothing to do with us," he said. "We have to do this by law."

Then three doctors pulled into my driveway.

"I don't want you in my house," I yelled through the door. "Go in the garden and I will talk to you there."

They were firing questions at me:*"Where had I been that day and how was I feeling? Was it true I was no longer taking my medication? Could I tell them the time?"*

It was a load of rubbish but I listened carefully. I was trying to be coherent. I was answering the questions slowly.

I knew they would be looking for any sign that I should be put in an ambulance and taken away again. The questions were so ridiculous – like could I tell them what day of the week it was? – that at one point even the sergeant laughed.

Straight away I stopped the conversation and said to him: "Officer, do you know these people have come to section me? Laughing at them isn't going to help me. This is my life."

He looked to the floor. It was the closest I'd come to crying since the doorbell rang. Eventually they finished their questions, then they said they needed to have a chat with the people back in their office.

As they stood in a circle deciding what was going to happen to me I went off to the garden and mowed the lawn. I don't know why, it just took my mind off the nightmare that was coming alive in front of my eyes.

Running did cross my mind but I knew it made no sense and being chased by the Old Bill doesn't look good on the CV.

I knew I had to stand and take whatever was coming like a man. From the lawn I could see Nina was speaking to the police and begging them to intervene so the doctors couldn't take me away again, but in the end they just stopped listening and started filling out their paperwork.

The longer it went on the more tense and stressed I became until, eventually, I turned off the mower and went back inside to confront them all.

"What the hell is going on?" I shouted. "Are you taking me away again or what?"

One of the doctors was just about to answer when I saw an ambulance in the distance coming down the hill. I kidded myself it might drive past my house, that it might be for someone else and that I would be all right.

Then it stopped outside my gate and I realised that Nina was punching the pass code into the security system so the driver could come in. I knew she had no choice.

The ambulance pulled into the drive, and the hands on the clock were about to stop. Again.

Chapter 7
ZOMBIE

I'm down on the floor and my face is pressed against the tiles. It is icy cold. I can move my eyes but I can't move my legs.

Where's George? He's normally here by now to lift me off the canvas, get me up on my feet and back to the corner of the ring.

"Thirty seconds," he'd scream in my ear, then squeeze that sponge in my face. It would bring me back to life and ready for the next round.

But George isn't coming. There is only darkness. It's quiet too: no-one is shouting at me to get up and no-one is willing me to stand. Then, finally, the silence is broken.

"Frank," says a voice. "Frank, you need to get up."

Oh the relief. It's George. He's there after all, he's always there. Good old George - I knew he wouldn't let me down.

But no, wait, who's pulling on my arm? And who's grabbing at my leg? George would never do that.

I can hear footsteps now. And I can see three people round me in a circle. Who are they? I narrow my eyes and try to focus. That's when I see the bed in the corner. Why's that there? Where's the stool?

"Jesus, we can't leave him here," says one of the voices.

Then one of them is right down on the floor with me and I can feel his warm breath against the side of my face.

"Frank, we need you to get up," he says. "We need you to get moving."

But I can't shift. I'm starting to get scared now. What if I never move? What if this is the end?

There's a bigger crowd of them, five at least, and they're all coming towards me now – all as one. Then they're pulling me up. Finally I am on my feet.

"Take it easy, Frank, steady," they say.

And they're guiding me, step by step. Then I'm down, on my back, on my bed and the nurse is whispering in my ear again.

"You need to sleep, Frank." she says pushing a glass of water at me. "You need to take them, Frank," putting the tablets in my hand.

"Oh, please God. No..."

I gulp them down, then everyone has gone, the door locks and there's only darkness. And I've no idea when I will see the light again.

Every now and again, flashbacks to moments like that haunt my dreams. Thankfully, these days, the nightmares are few and far between.

I thank God they are, because they take me back to the most terrifying time of my life.

The time, in May 2012, when I spent five weeks banged up in St Andrew's Hospital in Northampton. I say banged up because it was like being inside prison.

Thirty-five days? It felt more like a 10-year stretch.

There are large parts of my time inside that place I can't write about. It's not because I can't bring myself to talk about what happened. It's because there is a dark hole where my memories should be – the medication made sure of that. It left me feeling - and living - like a zombie.

There were times I feared the meds I was given were turning me insane and that I'd never come out the other side.

But those five weeks in St Andrew's shaped the rest of my life, so I have tried to piece together my hell in there the very best I can.

I arrived at the hospital on May 6 a broken man – a burning ball of anger and confusion. Two nurses were by my side in the back of the ambulance which took me from my house to the hospital.

I may have looked as if I was sitting calmly during the hour-long journey but I wanted to punch my way out. My head was telling me to stand up, smash down the door and jump out.

Yet, as I sat in the back of the ambulance, I didn't move an inch. I was frozen with fear about what was waiting up ahead.

I was gutted to the pit of my stomach. I'd only been out of hospital for 10 days. Now they were taking me back in. How could the dice be rolling this way?

I closed my eyes in the ambulance and tried to make sense of it all. OK, I'd not been feeling myself. There was no doubt I was bang in the middle of a whole new battle with my bipolar. Heading off to Scotland had not been the smartest idea but I didn't think that was enough reason to be locked up again.

I know the doctors had the right to take that choice away from me if they thought I was a danger to myself or to others. I'd heard that enough times in my life from a doctor holding a clipboard but, in my mind, none of it made any sense.

I hadn't terrorised anyone, I hadn't provoked anyone and I hadn't bullied anyone. And I was hardly a danger to myself, so I had no idea why my freedom was suddenly being stolen away.

But it didn't matter what I thought because everyone else had other ideas. The doctors were hell-bent on taking me back in and my family clearly thought hospital was the best place for me too. That stung and it left me furious and betrayed. I was scared stiff too.

WHY...? That was what I asked those nurses 50-odd times in the back of the ambulance. I bet it did their heads in, I was a needle stuck on the record.

"Why is this happening? Why won't you stop them from doing this to me?"

No matter how many times I asked, I didn't get an answer.

When I pulled up at St Andrew's the first thing that hit me was the size of the place. It was so much bigger than the unit in Basildon. The walls were higher and the hospital seemed to stretch for miles and miles.

It was as scary as the outside of a prison and every bit as bleak.

St Andrew's is built on about 135 acres of land east of the centre of Northampton. I've done a few shows in the town, I liked it and I liked the people. I'd driven past the hospital and always assumed it was a prison.

There's enough room inside for about 600 patients and, over the years, it has been home to some of the most troubled characters in the country. About 90 per cent have been sectioned under the Mental Health Act because they pose a risk to themselves or to others.

Men and women with severe personality disorders like schizophrenia, patients with psychosis and people with illnesses like mine are treated in low, medium and high-security wards.

Most are lost souls hoping the hospital will offer them a way out of their hell, but many end up staying for years.

A lot have scaled the walls and got out. One fella was recently caught by security when he ran out of breath after clearing the hospital grounds.

The Sherwood Ward, where I was treated, was pretty much an accident and emergency unit for the mentally ill.

The men who arrive can be brought in from anywhere – from home, the streets, prison – or straight from the dock of a courtroom on the say-so of a judge. Many patients arrive in handcuffs and never leave.

When I stepped out the ambulance I was just another number, the latest angry man to rock up at the door unsure what was about to happen next.

I hesitated and looked up. It was early evening, the sun had dropped and the sky above the hospital had turned grey.

It had been sunny when I opened my eyes in bed that morning. I closed them tightly as I stood outside the door, sucked in a deep breath and willed myself to hold it together.

The nurses guided me towards the main door and, as I stepped inside, I felt physically sick. It was like I'd been punched hard in the ribs. I slumped down and into a chair in the waiting room unable to take another step forward.

I could see the other patients eating their dinner behind a locked door. Then I heard what they were screaming.

"It's Bruno," they were saying. "Bruno is coming in here."

I slammed my back into the chair and held my head in my hands. Through the gaps in my fingers I could see the feet of a nurse walking towards me.

"Come on, Frank," she said. Dazed and numb, I was guided to a little room where a doctor said he wanted to check me over before I was taken on to the main ward.

He was an Indian fella with a strong accent and it seemed to me that he couldn't understand what I was saying, so I was getting more and more wound up because all I had were questions I needed answers to.

The nurse by his side didn't look interested. If they had really examined me they would have seen the fear in my eyes.

It seemed to me that all they wanted to do was prod me around, check my blood pressure, stick needles in me for blood tests and make notes on their paperwork. It was just the latest write-up in the Frank Bruno folder.

Pretty quickly I boiled over.

"Tell me why I am here," I shouted. "Tell me what have I done? Tell me now."

They both stopped and stepped back. They looked scared and fixed their eyes down and back at their paperwork.

I could feel my heart pumping out of my chest so hard I had to sit down. The least they could do, I said, was tell me why I was being sectioned. But they didn't say a word – they just kept ignoring me.

I was so angry by then I was close to hitting fight mode. I wanted them to get off me and I told them to back away.

Then I saw the doctor reach towards a button he had above his desk. I knew it would have alerted security and within a few seconds they would have been outside the door.

"Look," I said. "I don't want to cause any aggro. I just don't understand why any of this is happening to me."

The doctor had a blank look on his mush and still looked a bit scared. I sank back into my chair and stared at the wall. It was covered in hand prints and dirty smears.

They were the fingerprints of despair left by the patients who had arrived before me, but now I was no different to them.

Then I heard it – the noise that had been the soundtrack to my week in Basildon. First it was the sound of squeaky wheels as the nurse steered the medicine trolley. Then it was the clinking of glass bottles bashing against each other. Finally there was the click of the lid as the pills were opened.

I was handed some lithium and some tablets to help me sleep. I gulped them down. To be honest, by then I was glad of them. Anything to knock me out for a few hours and get away from this feeling. Maybe I'd wake up and find it had all been a bad dream.

But it was still feeling very real when the heavies arrived in the room to take me off to where I would be sleeping. As I walked into my room there was that sound again. Clink. The door had been locked on my world once more.

But I was glad to be on my own for a bit so I could try and get my head around what was going on.

Unlike in Basildon I was put in a room with a window straight away, but it wasn't one looking out on the world I'd been locked away from. No, it was a window for the nurses to look in on me and make sure I didn't do anything stupid.

I felt like I was back in a zoo. The room was a hellhole but I unpacked my suitcase and carefully put all my clothes in the wardrobe. I hadn't done that in Basildon, I had lived out of my case. This time something in my head was telling me that I was going to be banged up a lot longer.

That wasn't the worst of it though. Another thought whirling through my mind said I wasn't getting out at all. I desperately tried to block that one out. Then I placed a Bible under my pillow.

Lying in that bed with those plastic sheets under me again was the worst feeling imaginable. I pulled the duvet up to my chin and tried to control my fear. I was back where I had been just weeks earlier.

I kept my light on and stared out to the exercise yard wondering how the hell I had got to this point and how on earth I was going to get out.

As those first few hours went by the world slowly got hazier. Then, eventually, there must have been darkness. I say "must have" because I don't remember falling asleep. But God, I remember waking up the next morning.

I came round face down on the pillow with what felt like a rock strapped to the back of my skull. I tried to lift my head, but it was impossible. My bed sheets were drenched in sweat.

It was my first taste of what my life under lock and key would be like for the next five weeks.

As I lay there, I struggled to catch my breath and I quickly started to panic. It felt as if I was suffocating and it took all my strength just to sit up.

My head was throbbing, banging and hurting really badly. I looked down at my hands and they were shaking.

I can't remember another time in my life I'd ever seen them shake, not even before my toughest fights or after my most crushing defeats. But they were shaking now, and I couldn't make them stop.

How strong a dose were these lithium tablets they were giving me? Why were they making me feel like this? And why hadn't I put up more of a fight when the nurse wheeled in that trolley?

Damn. I clenched my fists, willed my hands to stop trembling and took a deep breath, but when I heard the footsteps outside the door and the shouting going on they were shaking again. I pulled the bedsheets up over my knees.

That's when I heard the screaming. It started softly but then got louder and louder until, eventually, it was unbearable. The guy sounded really young and totally terrified. Why wouldn't someone help him?

The last time I heard wailing like that was when a young kid at Oak Hall had been given a serious kicking by a load of older boys. As it had at the time, the sound made me feel utterly helpless.

I grabbed my pillow and tightly held it over my ears trying to block out the noise. I looked down and saw my Bible lying on the mattress with a little handwritten verse poking out the side.

It was the one I often used to say to calm myself before a fight. I dropped my pillow, clutched the piece of paper and recited the prayer out loud.

God, give me the grace to accept with serenity,
the things that cannot be changed,
Courage to change the things
which should be changed,
and the wisdom to distinguish
the one from the other.

I heard footsteps as a nurse walked towards my door. The shutter slid across and she looked inside. But I just started reading louder.

Living one day at a time,
Enjoying one moment at a time,
Accepting hardship as a pathway to peace,
Taking as Jesus did,
This sinful world as it is,
Not as I would have it,
Trusting that You will make all things right,
If I surrender to Your will,
So that I may be reasonably happy in this life.

And supremely happy with You for ever in the next.
Amen.

The *Serenity Prayer* had given me so much strength throughout my life. And as I sat on my bed I knew I would need every ounce of courage to get through the challenge ahead.

As I placed the Bible back under my pillow I could sense the nurse standing outside my door. She had been listening to me. I wondered what she was thinking.

I could hear some shouting now.

My name, like it had been when I arrived, was now ringing out around the hospital.

"Where's Frank, where's Frank?"

It seemed to be bouncing off the walls. I had no idea how anyone knew I was now a patient, but it was clear they did and all the other patients wanted me to do was to show my face.

But I wasn't ready for that, instead, I sank back on to the bed, grabbed my mobile and dialled the number. "Mum..."

I could hear the pain in her voice as she answered and I could sense her fear. It was how I felt in the pit of my stomach too and so, for just a few moments, I felt a connection.

I was a kid again and I suddenly felt safe – Mum was always able to make me feel that.

"What am I going to do now?" I asked her.

"Franklin, my dear boy, you will get out of this," she said. "You must not lose your faith. Stay calm, keep your head and don't let this break you."

But I was struggling to see a way forward. As I saw it, the doctors and nurses, the so-called experts, had locked the door on my life and now were in charge of it.

Then, right on cue, the door to my room swung open and the nurse stood there, staring at me.

"Come on, Frank, you can't mope in here all day on your phone," she said, ushering me out.

There was a harshness to her voice, an edge and a look on her face that told me she was the boss and I better get used to it. I didn't like it, but I couldn't hide away for ever.

I had no choice, so I stepped out of my room, feeling hopelessly alone. I dearly wished Nina, my mum or the kids were with me because I felt totally cut off from the outside world.

I was frightened about coming face to face with all the other patients again. As I walked into the main area of the ward everyone had stopped: all eyes were on me.

The ward was so quiet that I heard a bead of sweat that had dripped down my forehead fall on to the floor.

There was a smell of stale food and of unwashed bodies. Patients were wandering around aimlessly, many clearly in distress while others were looking numbly into the distance seemingly unaware of where they were.

There were about 20 guys in all – different sorts of characters: young, old, one or two clearly very troubled, with nurses sitting either side of them. It seemed totally chaotic.

Most of the fellas were confused, angry, unsettled and agitated. Like me, they'd had their rights taken away and, like me, they were fighting their own battle.

I sat down at a table where breakfast of toast and cereal was being served. The nurse brought me some plastic cutlery – real knives and forks were banned, she said. Just as well, after what happened in the last hospital, but they kept slipping out of my sweaty hands.

In the end I just gave up. My appetite had gone and the sick feeling I had in the pit of my stomach was still swirling round. Even though my hands were shaking I managed to force down a cup of tea and then I tried to chat to some of the other guys.

One was really making me feel nervous. He was a big fella who was just sitting and staring at me.

"Everything OK, boss?" I asked him. He didn't reply.

A couple of the guys asked why I'd been brought in and what had happened to me. I told them it was all a mistake and I'd probably be leaving in a couple of days. But I don't think they believed me. I didn't believe it myself.

"We saw you on TV with that Piers Morgan the other week, Frank," one guy said to me. "You won't be back on there for a while will you, mate?"

I forced a nervous smile. As I sat looking at my cold toast, I learned more about the other patients. They had all sorts of different problems. One guy told me he had been in and out of the hospital for the past five years. Big problems with booze had led to him losing his home and he ended up having a breakdown.

Another had lost a fortune gambling and his marriage ended up hitting the skids. Everything got on top of him and he ended up being sectioned.

There were addicts with drink and drugs problems, guys in the midst of severe breakdowns and a couple of blokes you could see straight off were never getting out. They were lost souls whose eyes told you that they'd given up. One or two didn't say a word – they just looked like the living dead.

After breakfast I was taken to a room where a doctor finally told me what was going to be happening to me. The first thing I asked about was getting a solicitor.

"I want to get out of here," I told the doctor. "I don't think it's right. Why can't I go home?"

But the doctor just let out a big sigh which really put my back up.

"Mr Bruno," he said. "Listen..."

"Er, for starters, sir, I'd rather you call me Frank," I said, butting in. "You are making me nervous."

"OK, Frank," he said. "You need to realise you are here because concerns have been made about you."

"What concerns?" I asked, demanding answers as ever. He looked at me and let out the same sigh. Inside I was getting more and more wound up, but I kept a lid on it.

"There have been concerns from your family, Frank," he said. "Concerns from the doctors who were coming to see you at home and concern from some of your friends."

Then his eyes were back down at his paperwork. He clearly didn't want to say anything else to me.

"Look," I pleaded with him. "Those pills were making me feel crazy after I got out of Basildon. Have you ever taken that stuff yourself?

"I didn't know my head from my arse half the time. If you let me go home I won't cause any grief or aggro. I'll chill out, I promise."

But the doctor wasn't having it.

"Frank," he said, placing my paperwork back into his filing cabinet: "You are not going anywhere. You need to get used to that. The sooner you do, the easier it will be for *everyone*. But here's the list of solicitors you can contact if you..."

"Forget that a minute," I said interrupting him.

"Everyone? What do you mean about this being 'easier for everyone'?"

He just looked straight through me. Then the penny dropped. It all started to click in my mind.

In the short time I'd been in that place I'd had the feeling that the doctors and nurses were on their toes around me – they were worried I'd smash the ward up and fight my way out.

They'd already decided my size and my history as a boxer made me a threat to myself, to the staff and to the other patients.

It was total nonsense. Why couldn't people see I didn't want to hurt anyone? I just wanted to go home. But that wasn't going to happen. I was locked up and no-one was listening.

The doctor went on to explain how life was going to work while I was inside. He said I was currently being kept in a low level of security, but I could be moved to the medium-secure part of the hospital if the staff thought that was more suitable.

I knew what that meant. I'd seen the people being taken upstairs. Most of them were handcuffed to someone who looked like a prison officer.

That terrified me: where I was was bad enough. The doctor explained how he believed I was showing all the classic signs of bipolar disorder and that it needed to be treated with strong medication.

He said I would be given a drug called Olanzapine, an anti-psychotic, to help treat and control my illness. As well as that I had to take Diazepam, mood stabilisers and sleeping tablets.

The words were like body blows. When I got back to my room I was up and pacing around like a wild dog. I was ringing everyone you can imagine. I'd packed two mobile phones and whenever I was on one the other would be charging up.

I called Nina, Dave, all the different people in my management team and my friends.

"You've got to get me out of here," I was yelling. "All they want to do is pump me full of drugs. I don't want to take them. This is no way to live. I can't train, I can't think straight, I can't find any peace of mind."

Christ, I was so desperate I even tried to get through to Prince Charles's office. Yeah, the nurses thought I was totally cuckoo when they heard me doing that.

But years before, I had worked for the Prince's Trust and I had the number saved in my phone. So I left a message and asked for them to help me get out.

The way I was behaving was crazy, it was ridiculous. I can see that now – but I was in despair.

Dave was the only person who could properly explain to me what was going on. He said from the moment I left Basildon there had been a lot of concern about the way I was behaving.

The main issue was that the doctors back in Bedfordshire were convinced it was no longer safe for me to be treated at home. They thought I'd become a danger to myself and to others.

"Frank, I am sorry but there is nothing else I can do," Dave said. "Your family have asked that they solely take things from here."

I was gutted. It wasn't Dave's fault – but I didn't feel as if I had anyone in my corner. I felt totally alone. I ended the call and tossed the phone on the bed.

"All OK, mate?" said a voice from behind me.

I turned round to see an old fella standing by my door. Like everyone else in that place he looked weary, worn down, but he had kind eyes.

He told me that he'd been inside the hospital for months. He was suffering from ME, which had led to him developing mental health problems.

I was gutted as I listened to his story. For weeks and weeks on the outside he was always feeling in pain, dizzy and exhausted, but the doctors couldn't work out why. By the time he was diagnosed with ME his mind was shot to bits. He'd been driven insane by the way he was feeling and he ended up being sectioned and taken to St Andrew's.

He said being in the hospital wasn't doing him any good and he'd been fighting for weeks to get out, but the doctors kept refusing him permission.

It was terrifying to listen to what happened to him. I explained what was going on with me and tears filled his eyes.

"Listen, Frank," he whispered to me, as he looked over his shoulder. "You have no chance of getting out of this place unless you get a good solicitor. Have they given you a list yet?" I reached into my pocket and pulled out the piece of paper I'd been given.

"This guy's the only one I'd trust," he said pointing to a name near the bottom of the list. "They don't like this one in here."

"Why?" I asked.

"Because he tends to win his cases, Frank."

As soon as he left, I grabbed my mobile off the bed and dialled the number. The solicitor picked up after one ring and I felt such a surge of relief.

"Sir, sir, can you help get me out of here," I pleaded breathlessly. "I need you to come down right away."

I hadn't even given him my name, the words were just spilling out. We spent a few minutes talking and I knew straight off I'd found the right guy.

He said he was working on lots of cases to help patients like me who were applying to get out of mental health hospitals across the country, but, thank God, he was happy to take on my case, too.

There was only one small snag – he couldn't get in to see me for 24 hours.

"Can't you come now?" I begged him. The thought of spending another second in the place was making me feel sick. But there was no way he could see me any quicker. I'd have to wait until the next day to meet him so I needed to keep my mind busy.

The next call I made was to my kids. My hands were sweating as I dialled the number.

I was still hurting like hell about what had gone on and felt like my pride had been shattered.

I was their dad, for goodness sake, but here I was sitting in a dingy room waiting for them to pick up the other end of the line.

When Nicola answered, I had to grip the arm of the chair and force myself to stay strong. I had my say. I told her that I believed the best place for me was at home.

I knew I had to be careful about what I said because my every move was being monitored. The nurses were walking past every few seconds for a reason.

Even so, a lot of emotion came out: hurt, anger, upset. I know it was hard for the kids to hear it but I couldn't keep things bottled up.

I thought if I was honest and open they might be able to get me out, but the kids insisted that me being in hospital was for the best.

"Surely you can see that, Dad?" Nicola pleaded.

But, at that moment, I couldn't. I was simply not able or willing to try to put myself in her shoes, to see me as she did.

I put down the phone and the fear started to rise. Fear of the future, fear of not getting out, but right then, more than anything, fear of being alone.

I missed hearing my children's voices and wished they could be sat by my side. I loved them more than anything in the world, but I was scared they were slipping away from me. As I slumped down on my bed I knew I was fighting for so much more than just my sanity. I was fighting for my family, for all of us.

I stared at the clock and willed the hands to move forward 24 hours so I could meet my solicitor and come up with a plan to get out of the place.

Then I heard that sound in the corridor, and seconds later the trolley was at my door.

Suddenly my mind was racing and I was struggling to breathe.

Before I knew what was happening, I was down on my knees. Panic had set in. I felt weak and dizzy. The next thing I knew my face was pressed against the icy cold tiles and then came the darkness again.

Chapter 8

WHERE DID IT ALL GO WRONG, FRANK?

I was pacing up and down the room in my bright yellow three-piece suit like a man waiting to be taken off to the gallows.

Yeah, I was wearing a whistle: I'd phoned Nina and asked her to drop one off at the reception of St Andrew's ahead of my meeting. There was no way I was going to sit down across the table with my solicitor without one.

I may have been stripped of my dignity but I was not going to let anyone strip me of my self-respect. I was nervous as hell as I waited for my solicitor to arrive, but as soon as he walked through the door I felt a surge of relief.

At last I had someone in my corner again. My solicitor was finally able to tell me a little bit more about what was going on and, straight off, I didn't like what I was hearing.

"Frank, you have been detained here under Section 3 of the Mental Health Act," he said.

"What the hell does that mean?" I asked, standing up and pacing the room again.

"It means things are a lot more serious now than they were a few weeks ago," he replied.

"At Basildon you were being detained under a Section 2. Then, the doctors were looking to see if you had a mental health condition and if you required treatment. But a Section 3 means you are here for a long programme of treatment and..."

I cut him short: "How long?" I snapped, sounding a bit like someone asking when their cancer was going to kill them.

"Could be at least six months, Frank," he said. "Maybe more."

That knocked the wind clean out of me.

I wasn't sure I'd heard him right. "Say that again," I asked, sinking into the chair opposite him.

"You could be here for six months, Frank."

The bile shot up from the pit of my stomach and a pain ripped through my chest. I was struggling to breathe. That familiar panicky feeling had me in its grip and I was frightened I was going to collapse like I had the night before.

I must have looked a mess because the solicitor walked round the table and put his hand on my shoulder.

"Stay calm," he said. "Listen to me – I am on your side. I am going to do my best to get you out of here as quickly as I can. But I must warn you: everything you do in here from this moment on is going to be monitored. So you need to play by their rules.

"What rules?" I asked.

"Well, for a start, whatever else you do you MUST take your medication. If you don't, there's no chance they will let you home. And try to stay as calm as you can – if you lose your rag it will be curtains."

"I can't cope," I pleaded. "The medicine is turning my brain to mush. I can't keep on taking it. I just need to get home. You've got to get me out as quickly as you can."

The idea of six months in hospital left me reeling, but thankfully the solicitor had a plan. His next move would be to tell the hospital I wanted another tribunal hearing. In it, he said, he would be able to argue the case for me to be discharged.

"Can we do that today?" I asked, realising straight away it was a daft question, but I was desperate.

"Sadly not, Frank," he said, taking a load of papers out of his briefcase. "First, I need you to sign this."

It was a form that said I agreed for him to look at my medical notes. "Why do you need to see them?" I asked.

"Frank, it will tell us both a lot more about why the doctors sectioned you in the first place, and it will spell out what the concerns are surrounding your safety."

"I need to know," I agreed as I signed the papers. "I've asked the doctors again and again but nobody will give me a straight answer."

The solicitor reassured me he was going to do all he could over the next few days to get things moving. Then he put down his pen, pulled out a notepad and took off his jacket.

"Right," he said. "Before we move forward here I need to know everything."

"Everything?" I asked.

"Yes. *Everything*." he said.

"How long have you got?" I said back.

"As long as it takes – I need to understand how and why things went wrong."

With that he pulled out a fat file of notes and photocopies of newspaper stories he'd collected. He'd obviously been doing his homework and I could see he meant business.

I glanced at the nurse sitting in the corner of the room and back at my solicitor.

He must have read my mind because he was quickly up and asked her if we could have an hour on our own. She left the room...

"OK, Frank," he said. "Here's what I can't get my head around. I remember that night in September 1995, watching TV, like everyone else, when you beat Oliver McCall.

"There you were in the ring, your family around you, holding the belt. And the whole country was celebrating with you and..."

"Yeah," I interrupted. "I know. I had it all, didn't I? Millions of pounds in the bank. Flash cars in the garage. Hundreds of designer suits hanging in the wardrobe. A beautiful wife and three amazing kids. The world title belt sitting on my mantelpiece. But after I lost to Mike Tyson and announced my retirement none of it was bringing me any happiness."

"How d'you mean?" asked my solicitor.

"Look, the way I saw things, I was a 35-year-old man with no job. Actually, it worse than that – I was a 35-year-old who couldn't see straight.

"I'd been to see a doctor who told me I had a torn retina which would need sorting. He said there was no way I could fight again. He said: 'Go home and put your feet up, Mr Bruno'."

"That was OK though wasn't it, Frank? You'd already won the title?" my solicitor said.

"It should have been," I replied. "Blimey, come the end of 1996, I read one poll in a newspaper which had me down as the second most famous person in the country behind Princess Diana! I'd achieved what I wanted and people were calling me a national treasure."

"They still are you know, Frank," he told me.

"Yeah," I replied, leaning forward. "But people don't know what goes on behind closed doors. After I retired, as far as the world was concerned I was living the dream, enjoying my life and making the most of all that money in the bank.

"But it was only a few months after losing to Mike that I started to feel low and the world seemed empty. I'd spent my whole life chasing this one thing. And suddenly I was like: right, what am I supposed to do now, then? I had no plan B."

"So what did you do, Frank?" he asked.

"At first I turned to the gym." I said.

"But you weren't fighting?"

"No, there wasn't a fight to prepare for. But I was still working out a hell of a lot. I had a gym at my house in Stondon Massey in Essex and I didn't want to let myself get out of shape. I stuck to the same training regime as when I was boxing. Running. Weights. Skipping. Sit-ups and press-ups. Hundreds of them. But..." I couldn't find the words to describe the emptiness.

"But what?" he asked, looking up from his notes. He seemed genuinely interested in my story.

"I just desperately missed the gloves," I sighed. "I felt like someone had cut my arms off. Some afternoons I asked my mate Danny Salmon, who I've known most of my life, to come over and spar with me."

"Spar where!?" asked my solicitor, looking a bit alarmed.

"Well, one session I pulled a canvas cover across my indoor swimming pool," I said.

He gave me a funny look.

"Hear me out," I asked. "The company who sold it were saying you could park a Bentley on the cover and it wouldn't split.

"So I looked at Danny and said: 'What d'you reckon, Danny Boy? It should take a bit of sparring from us two ol' geezers, shouldn't it?' "

"And what did he say?" the lawyer laughed.

"He didn't answer! I think he was worrying about getting wet. But, for half an hour, we slogged it out on there. It felt like being back in the ring again. Having that canvas under my feet was wonderful."

"But it wasn't enough?" the solicitor suggested.

"No. No way. Nothing was enough to stop the negative vibes in my mind."

"How were they making you feel?" he asked, picking his pen back up.

"Uptight. Angry. Restless – and pretty quickly it had a knock-on effect on my behaviour and my marriage."

"Tell me about the marriage."

"I don't really want to," I said, hesitating. "Look...it was tough. Laura and I were going through some personal problems and by the middle of 1997 the newspapers were getting hold of the story."

"OK, Frank," my solicitor said, digging out a newspaper cutting from his bundle.

"Is that when your lawyer released a statement saying you were 'having difficulties' but were not contemplating divorce."

"Yeah, that's right," I replied. "But all hell broke loose after that."

"How do you mean?"

"Well, for the newspapers, it was the first sign the Frank Bruno success story was crumbling," I admitted. "I tried my best to carry on as normal."

"How do you mean, normal?"

"Well there were still loads of offers coming in to appear on TV shows and I took a lot of them."

"But I guess it didn't replace the buzz of fighting," he said.

"Boss, nothing could," I replied, sinking back into my chair. "And I started to miss it more and more. You see, I never actually retired on my own terms."

"I don't follow you, Frank," my solicitor said. "You gave a press conference. I remember it. There's a newspaper cutting here and..."

"Yeah, I know, but it was the doctors who told me to jack it all in because of my dodgy retina," I explained. "Deep down, I struggled to accept that. I used to tell my mates all the time that boxing fans might not have seen the back of me, just yet."

"And what did your friends say when you said that?"

"My true mates told me to stop talking daft. But I was hanging around with them less and less. I was spending time with hangers-on who..."

"Who were only interested in hanging on?" my solicitor cut in.

"Exactly, chief. I took up DJing and spent tens of thousands on the very best kit out there.

"I had my own little studio at home. I'd been in love with music since I was a kid so when the first offer came in to appear at a nightclub I was delighted."

"Where was your first gig?" he asked.

"Hollywood."

"Not a bad start," he said, looking impressed.

"Er, Hollywood, the nightclub in Romford, boss."

"Oh, right."

"Yeah," I said. "You see that was the problem. I'd gone from selling out fights in Vegas to playing to a half-full nightclub in Essex. But the people around me were saying I was the bee's knees. And I believed it. I was throwing around money like confetti."

"On what, Frank?" he asked.

"All sorts. My son Franklin's christening was a pretty big deal," I said, closing my eyes and thinking back to that day in 1997.

"We had a fairground in the garden, a world champion trampolinist performing and two helicopters taking people for rides. We served guests the best Caribbean food and an endless supply of champagne and fine wine in marquees decked out with chandeliers."

"What do you think about that when you look back now?"

"Well, I just wanted to give Franklin a good christening but it was excessive and a sign of my illness taking hold a little bit."

"What else was the money going on?" he asked.

As I pictured the results of my spending sprees I felt embarrassed to admit: "I had so many clothes and gadgets in my house I had no recollection of even buying."

"How did they make you feel?"

"Empty."

"Empty?" he asked.

"Yeah, there was always emptiness. That and a constant nagging fear. I couldn't seem to escape it."

"What were you frightened about?" he asked.

"I don't know," I said helplessly."My brain was always racing so fast, and every morning I woke up with the same heavy feeling in my chest."

"What did that feel like?"

"It felt a bit like I did on the day I was sent home from school after my dad died. Silly, I know. I told myself that at the time. I was saying, 'Get a grip, nobody has died, Frank'. But looking back, maybe they had. Maybe the person I used to be had died and I couldn't handle it."

"So what did you do about it?"

"After a lot of persuading from my family and a lot of ranting and raving back from me I went to see a psychiatrist in 1998."

"And that's when you were first diagnosed with bipolar affective disorder?" he asked.

I nodded.

"So he prescribed you with medication and you went into the Priory Hospital for some treatment?" said my solicitor, looking at his notes.

"Yeah, but I spent less than 24 hours in there. It was private and they couldn't make me stay. So I checked myself out."

"Why did you do that?"

"Listen, taking pills and seeing a shrink was the last thing I wanted to do. I was in my prime. I'd just won the world title. I was still as fit as a fiddle. I had a life to lead. I didn't want to be lying in a bed all day having drugs shoved down my neck."

"What was everyone else saying?"

"My family and friends were worried sick. But I didn't want to hear it. When Danny used to come round to train I'd say to him: 'I'm not mad. It's everyone else who is mad, mate. It's you lot.'

"But I wasn't being true to myself, and then, well, then I did some really stupid stuff."

"Go on, Frank…"

I stood up and walked across to the other side of the room. I looked at the door and for a split-second I considered running. I pictured myself turning that handle, sprinting down the corridor and leaving all this behind: the hospital, the solicitor, all my past mistakes…

But I realised that running would get me nowhere. If I really wanted to get out, I needed this fella in my corner. So I clenched my fists, and then I turned and faced him.

"I regret it now, but I started to do drugs."

"When was this?" he asked, clearly relieved I'd decided not to leg it.

"Around the start of 2000. I remember that because it was the Millennium and I'd gone to Vegas. It was the first time I took cocaine. It was so stupid and I wish to God I'd never seen the stuff."

"So why did you take it?"

I looked at the wall, struggling to put it into words. This was tougher than I thought it would be.

"Frank," he said. "If you want to stop now, we can if you are tired. I know it's hard with the meds."

"No. I'd rather tell you everything now. I want to just get this all over with."

"OK, go on…"

"Look, with the coke, all I can recall is that the high took me to a new place. I was away from all my problems, but the next day there was always this terrible low. I was up, down, up, down."

"How long did it go on for?"

"About six months. I couldn't carry on like that so I just knocked it all on the head, but so many things were going wrong."

"At home?" he asked.

"Yeah. Laura and I separated shortly after I got back from Vegas. My solicitor issued a short statement and that was it – 20 years after we'd first met it was all over."

"How were you feeling about that?"

"I don't want to dwell on the past because it hurts too much, but Laura and I just drifted apart. It was impossible to work things out, but if I thought retiring had been tough then divorce was worse.

"Worse?" he asked.

"Absolutely. Laura had moved out with the kids and I stayed on my own at Stondon Massey."

"And how was that?"

"Terrible. The loneliness and emptiness felt a thousand times worse and my behaviour quickly became out of control. I was doing some strange stuff."

"Like what?"

"I was up to some weird bits and pieces. I started to spend a lot of time meditating in a boxing ring I had in the back garden.

"Why?" he asked, looking puzzled.

"It just brought me a bit of comfort and took away the emptiness. It made me feel closer to boxing. I was missing it so much, but nobody else could see that."

"How do you mean,'nobody else', Frank?"

"Well the newspapers were printing loads of stories about me being out of control. There were pictures too. There seemed to be a different story every weekend about my behaviour. It felt like I'd gone from a national treasure to a laughing stock. I felt mugged off every time I stepped outside my house. Then, when I thought things couldn't get any worse, they did. I got a call telling me George Francis, my old trainer, had taken his own life."

"Oh Jesus," the solicitor said. He looked genuinely sorry.

"I was stunned," I told him. "George was the hardest person I'd ever met, but privately, like me, he was having problems.

"His wife Joan had died of cancer and then his youngest son Simon died from cancer, too. It was too much. He couldn't handle it.

"So with first Laura and then George gone, I'd never felt so lonely."

"Did you do anything about that?"

"I threw myself back into the DJing to try and fill the void, but it wasn't helping me and, in the end, I started doing drugs again."

"Cocaine?" he asked me.

"No. It was skunk this time."

I noticed him writing it all down, which I found a bit unnerving.

"Look, I didn't enjoy it," I told him. "It wasn't for fun. I'd have tried anything to give me a break from the dark thoughts in my head. But every morning I woke up to find fear and emptiness was still there."

"Did you have anyone around you to talk to, Frank?"

I shrugged. "Not really. The kids were with Laura. That was tough. It was hard for them too because they were caught in the middle. Nicola tried to help. She moved back into the house around the spring of 2003. She was only about 20, bless her.

"She was worried and wanted to keep an eye on me, but I wasn't there much. I'd be out doing DJ sets at nightclubs or seeing friends.

"I knew people were whispering behind my back. They were saying that I wasn't right. That I'd lost it. That I'd gone. I covered my ears and closed my eyes, but they were right. It was only going to end one way. I was barely sleeping. I was rarely eating. I was running on adrenaline. I was shedding weight and I looked terrible. My illness was taking hold and I tried to hide from it."

"How do you mean, hide?" He was still scribbling away.

"I went into a shell," I said. "Voicemails would be left, texts and phone calls not answered. When the doorbell rang I stayed inside."

"Did you prefer being on your own?" he asked.

"No," I replied. "It was weird. I hated being alone, but I also didn't want people around, watching me, judging me."

I could see from the look on his face that he wasn't getting it.

"Yeah, I know," I said, standing up and pacing the room again. "It doesn't make sense, but nothing did back then. I thought everyone was out to get me. My friends, my family, everyone. In the end something had to give. But I didn't go quietly."

"Are you talking about the time you were put in Goodmayes Hospital?" he asked. "The first time you were sectioned?"

"Yeah," I said, flopping back down in my chair. "Christ. I will never forget that day – September 22, 2003. When I saw the ambulance pull into my drive, I flipped. I grabbed my mobile phone and I legged it.

"Who did you call, Frank?"

"Cass Pennant."

"The author?" he asked.

"Yeah, Cass and I go way back. Blimey, you'll find a few newspaper articles on him, boss," I said, laughing. "He stepped in to help when I was young and was having a bit of hassle from some kids on the street – and we stayed mates ever since. When I realised things were about to go badly wrong, it was Cass I turned to."

"So what happened?" asked my solicitor.

"I wanted to do anything I could to stay out of that ambulance. When it pulled into my drive I legged it. I was running to the bottom of the garden as I dialled Cass's number but it went to answerphone so I left a message. 'Cass, Cass!' I was shouting down the phone. 'I need you to get over here, mate. Quickly. The police have turned up and there's an ambulance waiting to take me to hospital. I don't want to go. I'll be waiting in the garden. All right, Cass. Bye.'

"Did he come?"

"Yeah. But there was no escape."

"So you got in the ambulance?" the solicitor asked me.

"Not without a struggle," I replied. "Nicola was begging me to get in. Cass was trying to persuade me too. 'Come on, Frank – it's for the best, mate,' he was saying to me – but I wasn't having it. In the end, it took half a dozen police officers and an injection in the backside."

"Now, Frank, am I right in saying that when you were sectioned last week you got in the ambulance voluntarily?" the lawyer asked.

I stood up. Just thinking about it got me wired.

"That's right," I told him. "I didn't want to, but I didn't want to cause a scene either. When they arrived the other night at my place there were loads of coppers. It was the same when they carted me off to Basildon. It was humiliating."

"I know, Frank," he told me. "I will make sure the authorities know how you feel about that."

I sat back down. It was hard to keep calm.

"Let's get back on track," he said. "What happened after they took you to Goodmayes?"

"I remember being put in the ambulance," I said. "Then the next thing I know I am lying on my back in a hospital bed. That was hard enough, but then I saw the papers."

"The Bonkers Bruno headline in *The Sun*?" he asked, grimacing.

"You saw it, then?"

"I did, but how did it make you feel?"

"It was terrible," I told him. "I was off my head on medication but I still remember how angry I was. Where was the respect? Is that what I had become? I'd gone from national treasure to a flipping laughing stock."

But I had to admit that the six weeks of treatment I got at Goodmayes had rescued me. My solicitor nodded, and turned to a new page.

"And what happened when you got home, Frank?"

"I had to face up to something even more scary – that I had a mental health condition."

"And did you face up to it?" he asked.

"No. I couldn't. I didn't want to. I just blocked it out. I wanted people to think I'd come through the storm and was now fine, so I threw myself back into my work."

"You went straight back to work then?" he said, raising his eyebrows.

"I gave myself a few weeks. I was living at Champneys most of the time."

"Why didn't you go home?"

"Too many memories there, boss. When I was at home all I could think of was the ambulance arriving. I had to get out. I had my own room at Champneys so I could just chill out. But there were still problems. Just different ones."

"Like what?"

"A lot of celebrities used to hang out around the place so there were always media people about. I remember one afternoon me and Danny were booked in for a treatment in an ice room."

He looked confused.

"It's brilliant, boss," I told him. "You sit in it for a bit and it's, well, bloody freezing! But you step out feeling amazing.

"So we were hanging around waiting because there were three people booked in for the session. Then, all of a sudden, these two massive geezers who looked like undercover cops turned up.

"For a minute I thought they were taking me back to hospital, but then Cherie Blair walked out of the female changing room in her dressing gown."

"The Prime Minister's wife?!" He was laughing now.

"Yep. She was a lovely lady but it was a bit strange. I'd gone from being locked up, to chilling out with Mrs Blair. We ended up having a little competition to see who could last the longest. Cherie was in for a few minutes, Danny was out not too long after that. I think I broke the record!"

"So, tell me about you returning to work."

"A couple of months after getting out of Goodmayes I went to the Royal Variety Performance in Edinburgh and got a standing ovation, which was very humbling. Then, a few months later, my friends and family threw a big tribute lunch for me at the Dorchester Hotel in London. Audley Harrison and Michael Watson were among the boxers who turned up."

"How was that?" my solicitor asked.

"It was amazing. To see Michael there, smiling, after all he'd been through, when he'd nearly died after that bout with Chris Eubank, gave me so much inspiration.

"I thought if he could cope with the way the dice had rolled in life, then I could too. But the truth was I was still deeply unhappy. I tried to go on holiday to get away from it all."

"How did that work out?"

"Danny took me on a Caribbean cruise with a couple of pals," I said. "We visited Miami, the Cayman Islands, St Thomas, St Martin and Mexico."

"Sounds good," he said.

"Amazing. Apart from Mexico, boss."

"Go on..."

"I'd had enough by then, to be honest. We had got off the boat and boarded a coach into the centre of Cancun for a bit of sightseeing. The four of us were relaxing, having a drink of Coke in the sunshine when I took off."

"Took off?"

"Yeah, I just wanted to get back on the boat," I said. "Danny was going crazy. 'It's miles away, Frank,' he was saying to me. 'Nah, it's over there,' I shouted back, pointing towards the sea.

"Danny was telling me we'd been on the coach for half an hour and reminding me all my money and my passport was on the boat. 'If you get lost, you are done for, Frank,' he told me. But I wouldn't listen. I can be a bit stubborn. You'll find that out, boss."

"So what happened?" said the solicitor, smiling.

"Well I got bloody lost didn't I!"

"What? No! So then what...?"

"When Danny got back to the coach he said to the driver: 'Senor, I just wanna check – is the boat that way?' and he pointed in the direction I'd gone. The driver just shook his head. I'd gone totally the wrong way.

"Danny had to explain to the driver I was missing and slipped him a few quid."

"What, so they set off, a coach-load of holidaymakers, trying to find you?"

"That's it, boss. As I said, I can be a little bit stubborn now and then. By the time they spotted me I was taking a little rest under a palm tree. When I climbed back on the coach they were all giving it the old Bruno! Bruno! Bruno! chant."

"So the holiday did you some good?"

"Yeah," I admitted. "When I got back I felt loads better. In the summer of 2004 I took part in the British Olympic torch relay through London."

"That must have been amazing," he said.

"It was. There were thousands of people cheering me on. It reminded me of the day I had gone round London on an open-top bus showing off my World Title belt."

"What were you thinking, Frank?"

"That maybe my best days were not behind me after all. That maybe it was all going to be OK. I didn't know then that I was gonna be knocked sideways by a terrible betrayal."

I stared at the floor. I couldn't quite find the words.

"You don't have to tell me anything else, Frank, we can stop now," he said, "and you can go back to your room."

That made me focus. "My room? It's not my room. It's like a prison cell. I just want to go home," I hissed, slamming my fist on the table.

"I shouldn't be here. Maybe I wouldn't be here if it hadn't happened."

"Tell me as much as you want, Frank," he suggested.

"OK. It started with a call from my accountants. I can't remember the day. All I know is it was a fair few months after I'd got out of Goodmayes. My accountant says to me: 'Frank, can you come into the office, please. We need to talk to you about something urgently.'

"I knew it must be important because my management never usually bother me about money, but when I sat down in the office that day nothing could prepare me for what came next.

"They said that there'd been a hell of a lot of money leaving my account. They asked me to talk them through what I'd been spending."

"How did that feel?" my solicitor said.

"I was a bit miffed. I'd hardly bought anything. Look, as I said, at the height of my illness before I was sectioned, I'd been blowing quite a lot of dough, but since checking out of hospital I'd been keeping my head down. Even the cruise had been a freebie from Carnival!"

"So you told the accountants that, and what did they say?"

"They didn't need to say anything. I knew from just looking at their faces something really bad was up. At one point I asked them if I was bleeding bankrupt or something.

"Then my accountant pushed a file of papers across the desk. There were bank transfers and transactions which had been highlighted. There were loads of pages.

"I was asking them what it all meant. I was confused. They said to me: 'Look at the dates.' Suddenly I got it – and the world went black."

"Go on …"

"Well, I recognised the dates straight away. How could I ever forget them? Some of these big payments had gone out while I was in Goodmayes."

"But how could you have been spending money while..." the solicitor asked, then drying up as he realised the answer to his own question.

"Bingo," I said.

"My accountants explained that I couldn't have been responsible. They said that somebody else had been spending my money and that it had been going on for a while.

"I demanded that they tell me who it was. But when they told me the name I had to leave the room."

I paused for a moment and looked to the floor.

"I didn't want these moneymen to see me get upset," I told him. "My heart had been broken. The person was someone I had trusted to look after my affairs after I was sectioned. Instead they had been stealing money from me again and again and again as I lay in a hospital. Coming so soon after the split from Laura and losing George, it was another blow I just could not take."

"What did the accountants say?"

"That they would get the money back, but it didn't matter."

"Did you get the police in?" my solicitor asked. This had clearly shocked him more than anything else I'd told him.

"No. We could've, I know that, but it would've meant a trial and the press finding out and I didn't want any more heat coming down on me. I just wanted to put my life back together.

"And calling the law in wouldn't have taken away the anger or hurt. Neither did the letter of apology the person who did this sent me. The damage had been done."

"What happened after that?"

"I tried to put it behind me," I told him. "I sold the house in Stondon Massey. I moved 60 miles away to Bedfordshire. I bought a five-bedroom pad in the middle of the country and the day I moved in I sat in the lounge and told myself it would be a fresh start.

"I was determined to leave my illness firmly in the past where it belonged and..."

I didn't get a chance to finish the sentence because the nurse appeared at the door and gave us a look to say our time was up.

My solicitor stared at me and I could tell he understood a lot more now than he had when he first walked in. As he got up, he put his hand back on my shoulder.

"Please get me out of here," I said.

"I will, Frank," he told me. "I will."

But then he was gone and I was all on my own with my thoughts. Again.

Chapter 9

EXERCISING MY DEMONS AWAY

Before the solicitor left he made me this promise: he was going to do all he could in the days ahead to get things moving and to get me out.

In the meantime, I had to get used to life inside the hospital. I did my best to grit it out but the first few days were a living hell.

The weather outside St Andrew's was gorgeous as the first signs of summer started to show. Yet, for me, life had descended into a world of darkness. And it was the meds which turned out the lights.

Every morning, afternoon and evening it was the same mantra: "Take your medicine, Frank."

I'd be up at 7am and was taken into the breakfast room where the doctors and nurses would dish out the pills. There was no point complaining. The nurses insisted I had to take it and I kept the advice my solicitor gave me at the front of my mind.

"Do as they say, Frank," I told myself when they came round with the trolley. "Keep calm."

Each day one of the staff carried out an assessment on me. I'd be physically examined and then a doctor or a social worker would ask a load of questions. They were always the same:

Hello Frank, how do you feel today? Are you depressed? Are you hearing voices? Have you been sleeping? Are you accepting your medication?

Everything was noted down. Everything was put on a chart to see what progress I was making. A tick or a cross was the difference between taking another step towards my bed or towards the exit.

Patients were allocated time for sessions with a psychologist and for activities like arts and crafts. If you showed signs of getting better then the doctors would sign for you to take part in the sessions. Other times you'd be allowed to go outside or into the wider hospital grounds.

I wasn't interested in speaking to counsellors. I know that probably went against me. The doctors thought by not opening up I was running away from my feelings, but I didn't feel comfortable talking to a stranger.

I'd not found anyone in the hospital who I felt I could trust. So, instead, I kept a lot of what I was feeling bottled up. In the end, it wasn't just my feelings that were kept inside: I was too.

The doctors decided that in my first few days I should be severely restricted in what I was allowed to do. I spent most of the first week in my room and wasn't allowed any visitors apart from my solicitor. The doctors said it was important I had time to rest and get better but being kept inside one room all the time left me feeling suffocated.

I found out the hospital had a little gym so I begged the nurses to let me use it. I explained how important training and keeping fit was to me and how it helped with my condition.

"Sorry, Frank," they'd say. "It's too soon."

A cross would go in the box, because the doctors decided I was not ready, so it would be back to my room.

Then I saw some of the other patients being given escorted visits to the nearby town centre. I asked to be allowed to do that and there was a big meeting, but they decided the risk of me legging it was too high.

So, again, it was a cross in the box. Instead my time was mainly spent pacing the ward, like a wild animal trapped inside a cage.

Keeping calm wasn't easy. The side-effects of my medication quickly became unbearable: all the structure had gone out of my life. When the meds kicked in it felt like electric shocks to my brain.

I'd be left with pins and needles in my face and have terrible panic attacks where I'd be left shaking and sweating. My legs would go into spasm and I could hardly walk. Other times, I couldn't stop my feet from tapping. I was swinging between paralysis and break-dancing.

I was a total car crash. The drugs were making my mental state worse. Some afternoons I'd have blackouts and come round crouched in the corner of my room – totally unaware how I had got there.

I was struggling to stay awake, I was slurring my words and dribbling.

Some mornings after I took my pills I'd be trying to bite my tongue.

The drugs left me feeling like I was locked inside a maze which I had no chance of escaping from. Everywhere I turned in my mind there was a blocked passage, bolted door or dark corner which offered no way out. Right, left, up, down. Wherever I looked there was only darkness. These were the hardest moments and the moments I feared I would not get through. I felt as if the meds were making me go insane.

The blackouts were awful. When I was eventually allowed visits I'd often totally forget that I'd had them.

Apparently, I used to spend hours watching the telly when I first arrived. But I couldn't tell you what programmes I had seen. I'd read a book but my eyes would glaze over the words. I was breathing, I was moving, I was existing. But I didn't feel alive.

It was rare for me to get past lunchtime without needing to be in my bed to get some sleep. I was exhausted all the time. Ever since my Oak Hall days I'd been superfit but in St Andrew's I felt shattered if I walked down the corridor to the toilet. At times, I was unsteady on my feet. Bed became my salvation, in there my mind wasn't racing and I could escape the thoughts in my head.

And those thoughts were increasingly negative. They were telling me I was never getting out of hospital and that I may as well just accept my fate.

It was so terrifying that sometimes I'd cover my ears with my fists.

Most nights I'd be tortured by the same hellish dream. I'd be walking through the street and then all of a sudden I'd be climbing to the top of a building. Then I'd watch myself fall through the air, hurtling towards the ground.

I'd always wake up just before I hit the pavement, then realise I was sitting bolt upright in my bed shaking and dripping with sweat. It didn't matter how often I had that nightmare – every time it scared me senseless.

Relief always swept over me when I realised it was my mind playing tricks on me but then, when I looked around me and remembered where I was, I felt trapped all over again. I was back in the maze.

But even in my lowest, darkest moments I never considered ending my life. I felt there was so much I still had to live for, so much to do.

During the worst points, I thought of George and what he had done, and I thought of other friends over the years who felt they had no choice but to end things.

I often reached for my Bible. My prayers to God provided me with the strength that helped me through.

Even so, those first few days inside St Andrew's were the toughest of my life. Each day when I woke up I knew I was fighting for my survival. The medication would leave my mood swinging so rapidly from high to low that some days I was frightened to move at all. Instead I'd spend hours sitting on my bed trying to pluck up the courage just to set foot outside my room. When I eventually did get moving I just wanted to be on my own, away from people and to have my own space.

I withdrew into myself because I was unable to cope with the thoughts that were going through my mind. Some days, there were no thoughts at all. Those were the worst. Those were the days where my mind was a blank – completely empty of any emotions or feelings.

I would be walking around the hospital for hours in a daze trying to make sense of where I was. *And who I was.*

I complained over and over to the doctors, urging them to look again at the medicine they were giving me.

"This stuff is driving me mad," I would say.

But the response would always be the same.

"Things may get a little worse before they get better, Frank," they'd reply.

The darkness just never seemed to lift. Those small pills I popped into my mouth every morning were going into my bloodstream and completely shutting down the world around me.

With every passing day I felt I was moving further away from the man I once was, and I was terrified I'd never find my way back.

I spoke a lot on the phone to Dave. Sometimes I was ringing four or five times a day just asking for him to tell me what was going on in the world outside the hospital.

The other thing that kept me going, that stopped me from losing all hope, was the contact I had with my solicitor via meetings and phone calls. I knew that was my only chance of getting out and getting my life back but they weren't always easy conversations.

The second time I saw my solicitor I didn't enjoy what he had to say at all. We went through my paperwork which explained why the decision had been made to section me.

"It basically shows the doctors in charge of your care no longer believed you were taking your medication, Frank," he explained.

"They say they raised concerns before you went to Scotland but then they grew more and worried while you were away. Basically, in the eyes of the doctors you'd stopped playing by the rules. They felt you'd failed to do what you had promised to when you were discharged from Basildon."

That wasn't all. The paperwork mentioned an incident where I had been accused of leaving my car parked in the middle of the road near where I live. The notes said it had put myself and others in danger. I couldn't believe what I was hearing when the solicitor read that out.

It was total rubbish! But that, along with the worries about my medication, was seemingly enough for the doctors to cart me off.

As I sat listening to it all I just held my head in my hands. It was one big mess.

"How are we going to sort all this out?" I asked my solicitor.

"It's not a disaster," he said. "The concerns being raised about the risk to yourself and to others is actually very slight compared to many cases I work on."

"How can they be allowed to do this to me then?" I protested.

"Frank, the way the doctors have acted is completely lawful. All we can do now is demonstrate you are better and willing to do things by the book this time if you are treated at home.

"Now, listen, we have applied for an initial hearing to take place, but it can't happen until you have been here for a fortnight."

"Two weeks!" I yelled. "I'm not sure I can cope that long. These drugs are sending me mad. I have told them again and again...but they won't listen. Please. I can't do this."

"You can, Frank," he said. "Take the chance to rest. We are working flat out to sort this."

It wasn't what I wanted to hear, but at least it was something to focus on and I knew he wasn't mugging me off when he said he was doing all he

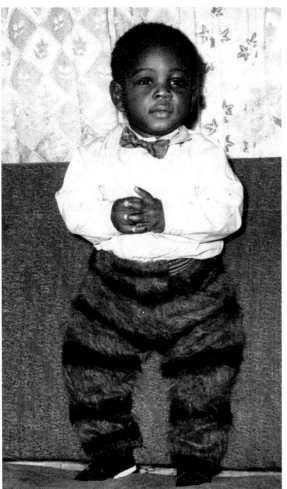

Family has always been so important to me. At the top are my wonderful parents on their wedding day.
Left: That's me suited and booted age three – not sure what's going on with the trousers.
Above: My beloved Dad. He was taken too soon – I still miss him every day.

At home and on the box.

Above left: My eldest daughter Nicola and I smiling alongside my daughter Rachel in her baby bouncer at Christmas.

Above right: My grandmother Teta and my niece and nephew make their entrance for my This Is Your Life episode. That was such a special day.

Right: A trip to Jamaica to see my grandma Teta. Here we are relaxing with Rachel and her cousin.

Below left: Proud dad with Rachel and Franklin.

Below right: My beloved mum – she was a tower of strength in my darkest days.

From Oak Hall to Buckingham Palace!
Left: Here I am after receiving my OBE.
Above: "Can't you get a proper job, Mr Bruno?"
– Prince Philip always had the best lines.
Below: With Princess Diana, a very special Lady
who I was honoured to meet many times.

Above: I've always been proud of what I achieved in my boxing career. Here I am at my old home in Stondon Massey surrounded by some of my treasured awards. Below: Henry Cooper and I in the early years. He was a special man who gave me lots of advice and support.

Two of the most important people in my career – Harry and George. Left: BBC commentator Harry Carpenter and I fooling around before an interview. Above: My trainer George Francis and I out running. He was with me on every step of my journey to the top. I miss him so much. Below: The Boys in Blue. Me with my manager Terry Lawless, George Francis, and the promoter Micky Duff, it was taken in Arizona at a training camp for my first Mike Tyson fight.

Above: Down but not out. Terry Lawless and I return home after the first Tyson fight. I lost, but proved to the world I had what it took to become a Champion. Right: that man Mike. He beat me twice and deserves his place in history as one of the great fighters.
Below: The one and only. The Greatest. I treasure this picture of Muhammad Ali and I.

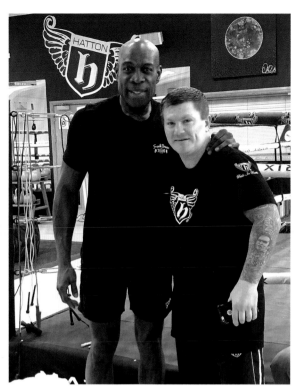

Left: We've both had our fights in and out of the ring. But we've come out on top. My friend Ricky Hatton and I after a session at his gym in Manchester.
Above: Meeting Mike... Tyson and I were pictured at Wembley after I beat James Tillis in 1987. We'd fight two years later.

Above: Suited and booted. At a boxing dinner with George Francis and the promoter, and my friend, Barry Hearn.
Right: The road to the top was long and tough but it was worth it.

Above: Swede success! Beating Swedish boxer Anders Eklund in 1985 to become European Heavyweight Champion.
Below: Sometimes you have to fall to rise. My defeat against Tim Witherspoon was so tough to take. But I refused to give in.

Above: Head bowed after my defeat to Tim Witherspoon. I needed picking up after that fight but I knew I had what it took to become a Champion. Below: Under attack. Tyson was a ferocious opponent but I was never scared of Mike.

Above: I was in control of the Lennox Lewis fight for so long. But then he caught me with an amazing punch and my dream was over. Again. Below: Moving in on McCall. I boxed the fight of my life to beat Oliver. Nothing was going to hold me back that night.

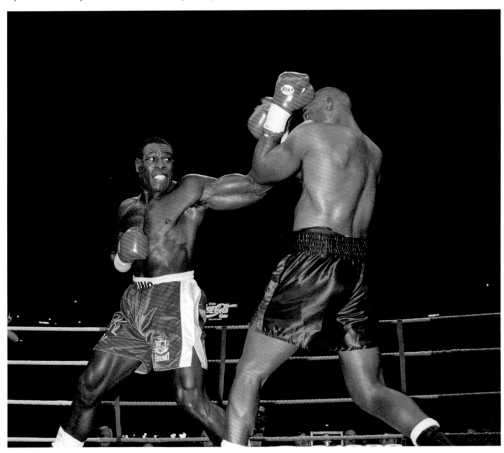

Above: Yes! I did it. My life's dream comes true as I win the World Title. I will never forget that feeling.
Left: From high to low. Mike Tyson takes my title in my final fight in Las Vegas. Defeat was tough to take but I don't regret accepting the contest.

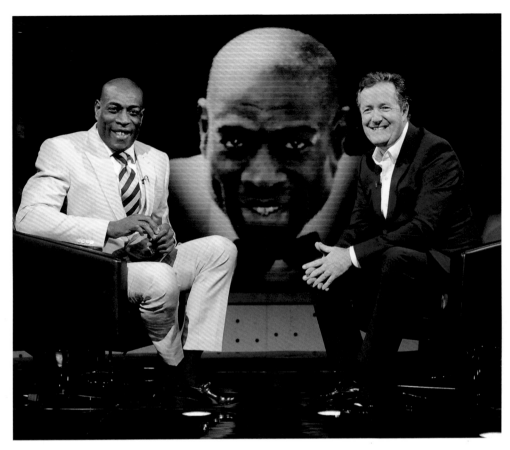

Above: My interview with Piers Morgan was supposed to mark the start of a new chapter in my life. But within weeks I was back in hospital. Below: Posing for the photographers at the Great North Run in 2015. Days later I made the decision to readmit myself to hospital. I've not looked back since.

Left: The papers break the news that I am back in hospital. Thankfully this time the newspapers were more understanding. Above: I'm behind you! My agent and dear friend Dave Davies relaxing in his garden. Below: My new toy... the caravan. I feel so happy and content here.

Top: On the campaign trail at the 2017 General Election with Norman Lamb MP. He's become a good friend. Above: Meeting Norman at his offices in Westminster. Right: A whole new fight. With members of the Frank Bruno Foundation team. We have big plans.

Top left: Proud dad. Nicola and I on my daughter Rachel's wedding day. Top right and right: Franklin and I at my daughter's wedding and ringside for the Tony Bellew vs David Haye fight. Above: My world. Here's me with Franklin, Nicola and Rachel after a spot of dinner.

Wow. To see my little girl looking like this on her wedding day and walk her down the aisle was one of the most incredible moments of my life. I will never forget it.

could to get me out. It was just that I was desperate to get home.

I was locked up with some really ill people and it was so sad to see, but what was even more heartbreaking was how everybody just seemed to be left to their own devices, to get on with it. The staff didn't seem to know what to do with us beyond giving us drugs to keep us quiet.

Yes, we were patients, but I felt as if we were being treated as guinea pigs. It was as if they didn't really know what the drugs were doing to us, but as long as we were no trouble that was fine.

I found things really tough, but I could see that for many of the other patients things were a lot harder. Many had been on meds for 20 years and couldn't see a way to get off them.

Some days I'd be having a conversation with a patient and they would be talking normally. Then they would be given their medication and 15 minutes later they were taking their shirt off, talking to the ceiling or falling asleep in their chair.

The change was so quick and so shocking. At the time it seemed awful to me, like a scene straight out of One Flew Over the Cuckoo's Nest.

I used to challenge the nurses about it, go round like a detective and speak to patients. The nurses didn't like that. They saw me as being a bit of a troublemaker, but I didn't care. Nobody else seemed to be putting up a fight.

I would ask the nurses: "How can this be any good? How can this be right? People are being turned into zombies. We have our human rights, you know."

The medication would make some people's behaviour change so rapidly. Ten days in I nearly had a fight with a young guy from the Midlands who was tough. Well, he thought he was tough. He was the one I had clocked the very first day staring at me.

I was right to have been on my guard. He had a bad temper and I could see and feel his bad vibes every day.

To look at him reminded me of my time back in Oak Hall and the bullies I'd come across in there. I had to remind myself he was very ill like the rest of us but, at the same time, I had to make sure he didn't cause me any hassle.

He was a big old lump, about my size, and I could see that he was watching me everywhere I went. So I had to be on my toes, ready for the moment he finally went for me. I knew he would.

On the afternoon it happened I was minding my own business in the dining room when, from out of nowhere, he was in front of me spitting and swearing. His eyes had gone and I could see he was about to try and be brave. We exchanged words.

"Let's take it outside then," he screamed.

"OK," I replied.

The guy was making such a racket that everyone else in the unit stopped dead in their tracks. A nurse spread herself in front of him but she couldn't hold the fella back. Suddenly he was pushing past her trying to get at me. His mouth was moving 10 to the dozen but his feet stayed anchored to the floor. I stood my ground.

"Please don't do it, Frank, don't do it," screamed one of the doctors.

I didn't lay so much as a finger on him, but the panic button was hit and all hell broke loose. Staff burst in from all angles and bundled the geezer to the ground.

He was kicking and screaming as they dragged him away. The adrenaline was pumping through my veins and my mind was racing.

I never saw the guy again. He was moved to a different part of the hospital for his own safety, apparently. Off to the floor upstairs with the guys in the handcuffs probably.

The nurses must have been worried I was going to give the poor fella a good hiding but I'd have been looking at a much longer stretch than six months if I landed one on him.

There was no way I was going to hit a man whose only crime was to be fighting for his sanity like I was.

I felt nothing but sadness. Sadness for him. And sadness for the hell I was trapped in.

Sometimes in life you have to take a punch. It might knock you off your feet. It might knock you out. But the real test is what comes next. It's how you react.

When Jumbo Cummings landed that punch on my chin it shook me to the soles of my feet and if I hadn't fallen into the arms of the referee I might have been out cold.

Where the Frank Bruno story would have gone then is anyone's guess. But I went to my corner, took 30 seconds to sort myself out, stood up and beat him.

On Day 15 in St Andrew's I woke up and sat bolt upright in my bed. I knew I was two weeks in because I used to mark each day off in the front of my Bible. Another swipe of the pen, another day. But that day something felt different.

Something inside my head was saying things were finally about to turn in a new direction. The feelings in my mind were as clear as that night I slumped down on to the stool in the fight against Jumbo.

I'd taken a lot of punches – to my health, my freedom and my sanity – in that hospital but I couldn't allow myself to keep getting punched for ever. I had a choice – go under or wrestle back my life.

I looked at the other patients in the hospital and I could see many were lost souls, caught up in the system and unable to get themselves together. If I didn't stop and change I knew I could end up the same. I had to lose in order to win.

Day 15 also brought news I had been waiting for...

"Frank, it's D-day tomorrow," my solicitor said, when he rang that morning. "The hospital has agreed to hold a hearing to decide if you can go home."

Sleep didn't come easy the night before the meeting. Instead I lay in the dark planning the things I wanted to do when I got out.

Get myself home. Rest up. Spend some time with Nina. Get back down the gym. Have the kids over. Eat some nice food. See my mum. Play my music. Catch up with my brother. Chill out.

I wasn't asking for a lot. I was just asking to live my life again.

As I walked into the hearing the following morning I knew the chance to get my life back was out of my hands. It was down to three hospital managers in suits sitting across the table.

My heart sank when I looked around the room. I saw one doctor sitting there who always seemed to be on my case. Next to him was a social worker who I just wasn't getting along with at all.

When I was told that the five of them were going to talk through how I was doing I was frantic. I didn't fancy my chances much.

But my solicitor urged me to let him do the talking. The next half an hour was like a tennis match and my life was the ball being whacked around the room. On one side, the doctor and the social worker were explaining why I needed to stay in hospital. On the other, my solicitor was arguing why I should be allowed to return home to have my treatment there.

The three guys in suits who, my solicitor explained, were hospital managers, listened to all the evidence and looked through my paperwork.

Eventually, after what seemed like for ever, one of the people in charge said his piece.

"OK, Mr Bruno," he said. "We believe there are grounds for your release, but you are going to need to meet us in the middle on this. We will recommend a delayed discharge for three weeks' time."

My solicitor explained that meant I was going nowhere for now. He said I needed to spend another three weeks in the hospital then, at the end of that time, they would meet again to discuss my discharge.

I felt totally deflated but my solicitor said it was probably the best result we could expect. He had a word of warning, too.

"Frank," he said. "Over the next three weeks they will watch you like a hawk. This is all about assessing whether you are ready to go home. You need to prove you are."

The solicitor could see how distressed I was and grabbed my shoulders.

"Listen to me, Frank: Take your medicine. Follow orders. Keep your head down. Then we will be able to get you out of here."

It was just what I needed to hear. My mind flashed back to my days in the ring. When I sat on that stool in the corner of the ring I needed clear instructions and George always had them. It always helped me to fight.

Thankfully, it was around this time I finally found a doctor in the hospital I could trust. I am not going to give his name in case I get him in trouble, but he knows who he is.

If he hadn't come along I may never have got out of St Andrew's – that is how important he was to me. He was one of the good guys and when he spoke to me I felt as if he was chatting to me like I was an equal.

When I explained I felt I was better off at home, where I could rest and get better, he listened and said he agreed. But he warned me, like my solicitor had, that I would need to keep my nose clean if I wanted to get out.

He said my behaviour was being closely monitored and I needed to prove to everyone I was well enough to be allowed home. It was the same line that everyone else was giving me in that place, but for some reason I knew this doctor had my back. I was able to explain how my medication wasn't agreeing with me at all.

He listened and arranged for me to be switched to a drug called Quetiapine. It wasn't easy changing meds, but I was able to talk through how I felt with this doctor and manage the side-effects that came with this particular drug far better than I had in the first two weeks.

He would come in every morning and evening to give me my tablets. He'd even pop in on weekends to make sure I was OK. He was also able to persuade the manager of the ward that I should be allowed to use the little gym. That was a massive turning point for me.

"Don't overdo it, Frank," the doctor said, as I left his office. "But I know how important exercise is to you so I have cleared it with the managers that you can use the gym."

"Thanks," I replied. "You don't know how much this means to me."

They wouldn't let me go there every day, but on the days I was refused permission I would go outside to the basketball court instead and do my exercise there.

I had my iPod on and in the morning, after breakfast, I would drop down on my fists and do 1,000 press-ups. In the afternoon and evening I'd do the same again. Some days I was doing 4,000 press-ups. It was so nice to be out in the fresh air. I felt suffocated stuck inside the hospital for hours on end. I spent hours outside on that court.

A couple of times I grabbed a feather duster off the cleaner to give the court a bit of a spruce-up to give the other patients a laugh. When the nurses saw me doing that they must have thought I'd totally flipped but I've always enjoyed entertaining people. I was just doing anything I could to pass the time and to get me through the day.

Being able to exercise gave me strength, and the music in my ears helped drown out the negative thoughts in my head. Otis Redding, Bob Marley and Michael Jackson became the soundtrack to my world. I'd close my eyes, listen to the songs and imagine being free.

Over my shoulder I carried a little bag with a self-help book called *The Four Agreements* by Mexican author Don Miguel Ruiz in it.

Nina had given it to me as a gift. I have never been a great one for reading but the words in the book gave me so much strength to cope with the fight I was in. Some afternoons I read it to a couple of the younger guys on the unit who were really struggling.

The Four Agreements (stick to your word; don't take anything personally; don't make assumptions; always do your best) became my rules for getting through the day.

It wasn't always easy. As my solicitor had warned me, there were often tests that came my way. I felt that some of the staff were trying to wind me up to see how I would react.

One afternoon, when I was having a really tough day on the meds, the social worker who had sat in my tribunal was in the lounge demanding to speak with me.

I was polite, like I was with all the staff, but I begged her to give me some space.

"Please ma'am, can you leave me alone for a bit?" I said. But she wouldn't stop – I felt she was in my face, demanding I go with her.

"No," she said. "I want to talk with you."

I could feel myself getting more and more tense.

"You are making me nervous, ma'am," I pleaded. But she didn't want to hear it.

Eventually, a doctor came over and ushered her away. I was glad he did. I felt as if I was being poked to see how I would I react. I knew the threat of being moved off the unit and to a more secure part of the hospital was hanging over my head like a dark cloud.

It wasn't the only occasion I was pushed close to the edge.

One afternoon I was taking a crap and two nurses looked over the door. I begged them to leave me alone, to give me some dignity. They just stood their ground and I realised all dignity had been stripped away.

The only way I could keep my emotions in check was by training. It helped to clear my mind and focus on the tribunal. Just like I had during my days in the ring I used my training to prepare me for the challenge that lay ahead: *I was exercising my demons away.*

The doctors and the nurses weren't the only ones who'd noticed my sessions in the sunshine. On some of the days when I was working out I looked up and saw the faces of patients pressed against the window inside the lounge of the Sherwood Ward.

Many of them had huge smiles on their faces as they watched me work up a sweat. It got me thinking.

One afternoon, when there was a line of half a dozen patients looking on, I managed to persuade the nurses to let them all outside and we did a little keep fit session on the court. It was nothing much, a bit of running, stretching and some exercise. The nurses didn't want me to do it.

"Look, don't worry – we aren't all going to hold hands and run away like Forrest Gump," I said. "All anyone wants to do is feel human again and get a bit of a break from the ward."

Then, under the sun on the basketball court, I watched those patients who had been reduced to zombies turn back into men. For half an hour or so we all felt alive. It was the only time I saw a lot of them smile.

Every time I saw my solicitor or spoke to him on the phone I would make the same promise.

"When I get out of here, I am going to help people with mental health problems like me," I'd say. "This can't be allowed to happen to others."

But as time passed I learned to let the anger about being locked away wash over me a little. Rather than kicking off, I just let it go the best I could. I'd listen to my music, meditate and relax.

I took the rest, took the chance to recharge my batteries and allowed my mind to stay calm. Finally, after weeks and weeks I was beginning to find some sense of a peace of mind.

There were still times the drugs got the better of me and the blackouts would come. One morning when an old mate came to see me I stood up to give him a hug and my legs just went from underneath me. I cracked two of my ribs and was in agony for days.

But rather than getting angry I just stepped back and thought it was all the more important to get away from the nightmare I was in.

Nina came a lot too and that always gave me a massive boost. She reassured me she would be waiting for me when I got out and that going forward she'd support me 100 per cent.

It was always so tough after she left, a sadness would come over me again because I was back on my own. But she'd agreed to give evidence in my hearing at the hospital and I was so proud of her for doing that.

The kids visited twice. The first time wasn't easy, I was pretty blunt about the decision to lock me away, but they made it clear they believed hospital was the best place for me. I said I was doing my best to get out and I could see that worried them. It was obvious we were never going to agree.

After they left I was able to start seeing that they were acting only out of love and concern. I wanted to prove to them and everyone else I could come out the other side stronger.

When they came the second time, things were easier. We stopped talking about the past and tried to focus on the future instead. There were still lots of things I wanted to say to my family. There were things I needed to get off my chest, that I had been bottling up and keeping to myself. But those conversations could wait. It was not the time. My focus was on getting out and trying to move on.

I called my brother Michael a few times, too. I didn't want to bother him too much. He had his own illness to fight but I didn't want him to think I had forgotten about him. I felt a bit angry we were being denied precious time together as it was unclear how long Michael had left to live.

One person I didn't want to come and see me was my mum. I knew her heart was breaking so, instead, I spoke to her two or three times a week on the phone. She knew what I was going through and was always very honest with me. She didn't like me being in hospital but felt, like the doctors, I needed some sort of medication to calm the anxiety I was going through.

When I had a wobble in those final days in St Andrew's, it was Mum I turned to. When I told her I felt degraded, she told me to have faith. When I told her I was scared, she urged me to be brave. When I told her I felt weak, she reminded me I was strong. Mum told me to use all the skills and strength I had in the ring to make sure I won this fight, too.

Then, four weeks in, I got the news I so desperately wanted to hear. My doctor called me into his office and said a date had been set in a few days' time for my tribunal hearing. He told me he believed I had a good chance of being discharged. Finally I had a goal, something to aim for. I'd been set a challenge: prove to everyone I was ready to go home.

I kept my nose out of trouble in the days before the hearing and made sure I ate and slept well. I trained more than I had at any point while in hospital.

On the morning of the tribunal Nina brought me a suit to wear and I felt like a proper person again as I put it on. When I looked in the mirror that morning I was a man again. As I walked into the hearing I knew I was a different person to the guy that had arrived at hospital five weeks earlier.

Then I was angry, frustrated and ill. Now I was ready to go home and ready to try and beat my illness on my own terms.

My solicitor had brought in a barrister for the hearing and it quickly became clear why. My team was going to need the big guns as the hospital didn't seem that keen on letting me go home.

As I sat in the room listening to the discussion going on around me I felt as if I was being transported back in time. It was like being in the headmaster's office at Swaffield Primary as I waited to hear if I was about to be expelled. The doctors were doing all they could to persuade the panel I should be kept in longer. They were saying that during my five weeks locked up I was often agitated and the only way they could get it under control was with drugs. As the doctor yapped on and on I tried to butt in. But my solicitor shot me a stare my mother would have been proud of. So I kept it zipped. Then they were bringing up Scotland again and how it showed I couldn't be trusted to take my medication. According to the social worker I had been telling other patients I wanted to fight when I got out.

"Mr Bruno has said he wants to box in a big comeback fight at Upton Park," she said. "These delusions of grandeur show he is still not in control of his illness."

If I had been talking about that I certainly didn't remember it, but then large parts of my time in the hospital were a black hole. All I could do was sit, listen and keep my fingers crossed things went my way.

Then it was my team's turn – and they didn't let me down. My barrister went through the way I had behaved since the day I arrived. He explained how I walked away when I was the victim of an unprovoked attack. He told them how I had been taking my medication and would continue to do so at home. He also recalled the day I was attacked in the market and had gone off without laying a finger on the person responsible.

"This is not a person who is a danger to himself or to others," he said. "He is more than capable of going home and living his life again."

Nina spoke next and explained how, when we'd been in Scotland, I'd not let myself go off the rails. She told them how we had visited the doctors in Scotland and that if I was released I'd be fully supported at home.

"All anyone wants," Nina said. "Is for Frank to get back to his best."

There was a lot I wanted to say about my treatment and the standard of nursing at the hospital. I forced myself to keep my mouth shut, but it wasn't easy staying silent and in the end I found it impossible to sit and listen.

I went back to my room, changed into my tracksuit and went outside to the exercise area. Standing there, smoking a cigarette, was a patient who I'd become quite close to. He was in his late sixties, had no family and had been in and out of the unit for the past 15 years. The guy had become institutionalised and unable to live his life beyond the walls of the hospital.

He said the last time he had been discharged he had no idea how to use the internet. It was as if time and the world outside the unit was alien to him.

"How do you think you will cope if you get out, Frank?" he asked me. It broke my heart to hear him asking a question like that, but there was no time to reply. I looked up and saw Nina at the door telling me it was time to go back in. It was decision time.

I felt sick as I walked back to the room. I expected them to stamp my paperwork "reject" and send me back to my room. But as I sat down, one of the doctors stood up with a face like thunder. He took his paperwork and stormed out.

The look on my solicitor's face told me we'd done it.

"Frank," he said, putting his hand on my shoulder. "It's over. It's time to go home."

Chapter 10

THE DRUGS DON'T WORK

I could see George's lips moving but the sounds weren't making sense. He put his hands on my shoulders then whispered in my ear.

"Frank, it's over," he said. *"It's time to go home."*

But what did *home* mean? That night, for me, going home meant facing up to the fact my dream was over.

George was standing in front of me as I slumped on a stool in the corner of the ring at Cardiff Arms Park, beaten up and demoralised. Lennox Lewis had just ended my hopes of becoming world champion.

"Are we looking at the end of Frank Bruno?" screamed Ian Darke, the Sky Sports commentator, watching me climb out through the ropes.

As I made my way back to the dressing room in the early hours of October 2, 1993, everyone was telling me the game was up: the press, my family, my fans. There was one single message: *"Frank, it's over. It's time to go home."*

My life was at a crossroads and I had no idea where I was going to end up.

It felt much the same as I left that tribunal at St Andrew's on June 15, 2012. One day was a defeat and the other was a victory of sorts but they both put me on the spot, wondering which way to turn and how to prove those who didn't believe in me that they were wrong.

I walked back to my room in the certain knowledge that I still had a long way to go. My hell inside that hospital had driven my mind into its darkest corners but finally, after five weeks, my destiny was back in my own hands. I'd won back control.

The doctors weren't doing cartwheels, though. There were no high fives or fanfares and I quickly realised why. After the hearing, my solicitor told me the hospital was receiving a lot of money from the NHS for my care, which left me wondering if my time there was as much about money, power and control as anything else. There must have been a reason why the doctor slammed that door so hard at the end of my hearing.

And while I may have secured my freedom, I couldn't help feeling worried for those I was leaving behind. Many of the patients didn't seem to be getting any better and were trapped inside a system which didn't look to me as if it was offering a way out. I was walking away from a hospital full of zombies who'd been stripped of all emotion. I could see in their eyes how badly some of them were hurting.

Their despair and hopelessness broke my heart. A lot were very bright people who had been stuck inside the system for so long they had lost the confidence to fight. Before I left I said I was in their corner and I promised to try and do something to help. I pleaded with one or two, who I'd become close with, and told them to look after themselves.

But as I stepped out of the unit and heard the door lock behind me I was simply glad to be free. The sun was setting but there was a clear blue sky overhead. Nina was waiting by the car and I didn't look over my shoulder as I walked away. I was determined to leave St Andrew's in the past.

"It feels so good to be out, Nina," I said, gulping in a breath of fresh air. "There were times I thought they'd keep me banged up for months."

Nina gave me a look which said she'd been worried too.

"Come on," I said putting my arm round her. "Let's go home."

It was so good to unlock my own front door again. I was back in my castle and this time there would be no running away. I had to stand and fight and try to get better.

I'd begrudgingly accepted that I had to let the doctors into my world – I had no choice. My lawyers had promised the doctors at the tribunal that I would agree to be cared for at home. If I didn't hold up my end of the bargain, I'd be carted straight back in. They were the rules. For the past five weeks I had ranted and raved about how everything would be better if they let me go home: now it was time to put up or shut up.

My treatment was placed in the hands of a team of doctors from the

Bedfordshire and Luton Mental Health and Wellbeing Services Trust. I was told that I had been released as part of a Community Treatment Order which meant that I had to accept home visits from doctors.

"How long will that be for?" I asked my solicitor.

"For as long as they want," he said.

I'd also have to attend regular appointments with a consultant near to where I lived so he could keep an eye on how I was getting on. From the very start it was made clear my care plan at home would revolve around taking medication just like it had in hospital. I'd been back indoors less than 24 hours when the doorbell rang for the first time. My stomach turned when I looked at the CCTV and saw a doctor standing there, but I had to let him in.

"Remember the rules, Frank," I told myself as I walked to the front door. "Keep it together."

He took me into the kitchen and put his bag down. Then he pulled the blinds and asked me to strip. I was injected with a powerful dose of a drug called Olanzapine Embonate.

"You'll need one of these every two weeks, Mr Bruno," he said as the needle went in.

I grimaced, clenched my fists and looked down at the floor. After everything I had achieved in life, there I was, gripping on to a chair with my backside in the air. It was completely humiliating.

But it was still better than being locked up.

The doctor insisted I had to have the injections – called depots – because nobody trusted me to take tablets.

"This will keep the medication going round your body all the time," the doctor said as he packed up his bag.

When I watched him leave I felt a surge of relief. It wasn't that bad, I told myself. I thought, a few days' rest and I'd be right as rain and back to my best. It was no biggie.

But I couldn't have been more wrong. Once the medication started to kick in I felt as if someone had pulled the curtains in on my world. Summer was in full flow but my life had yet again descended into darkness.

I didn't know it at the time but the drug I'd been injected with was the same one I'd struggled with so badly in the first couple of weeks at St

Andrew's. I may have been home but I was trapped in that drug-fuelled maze again – and everywhere I looked I saw despair.

Some days the side-effects were so awful I couldn't get out of bed. I would spend hours under the covers, desperately trying to sleep and blocking out the horrible thoughts racing through my mind. I was trapped in a cycle of negative thinking and I wasn't saying nice stuff to myself. I was constantly worrying that I was going to be put back in hospital. I was terrified that when I started to try and live my life again I'd be judged and I became paranoid about what everyone was going to think of me.

The racing thoughts and noise between my ears became exhausting. At times my head would ache as I tried to push the feelings away. I'd find respite by sleeping but my dreams were regularly being invaded by those nightmares where I'd see myself falling. Daily life inside the fog of medication was unbearable. I couldn't dress myself, I couldn't wash myself, I couldn't make a cup of tea for myself. Even getting up and downstairs became impossible.

"Please don't make me take these injections," I begged the doctors when they knocked on the door. "You need to get this stuff out of my system," I said. "It's making me go crazy."

But they made clear I had to stay on it.

"Frank, you must," they said. "It's the only way you will get better."

Some days, when the doctors rang the bell, I didn't answer. I just couldn't face it. But then, when they'd gone, I'd be up pacing my room for hours, petrified an ambulance was going to come and take me back to hospital.

Thankfully, that never happened, but deep down I knew I was starting to push the doctors away and out of my world. That would come back to haunt me big time.

As well as the injections I was placed on a strong dose of another drug called sodium valproate which, the doctors said, would help control my moods. I was also left with enough sleeping pills and multi-vitamins to open my own health shop. I needed them because some days I barely had the energy to lift my head, let alone eat. I was on so many different tablets I lost count of the number I took each morning.

My mind was racing. I'd have moments in the day when I was bursting with energy, others when I was flat on my back. When I told the doctors about that they said that was why it was vital I took my medication. My bipolar, they said, had to be controlled. I couldn't convince them that the medication was only making things worse. It was a scary feeling.

Nina was a godsend in the first few days. She took some time off work and stayed at home to keep an eye on me. There was no big family summit in the days after I came out of St Andrew's. There was no meeting round the kitchen table where I demanded to know why things had turned out as they did. There was no screaming on either side. No, that's not really how the Bruno family do things.

Instead there was this stand-off between us all.

Part of me wanted to let loose, to rant and rave about how upset I was feeling about everything that had happened, particularly when I was up in Scotland, but I kept it zipped. I knew my behaviour was being closely monitored and I didn't want to say or do anything that would lead to an ambulance arriving back at my gate.

I knew I should have been more open but I was scared about what could happen if I told everyone how I really felt and how badly I was struggling.

I sensed there was a lot the kids wanted to say too, but they didn't. It was as if we were all trying to carry on with our life without really talking about what had happened in the past few months.

"Why is it, Frank," the medics had often asked me, "that you can go out there and stand up in front of a group of strangers and make speech after speech about how you feel but you find it tough to tell the ones you love?"

I had no answer to that. But they were right about one thing – I loved my kids, I adored them and nothing would ever change that.

The relationship with my family would need putting back together, but that would have to wait. I needed to get my head straight before I started to build those bridges. I was ashamed of the way I looked and knew it was going to take time to be able to face everyone again. The drugs made me feel like someone had taken half my brain away. I couldn't understand how people expected me to live this way: unable to talk, unable to stay awake, unable to find any peace of mind.

It was the worst I had felt in my life, but the doctors insisted I had to keep taking the medicine. I would challenge them when they told me things would improve.

"Have you taken this stuff?" I would ask the doctors.

They looked at me like I was crazy.

"Do you know how it makes you feel?" I said repeatedly.

They never gave me an answer, from which I assumed they didn't.

I cut myself off from my friends and stayed indoors. On the rare days I found the strength to get up, I was shuffling around my big, five-bedroom house like an old man. My shoulders were slumped, my head was down and I was shaking and dribbling all over the place. I was slurring so much I struggled to put two words together most of the time. I couldn't talk to people on the phone or hold a proper conversation.

Nina was frantic with worry. Some mornings she would beg me to let her ring the doctors and get them round to review my medication, but I was paranoid about what would happen if we did. I pictured myself being carried out of my bedroom on a stretcher and carted back to hospital.

The doctors always insisted things would get better and the side-effects would clear.

I prayed each night they would, that I'd wake up, pull open the curtains and sunlight would burst back in. Yet days passed and the fog was still there. I didn't even have the energy to go to the gym, it was the last place I wanted to be. The communication between my head and my body seemed to have stopped working. My arms and legs had become useless so, for the first time in my life, exercising and keeping fit was of no interest at all.

I far preferred to be in bed. Some days Nina would sit next to me and read letters that had arrived from my fans. They gave me so much strength. People would write and say they were going through their own problems and it willed me to keep going.

"Dear Frank, you've been a fighter from day one...don't stop now," wrote one woman who went on to explain how she was fighting her own battle with depression.

"I remember meeting you the day after you lost to Lennox," wrote another guy. "Even then you had time for me and my son, stopping for a photo and to sign an autograph. Everyone was willing you on to win the title. And they are willing you on now."

The media coverage was pretty positive too. It was obvious the papers had more sympathy. There was no scrum at my front door – finally it looked like I was being given the space to get better.

Three weeks after I was released I had my first appointment with the local consultant in charge of my care. It took all my energy to lift my head off the pillow that morning. But I thought about the hellish days inside hospital and told myself I simply had to get up.

I knew if I didn't make the appointment everyone would think I was running away from my illness and I'd be taken back to hospital. I felt in a daze as I drove the car to the centre of Leighton Buzzard to the clinic. The world outside was passing me by and I wasn't interested in being a part of it.

For weeks I had dreamed of getting out. But, once again, freedom was not feeling the way I'd hoped.

When I sat down in front of the consultant, I explained how badly I was doing and how difficult I was finding the medication. Then he hit me with it.

"Look, Frank, you need to realise you will be on these drugs for the rest of your life," he said.

I didn't take it in at first. I thought he'd said I could never come off these awful meds.

"Sorry?" I replied.

"You will need to take these tablets for ever," he repeated.

It was like someone had turned the lights out on my life – a hammer blow. What had been the point of getting back control of my life if I was being turned into a zombie – for good?

"But I can't live this way," I protested. "It can't be right. These drugs are making me feel so much worse, I need to get off them. They are messing me up. I can't go to the gym, I can't talk to people on the phone, I can't exist like this."

I was begging the doctor to help me because I was frantic with worry. I explained how after coming out of Goodmayes nine years earlier I'd managed to get off the medication and I was determined to do the same again.

"Just give me a chance," I pleaded. "Please, please let me try. I will do anything."

Thankfully, he did.

"I will reduce the dosage of the injection you are being given and I am cutting back on the amount of the tablets I recommend you need to take," the doctor said.

"We are trying to keep you out of hospital here, Frank," he warned me. "But you have got to take things slowly and if you feel like you are slipping back you must say."

"Slipping back?" I said. "It's the meds that are holding me back."

I left feeling like I had won a little victory. I went home, looked in the mirror and told myself I had to start fighting.

Cutting back the amount of medication I was on was the little kick-start I needed. Within days I felt my energy levels returning. My mind was more focused. The fog was lifting. Where there had been an endless cycle of darkness and negativity, my mind was starting to let in happier, more positive thoughts. It was as if someone had turned a key and unlocked a part of my brain that had been put to sleep for too long.

I started forcing myself to go to the gym. It was nothing heavy at first, just two or three sessions a week at Champneys doing some light weights and gentle jogging, but I always felt so much better afterwards.

Getting back to the gym was only one small battle though. I desperately wanted to return to work as well.

But Dave told me to take things steady. I started by attending a photoshoot for Getty Images at a gym in Rayleigh, Essex.

"You don't look so good, Frank," Dave said to me that afternoon.

We hadn't seen each other for weeks and he was shocked at how hard I was finding the medication.

"Nobody knows what it is like, Dave," I said. "I have got to get off this stuff."

When I saw a video of the event a few days later I was shocked. My speech was all over the place and I didn't like the person I had turned into. I had lost my sparkle. I tried to attend a few events but some days it was just too difficult.

I felt embarrassed and ashamed about the person I had become. In an attempt to try and move forward I decided to try and get some counselling for the first time.

For me, it was a big step because opening up to someone I didn't know felt very frightening. But I was introduced to a lady called Dr Lucy Porter, who I'd previously met at an event with the mental health charity Mind, and I felt I could trust her.

Dave arranged a couple of sessions. It wasn't easy plucking up the courage to talk to a stranger at first, but I managed to get through it and express a little about how I was feeling. I knew deep down there was still a lot I had not come to terms with. I was still bottling up so many emotions. In my heart I was yet to accept my illness but I didn't want to face up to that reality.

The fortnightly appointments with my consultant became the big things to focus on. Each time I saw him we would talk through how I was doing. After a couple of months out of hospital he agreed to reduce the amount of medication I was on a second time. But he still insisted I needed to get my head around the fact I would be remaining on the medicine for the rest of my life.

"Please don't say to that me," I begged him. "I want to be able to live my life without it. I have done it once and I will do it again."

Every time the medication was reduced I started to feel so much stronger. Slowly I could sense the fog lifting. Each morning the light coming through the curtains felt a little brighter.

It made me want to exercise a lot more. I wasn't overdoing it, I had learned my lesson there, but being down the gym made me feel so much stronger in body and mind.

I now know that these good feelings are triggered by endorphins – hormones your body produces when you exercise. In my opinion they worked better than any drug the doctor was prescribing. I was regaining the confidence I needed to finally get out and about a lot more and return to work. Again, I didn't overdo things, but I felt myself slowly coming back to life.

One of the most important jobs I attended after I was released from hospital was an event to support Mind.

It was a stepping stone on my road to recovery but I was nervous and anxious when I drove to Dunston Hall Hotel in Norwich on September 23, 2012, for the gig. It was my first major public appearance since my discharge and I was wary about what people would say and how they would treat me. I was going to be interviewed by the TV presenter Trisha Goddard so I had butterflies swirling around my stomach.

I was still heavily medicated. But I was determined to get through the interview and prove to myself I could do it.

As I walked into the conference room where the audience was waiting, people started to clap. Then, I realised, they were getting up on their feet, they were giving me a standing ovation. I looked around in disbelief. I'd been scared to come here and they were giving me a welcome like this. I was so touched – it was humbling.

Trisha gave me a warm welcome too and then started taking me through what I'd been through. As I talked it all through with Trisha, the people in the room seemed to be hanging on my every word. I explained the hell I had gone through in hospital and that I was trying to get my life back on track. I was open about the drugs the doctors made me take, but I didn't pull any punches either and I made it clear I was determined to get off them and fight the illness on my own terms.

As I spoke, I noticed many people in the audience were nodding. Some in the room were fighting their own battles with illnesses and when I spoke to a few of them afterwards they agreed with what I had to say.

I got another standing ovation when I left. I felt like I was floating, all the anxiety and tension in the build-up to the event had faded away and my chest was puffed out again. When I watched a video of my speech that a punter had put on Twitter I was no longer ashamed of the person looking back at me. I could see the old Frank returning.

The following month I knew I was ready to go further, which was why I made a decision to give a big newspaper interview about my illness.

It wasn't an easy call to make. When I was first sectioned, and *The Sun* said I was "Bonkers Bruno" on the front page, it left me feeling terrible. It was humiliating for my friends and family.

I knew the press still had a lot of power so part of me wondered if it was better to keep a low profile. As I mulled over the thought of spilling my guts to the papers, I knew it was a gamble.

What might people say about me? How would they react? Was I going to be mocked all over again?

Those dark thoughts were still there. But they were trumped by one thing – I desperately wanted to have my say about what I'd been through. I have always been a proud person and being sectioned had stripped me of my dignity. I needed to wrestle it back.

I wanted to make clear how unhappy I'd been about some of the treatment I'd received in hospital and the terrible things I'd seen. I wanted to speak out about my determination to get off the meds I was on. And I wanted to be open about how I'd not agreed with the decision made to section me.

I knew it could put me at loggerheads with my family and some of my friends, but to properly move on I was determined to set the record straight once and for all.

There were no shortage of offers for the newspaper chat. In the end, we decided to go with the *Sunday Mirror*.

I knew it was going to be a big deal. It was my first media interview since I'd appeared on Piers Morgan and in the days leading up to the meeting with the paper I kept the experiences I had seen in hospital at the forefront of my mind.

When I sat down and gave my story I was not just talking as Frank Bruno. I wanted to speak on behalf of the patients I had left behind. They did not have the strength to fight – but I did. So it was time to give them a voice. That's one reason I chose the Sunday Mirror. I was worried about giving the story to a tabloid at first but I wanted as many people to read my story as possible.

The paper filmed a big TV advert to trumpet the fact they'd "got the true story" on my breakdown. When I saw it on the telly on the Saturday night, bigging up the story which would be in the next day's paper, I felt anxious at the way, once again, my illness was about to become public property.

On the morning the newspaper came out I was quite nervous as I walked down to the newsagents. I went up to the counter and there I was on the front page...*World Exclusive: Frank Bruno – My Story.*

There was nowhere to hide now. I needed some space and peace of mind and I knew where I would find it. I headed straight to the gym, put on my iPod and ran for miles on the treadmill.

When I went back into the changing room I could hear a buzzing from my locker. I opened the door and my mobile phone was going crazy. Missed calls, unread messages, hundreds of tweets, more than a thousand emails… I flicked through them with a sense of fear. Were people going to be slagging me off?

The reality was the total opposite. The support was completely over-whelming. I'd not seen anything like it since I'd won the world title.

The days that followed were a real eye opener. People crossed the road to ask how I was, to wish me well and to say how brave they thought I was for speaking out. People genuinely cared about finding out how I was doing.

It was a world away from the treatment I'd endured after coming out of Goodmayes Hospital in 2003. Back then, people would cross the road to *avoid* seeing me. They'd sink their chins into their chests and walk on by. You'd have thought I'd grown horns.

This time though, there was real warmth and interest from people because they knew I was facing up to my demons.

The interview had given me a massive boost and was a shot in the arm for my confidence. In the space of four months I had come a long way. After standing at a crossroads I was heading back in the right direction. Nothing was going to stop me. Nothing was going to hold me back.

Well….that's what I thought. But sometimes, when you are so focused on looking forward, the ghosts from your past can come back and ter-rorise you.

And in the days, weeks and months ahead I was to discover just how true that was.

Chapter 11
STAGE, SCREEN... AND SAVILE

I grabbed the box from my dining room, pulled out the scrapbook and stuck the *Sunday Mirror* article inside. It felt weird at first to be back on the front pages of the newspapers in that autumn of 2012, but I soon got my head around it.

After more than 30 years of seeing my life splashed across the tabloids this was the latest addition to a catalogue of pretty colourful stories!

I guess I first became of real interest to the press boys that night I fought back and beat Jumbo Cummings in October 1983. It didn't just set me off on a path to become a world champion. It was the moment everyone in the country seemed to sit up and take notice of this bloke called Frank Bruno.

And, of course, it was the night my double act with Harry Carpenter was born.

I was delighted at the switch to celebrity status. It was my plan, right from the start, to try and do things differently.

Yeah, I wanted to be a world champion, but I also wanted to be famous so I could be sure of a regular income and support my family when my boxing years were over. I'd listened carefully to what Terry Lawless told me.

"You'll need more than your fists to survive in life, big man," he always said.

And he was right. I took a lot of stick for all the showbiz and TV work I got involved with in between fights. Journalists used to say the same thing over and over again – especially if I lost a bout: *"Who does Frank think he is, a celebrity or a boxer?"*

I was often accused of "selling out" and being more interested about life in front of a camera than fighting. The people spouting that rubbish couldn't have been more wrong. Boxing always came first. But I knew boxing wouldn't last for ever and that I would need something else to fall back on to make sure I could support my family.

It turned out that making people laugh came as easily to me as knocking out my opponents. If I could make use of my fists then why shouldn't I make use of my personality, too?

I was naturally shy, but I soon discovered being a showman seemed to come pretty easily.

My first real taste of the world of showbiz started with a single phone call in 1985.

"Frank," said the guy on the other end of the line. "We'd like you to appear in next month's *Comic Relief* show."

The caller was a bloke by the name of Lenny Henry...

I was totally starstruck.

"Great," I said.

"You'll be appearing on stage with me," Lenny replied.

"Fine, Lenny. I look forward to it."

"We're going to do the balcony scene from Romeo and Juliet," he explained.

"Err... great. You did say Romeo and Juliet, Lenny?"

"That's right, Frank, and I am going to play the part of Romeo."

"I see, Lenny. And dare I ask what you want me to do?"

"Well we don't want you to play the part of the balcony, Frank..."

"You aren't joking are you, mate?"

"No, Frank. It will bring the house down. And maybe the balcony, too."

He wasn't wrong. The show at London's Shaftesbury Theatre where I played Juliet went down a storm.

Lenny didn't tell me he was going to impersonate me while playing Romeo! His take-off was so good that if I hadn't been wearing a dress I'd have struggled to tell us apart.

We performed three nights at the theatre and it was the moment I really caught the showbiz bug. Hearing people laugh and clap and cheer was addictive. And I wanted it more and more.

That's why I didn't hesitate when offers started rolling in for panto. The interest really started after my first fight against Tyson in February 1989. I returned home to a load of messages from agents desperate to get me on the telly and I lapped it up.

There was a lot of criticism thrown at me and people like Ian Botham and Barry McGuigan at the time – sports stars who also decided to do a bit of acting. I didn't pay any attention to it. I still think my experiences working in the theatre gave me some of the happiest moments of my life.

I thought Lenny was the master until I played a supporting role to Michael Barrymore in my debut panto performance in Aladdin at the Dominion Theatre in London's West End.

It was a huge part – the Genie – in a big theatre, but it all went fine until about the fourth night, when I relaxed too much. I was supposed to magically appear from a trapdoor and do a "ho-ho-ho" and all that business. But, when I got on stage, I totally forgot what I had practised so I just froze. I stood there for about half a minute. It was the longest 30 seconds of my life. I didn't know sweat could come out of a body so quickly. The other actors really helped and went on as if it hadn't happened.

To see Michael perform was a lesson for me, what a pro.

Sometimes I'd go for a drink with Micky and the other actors after the show. In fact, it was on a night out with him that I got the closest I ever came to laying my hand on someone outside the ring.

This one night, after bringing the house down with Aladdin, Michael and I popped to a pub across the road with the rest of the cast.

Out of nowhere, a guy came up from behind, reached between my legs and grabbed hold of my Black & Decker. Those old instincts kicked in. I swung round and was about to land one on him. Then there was a moment of clarity, and instead I lifted him off his feet by the scruff of his neck and sat him on a bar stool.

His face was a picture. Michael and the rest of the cast were cracking up, but I had learned an important lesson – my star was rising and wherever I went people wanted a piece of me. They just weren't getting that particular piece!

I had no problem with autograph hunters and fans wanting photos. I'd stop and do that all day long. But every now and then I came across a geezer who fancied making a name for himself by trying to goad me into scraps.

There was one incident when I was out with my mate Danny Salmon. We'd been to a fight and had popped into a kebab shop close to Wembley and were waiting for our grub when a couple of other fellas in the queue got a bit lairy.

Danny told them to "leave it out" but then, well, I won't repeat here what they said...

My blood was boiling and I moved forward to have a word. Thankfully, Danny stepped in.

"Do yourselves a favour, chaps," he told them. "Sling your hook before you get hurt."

Their bottle must have gone because they left without taking the kebabs they'd already paid for! As we were driving back I was a bit annoyed with Danny.

"Oi, Danny, I don't need anyone to fight my battles, you know," I said to him.

But he was having none of it. "Frank, remember who you are now," he said. "If you slip up, you'll be all over the *News of the World.*"

He was right, of course. I knew if I didn't keep my nose clean they'd take my licence off me and my dreams of being a world champion would go up in smoke. I needed to be on my guard all the time, but it didn't put me off the showbiz life and, over time, I got more confident on stage and in front of the camera.

I impressed the BBC enough to get a contract to take over from Derek Jameson as the presenter of the People series, which was all about interviewing ordinary punters doing extraordinary things. I knew all about that – a boxer presenting a TV show!

I got a bit of stick at first for my performances. I did mug myself off a bit. I was as wooden as Pinocchio at the start. But as the series went on I relaxed and found my feet.

I was even catching the eye of film producers in Hollywood who offered me the chance to appear in Rocky V. At the time the papers said they were waving £250,000 under my nose. I wish! If that had been the case I'd have been there like a shot. Truth was, I lost all interest when they said I'd be playing a fighter who was knocked out by the American boxer Tommy Morrison.

I may not have been lucky enough to land a punch on Rocky's chin but I did get to work with so many amazing people.

The comedians I acted alongside stand out. Freddie Starr, Little and Large, Les Dawson, Frank Carson, Norman Wisdom and, of course, Lenny Henry were geniuses who could hold an audience in the palm of their hands.

It's so sad that some of those legends are no longer with us. I have so many photos around my home of me alongside people I'd met who tragically went way too soon.

In the spring of 1986 I was flying to Las Vegas to watch Marvin Hagler fight John Mugabi. I was just chilling in my seat when Terry said: "Frank, there's someone here who wants to meet you."

I grabbed a pen out my pocket expecting a fan to be walking down the aisle wanting an autograph, but when I looked up it was George Michael. We sat down and spent a couple of hours chatting about music. I've always loved music. I've spent an absolute fortune over the years on records and DJ kit. So to meet George was a huge honour. His death at such a young age is an absolute tragedy and I feel so sad for his family. I could tell from the way he talked that he adored them.

Another tragic hero I was lucky enough to meet was Michael Jackson. He performed in a concert in Marbella, where I used to own a house, and I was invited to spend a bit of time with him before the gig. Muhammad Ali may have been the king in the ring – but nobody comes close to Michael in terms of musical talent. He was a one-off, a total genius and his death such a tragedy.

The photos around my house also seem to suggest I have spent a lot of time with the Royal Family! I certainly never planned it that way but it's a huge honour because I am a staunch Royalist.

I was lucky enough to be invited to the Queen Mother's 90th birthday party at Buckingham Palace so I got to see for myself why so many people adored her so much.

I've struck up a particular bond with Prince Philip over the years, too. I'm not sure why that it is but I have always found him a very funny guy.

I remember at one function he said to me: "Mr Bruno, can't you find an easier job than boxing?"

I said I didn't have the brains to be a barrister and I wasn't good enough with numbers to be an accountant.

As he listened he laughed and said: "Oh, OK. Wicked."

I couldn't believe my ears.

"Pardon, sir," I said.

And he repeated: "Totally wicked, Mr Bruno. Have a good evening."

The Prince had just dropped an impression of the line Lenny Henry used in our Comic Relief ditty on me. It cracked me up. But that's just how he is. He's a real character, very outspoken and doesn't really care what people say about him. I always really respected that.

I was honoured to be invited to attend his 70th birthday on board the QE2 when it docked at Southampton. I almost died when I was asked to lead the loyal toast to Her Majesty the Queen. I had to have a glass of water to steady my nerves and I said to Prince Edward: "What happens if I go blank when I am up there?"

Edward smiled and then took a piece of paper out of his pocket and wrote down my words.

"Your Royal Highnesses... my lords, ladies and gentlemen... the toast is to Her Majesty The Queen."

Not bad having Prince Edward as your scriptwriter, is it? Good job he had neat handwriting because my hands were shaking 19 to the dozen as I read the toast out. I got through it. God knows what my old teachers at Oak Hall were thinking when the papers reported my royal role the next day!

I kept the memories of my school years close to me as I went about my business outside the ring. That's why I was so pleased to work closely with the Prince's Trust and the Duke of Edinburgh's Award scheme and other organisations helping kids who have not had the easiest starts in life.

The work has been very rewarding and I was lucky to meet so many amazing people.

My time working with the Prince's Trust made me realise that Prince Charles has inherited his father's sense of humour. They really are like two peas in a pod and I don't think people truly understand the real side of Charles. He's a warm, kind and funny man and I have been lucky enough to receive many personal cards and letters from him which I cherish.

But as much as it chills me to admit it now, when I look back, one person I worked with outside the ring was head and shoulders above everyone else in terms of raising money for good causes.

And that was a certain Jimmy Savile...

In the weeks and months after I was released from St Andrew's, all that time that I was working on sorting out my head, I also had to come to terms with a sickening truth – the fact that Jimmy Savile, a person I'd called a friend for more than 20 years of my life, was, in fact, a monster.

Like millions of viewers, I watched *The Other Side of Jimmy Savile* on ITV in September 2012. But unlike most of them, I thought I'd known the man.

I had to slap myself across the chops to make sure I wasn't having a nightmare. In front of my eyes Jimmy was being unmasked on the TV screen as a predatory paedophile.

But that turned out to be just the start of his depravity. More and more victims came forward and more and more stories appeared in the papers.

I was in a state of shock. I was still highly medicated and so, at times, I thought my mind was playing tricks on me. How could a man I spent so much time with, and who I had run marathons alongside, have abused so many innocent kids?

None of it made any sense. It still doesn't now. But I had to face up to the fact he fooled me like everyone else.

The first time I met Jimmy was in the mid-1980s. The first proper job I did for him was when I was asked to take part in an episode of his BBC series *Jim'll Fix It*.

I jumped at the chance. The show was a big deal and it sounded like a laugh.

He'd received a letter about how Christmas had been ruined for people living in Holyhead up in North Wales after a flu bug swept through the place. So Jimmy arranged for me to go up there in the middle of August dressed as Father Christmas, hand out sacks of pressies and spread festive cheer. I was sweating my nuts off dressed in that red suit but it made a lot of people happy so it was worth it and I was well pleased.

For the first time, I saw the power and influence Jimmy had. He was always the same. Always dressed in his tracksuit, always smoking his huge cigar and always with lots of people around him.

No matter where you were or what you were doing, Jimmy was always at the centre of things. I watched him at Buckingham Palace holding court among the Royals. In his mind he was the king. Jimmy was always in charge – he had more front than Sainsbury's.

From day one he called me Francis. I don't know why. Nobody else ever did, perhaps that was the reason – to be different. It stuck and he always referred to me that way. He would introduce me to everyone he met as: "The future heavyweight champion of the world."

After that first job in Holyhead we were back in Wales a few months later, this time attending an event for the Duke of Edinburgh's Awards. Jimmy just loved being around the Royal Family.

He enjoyed being in the company of politicians too. The more power a person had the chirpier Jimmy seemed to be and the wider the grin was on his face. I was a big noise in boxing at the time but I wasn't in Jimmy's league. Nobody was. Jimmy was a proper celebrity, a superstar, and all he seemed to want was to help those in need. The sheer number of people and good causes he supported was staggering.

Now I know the truth about Jimmy's real motives I feel sick – I can see it was all an evil cover. What makes it worse is the people who Jimmy said he was helping always seemed so vulnerable.

Over the years we did loads of things together for the Duke of Edinburgh's Awards and Prince's Trust to help kids really struggling to find their way in life.

Jimmy and I also spent many hours on the road running side by side. The first time I turned up to take part in the Great North Run with him I couldn't believe my eyes. The race was about to start and he was strolling around smoking a massive cigar. I'd heard he was a serious runner yet he looked as if he didn't give a monkey's.

"Are you not racing today, Jimmy?" I shouted out to him.

"Now then, now then, young Francis," he said gesturing his hands towards me and suggesting I calm down. "Don't worry, lad. You can count me in, I'll be along in a minute."

When he turned up at the starting line I looked at him in his shorts and shouted over: "Come on then, chicken legs – try and catch me."

The nickname stuck after that. During his downtime Jimmy was often around Champneys. It was a place Jimmy and I used a lot and for me it became a second home.

He seemed to know everyone and claimed to have contacts who could seemingly solve any problem. Just as he did on his TV show, whatever your problem was, Jimmy was able to fix it.

He would boast of having a direct line to Prince Charles and Margaret Thatcher and he wanted to go out of his way to help me. At one point during my career I was having problems with the sight in my right eye.

For a long time I feared I would not be able to fight again. As soon as Jimmy found out he was straight on the blower to me.

"I've heard about the injury, Francis, leave it to me," he said.

Within an hour I had a number for one of the best eye consultants in the country.

"Tell them Jimmy Savile passed on the number," he said, before hanging up.

But there was a controlling side to him that I only really experienced once and it upset me. It was because of Jimmy that I had to stare evil in the face.

It happened in 1991 when he asked me to go with him on a visit to Broadmoor Hospital where he was apparently doing a lot of work to support some of the patients.

Now I know it was another place he abused his victims it makes my stomach turn.

But the day he invited me there Jimmy walked through the entrance acting like a VIP, Mr Big Potatoes. The staff and the patients were totally mesmerised by him. He had everyone fooled.

I was a bit nervous going inside, and the feeling in my gut wasn't helped when one of the nurses pulled me over at the entrance and said: "Don't turn your back on anyone in there, Frank."

"What d'you mean?" I asked.

"Just be careful," she told me. "Some of them will poke your eyes out if you give them a chance."

I was on my guard, on my toes and on red alert. Jimmy had asked me to open a new gym but, after I cut the ribbon, he was leading me down a corridor.

Eventually, after going through a maze of locked doors, we were suddenly in a recreation room full of a load of strange faces.

"I want you to meet this man, Francis," Jimmy announced as he ushered me towards a guy standing in the centre of the room. As I looked up a fella was there with his hand outstretched.

"Hello, Frank, an honour to meet you," the geezer said.

I remember he had a really soft voice and sounded a bit like a young lady. I shook the patient's hand and we spoke briefly, but I couldn't wait to get out of there. It was giving me the creeps.

As we left, Jimmy was beside himself with excitement. He was even more hyper than usual.

"Do you know who that was?" he asked me.

I shook my head.

"Francis, that was Peter Sutcliffe – he killed 13 women, you know," he said. "They call him the Yorkshire Ripper."

"That was the Yorkshire Ripper?" I asked. "You are joking with me, right?"

But Jimmy just grinned and said it was time to go. I wasn't happy. When the pictures later emerged, I was furious. Dressed smartly in my Sunday best, there I was holding out my right hand. Standing in front of me in a bright pink and mauve tracksuit was Sutcliffe. And smiling in the background, a trademark cigar in hand, was Savile.

I rang Jimmy to ask what was going on. But he just chuckled and said not to worry about it.

"Look, I'm sorry, Francis," he said. "But it will be tomorrow's fish and chip paper, now chin up, young man," he said before hanging up.

Fish and chip paper? Another Jimmy lie. No, the picture has hounded me. I want to say sorry to every victim's family and anyone that was upset by that photograph.

I didn't recognise Sutcliffe and if I had even the slightest hint that I was about to meet a monster like that I'd have turned my back – not held out my hand.

There have probably been close to a million pictures taken of me throughout my life. Most of them I cherish, but I wish I could delete that one for ever because it makes my blood run cold. I hate it when it appears in the newspapers and am trying to get that stopped from happening in future.

Maybe that was the moment I should have seen the warning signs and kept my distance from Jimmy. But, sadly, I didn't and our friendship lasted two more decades in the end.

Jimmy had a way of making you listen to him. And I did.

Midway through my career, when I was spending a lot of time doing panto, it was Jimmy who pulled me aside and said: "Francis, do you want to be remembered as a pantomime fairy or a champion boxer?"

When the TV people surprised me with a *This Is Your Life* episode it was Jimmy who was one of the first people to be introduced by Michael Aspel.

He burst on to the set wearing a gold tracksuit, smoking a cigar and gave me a bear hug.

Then chicken legs dropped his trousers to reveal his running shorts and told a joke about how he wanted to be known as turkey legs from that day on.

Everyone roared with laughter and he got a standing ovation. It was my big night but he was centre stage – but that's what Jimmy did. He loved the adulation.

Eight months before he died I was told by my friend Stephen Purdew, who was also very close to Jimmy, that he was ill. It was late at night but I phoned Jimmy up.

"Only you would get away with ringing at this hour, Francis," Jimmy told me.

I said: "Look, Jim, I heard you are going through a bad time right now. I hope you can get better soon."

It was the last time I spoke to him. I went to Jimmy's funeral in November 2011, because, like so many other people, I believed he had done a lot of good things in his life and I wanted to pay my respects.

He was an unstoppable force of energy who only ever spoke to me about the money he wanted to raise to help others, but it's all tainted now.

I just wish there was a chance to speak to him again. If I could, I would ask him *why?* Why did he cause so much misery for so many very vulnerable people?

I find it hard to understand when I read all the terrible things he did. I find it harder to understand how he hid it from us all. I remember seeing his former personal assistant, Janet Cope, give an interview to the papers after he died.

Dear old Janet was Jimmy's best friend. She was the woman who mopped his brow after a marathon, lit his cigar first thing each morning and made sure his gold jewellery was always polished to perfection.

Janet worked with him for 30 years and she was probably closer to him than any other person. Janet must have thought she truly knew Jimmy, but she didn't have a clue about his evil crimes. If the woman running his life didn't know, what chance did the rest of us have?

I bet Janet did a lot of soul-searching after the documentary that exposed him. During those weeks at home, recovering from my time in hospital, I certainly did. I spent many hours lying in bed, thinking back to the times I spent with Jimmy.

I searched my mind for clues, for hints of anything he had said or done that may have exposed him for what he truly was. There was nothing. Not a single moment I could recall where an alarm bell rang in my mind.

When the truth about Jimmy emerged, I stood in my kitchen and ripped up a lot of pictures of the pair of us which I'd kept in boxes in my loft.

As I emptied out those boxes, I looked closely at the photos and newspaper clippings. They'd captured me in so many different moments in my life. In the ring. On stage. And those traumatic months when I'd returned to public life after leaving Goodmayes.

The photos made me stop and think. What would my legacy be when I was six feet under? Would I be remembered as a champion? Or would I be known as the guy who lost his mind?

I knew what I wanted the answer to be. Then, as the new year began in 2013, I got a new chance – a chance to change things and make it happen.

Chapter 12

FIGHTING FOR CHANGE

Savile wasn't the only ghost keeping me up at night.

The screams and faces of the patients I'd left behind were still with me.

I was out of hospital. I was starting to feel that I was going to be all right and I was trying to look to the future. But as I lay in bed trying to recover in the months after I came home from St Andrew's, I couldn't get those poor souls – who were still stuck in there – out of my head.

And I was beginning to realise they were not the only ones suffering. The two massive crates of letters I had in my dining room were proof of that.

Every morning I woke to find another big pile had been left on the doormat by the postman. Others were passed on by the *Sunday Mirror*. Some were words of support and encouragement from my fans – telling me how brave I'd been to tell my story – and wishing me well, but most were people writing to tell me about the terrible treatment they were receiving and begging for help.

As those letters stacked up I found myself getting more and more angry: I had to do something. It was clear my condition was far more widespread than I realised. All sorts of people were having all sorts of issues coping with the stresses life was throwing at them and they weren't getting the treatment they needed.

Many were from hospital patients who'd been locked up in units like the ones I'd left behind in Basildon and St Andrew's. Others were suffering in silence and telling me they were not confident enough to talk to their friends or family, let alone a doctor. The scale of their misery really upset me.

One woman who wrote to me apologised for her handwriting being so badly smudged saying the blotches were down to the fact she couldn't stop sobbing as she wrote the letter. As I held that note in my hand I wished I could reach out to the woman, talk to her and help.

There were so many horror stories arriving at my door that I could fill a book just with them. I won't name names, that wouldn't be fair, but I kept many of the letters in my bedside table as I recovered. I read them again and again.

Two stuck out. One was from a mum and dad whose 13-year-old daughter had been battling bipolar disorder for 3 years. She'd tried ending her life four times and they were so terrified she would eventually succeed that, in the end, one of them had to sleep outside her bedroom door each night to make sure she was safe.

When the NHS eventually found her a place in a hospital it was more than 150 miles from home. So every day her parents made a 300-mile round trip to make sure she was OK. I thought of how scared I'd been, a grown man, in Basildon and St Andrew's for all those weeks. How bad must it be for kids who couldn't be with their parents? It didn't sound like proper care to me. How could that be right?

Another letter that shocked me was from a man whose wife had tried to kill herself after being told again and again by her doctor there was nothing wrong with her.

"She felt like she had got over the biggest hurdle which was asking for help," the letter said. "Then the door was slammed in her face. In the end she felt she had no choice but to try to end things."

Thankfully, the guy had found his wife just in time and was able to save her.

But what about all the other people who weren't so lucky? Who was helping them?

The stories kept me awake at night. I replied to as many of the letters as I could, but I knew I had to do something else, something more.

I talked to my agent and we fixed up a second meeting with the *Sunday Mirror* in January 2013 to talk about this shocking response to my interview. We decided to launch a campaign, to start making some serious noise about the problems with the NHS treatment on offer for sufferers from bipolar disorder and other mental health issues.

For years I had fought like a lion in the ring to achieve my goals. Now I was determined to win a whole new one: *I was going to fight for change.*

I knew 2012 had been the toughest year of my life, but I was determined 2013 was going to be different. My New Year's resolution had been to stay well and to make a difference. Now I was going to go out and do it.

Round one, as I saw it, was to demand a sit-down meeting with someone in the Government. I wanted to tell them straight how poor I believed the services were that I'd received.

The paper set up a meeting for me with the Care Minister, Liberal Democrat Norman Lamb, in March 2013. I was delighted. I wanted to look him in the eye because he was the bloke in charge at the time I was sectioned and locked up.

The morning of the meeting was one of the first times in months I had put a suit on. I felt pumped up, there was a spring back in my step. I was still on high doses of medication to control my bipolar and there was still a long way to go before I could think about coming off it, but I felt as if I was at the start of an exciting new journey.

Then the phone rang. I saw it was a withheld number so I thought it was Dave ringing to check up on me.

"Yep, don't worry I am putting the tie on today, boss," I joked.

But it wasn't Dave, it was my sister.

"Frank," she replied. "Listen a sec, it's about Michael. Are you sitting down…?"

I knew what was coming next. I didn't need her to say it.

"When?" I asked, gripping a chair to steady myself. "This morning, Frank," she said. "He didn't suffer. He's at peace."

I put down the phone and sank on to my bed. As I closed my eyes I could picture Michael as a teenager writing that prediction of his on the wall of our kitchen. That swipe of the pen had created a bond between us that I thought would never be broken. Right from the start, when people laughed at my dreams, he was at my side saying I would do it. Michael had always believed in me.

Now my brother, my hero, was gone. After I'd called my mum and my family, I wiped away the tears with my fists and went to make a cup of tea. I reached for the piece of paper in my pocket with the minister's office number on it, grabbed my phone and dialled the number. I'd have to call off the meeting.

"Mr Lamb's office," the lady said.

"Er, sorry, ma'am" I replied, unable to think straight. "Wrong number."

I tried to focus. I couldn't cancel. Michael would be willing me to go. Willing me to carry on. And I knew if I didn't show up I might never get the chance again.

As I drove the Bentley to the Houses of Parliament that day I was only thinking about my brother and what he would want me to do now. I knew I was so very lucky. I was still alive and I had the chance to start making a difference.

My mind was all over the place when I arrived but I forced myself to keep it all together. I wasn't just there for me, I was speaking up for all the patients I'd been locked up with and for all those people who had sent me letters. I knew the average man and woman on the street wouldn't be able to get an audience with a fella in a smart suit from the Government.

"Don't balls this up, Frank," I was telling myself as I walked in.

I kept a couple of the letters in my inside pocket. I'd also written down what I wanted to say. When we sat down in Mr Lamb's plush office I reached for my notes.

As soon as the minister arrived I jumped up – I wasn't sure if I had to bow or something. But Mr Lamb put me at ease.

"Frank," he said, waving me back down into my seat. "It is a huge privilege to meet you. I want to try to help you today and listen to what's been going on."

The fella was making all the right noises but I was still nervous as hell. So I reached for my notes.

"Sir, this is the hardest fight of my life," I said reading out what I'd written. "I'm still trying to win it, but to have any chance at all I need a bit more help, and I am not alone."

I looked down at the piece of paper, screwed it up and stuffed it in my pocket. I didn't need it. I needed to talk from the heart like I did on the road in my speeches. So I just offloaded – I told him how angry I was, starting with the moment the Old Bill had arrived at my door 11 months earlier.

"There were six police officers and three marked cars," I said. "If I was a robber, a murderer or a serial killer I could understand it, but I wasn't. I wasn't being violent. It was bang out of order what they did."

I was surprised by what Mr Lamb said then.

"I agree," he told me. "You should never have been treated like that."

Then we moved on to life inside Basildon and St Andrew's. I told him how I felt that many of the staff had simply not given a monkey's and that I felt as if they had wanted to keep me locked up for as long as possible.

"Sir, do you realise people are being kept in their rooms all day and pumped full of drugs to keep them quiet? I saw some of the patients turned into zombies," I said. "It can't be right. What are you going to do about it?"

I explained how exercise had been helping me and being active and reducing my medication was a boost to my recovery. I talked him through the day in St Andrew's when I'd led the training session outside and the smiles it brought to the other patients' faces.

I noticed Mr Lamb taking a hell of a lot of notes. He seemed to be listening. Even so, as I got up to leave and he shook my hand, I didn't really expect a huge amount to come of it.

But I was totally wrong. Before I'd got back on to the M25 my mobile phone buzzed into life. I pulled over to take the call, and a woman on the end of the line said she was calling from the minister's office.

She put through Mr Lamb who said our meeting had got him thinking. He wanted to work with me, he wanted me to help improve services and bring about change.

The next few weeks were crazy busy. Me and the *Sunday Mirror* launched our campaign and worked really closely with an organisation called Time To Change (time-to-change.org.uk).

Our campaign demands weren't rocket science, which is a good job because I wasn't much good at physics at Oak Hall! The main aim was to get people talking about mental health a bit more. We made clear it was OK, especially for men, to talk about their feelings and to be open. The message we wanted to get out there was there is no shame in saying you are struggling. Then, when someone makes the step to ask for help, we said the care needed to be better.

The campaign really hit home. Tens of thousands of people got in touch with the *Sunday Mirror* to sign a petition. And I was getting hundreds of letters a week too.

I worked closely with Norman (we became mates, so I'm sure Mr Lamb won't mind me calling him that) and he asked me to become a Government ambassador. At the time he was putting together a scheme which was about trying to get people out of large hospitals, like the ones I was in, to be treated in the community.

I was delighted to put my name to it. Norman and I travelled a lot around the country speaking to doctors and nurses in charge of services, talking about the care I received.

I was able to go toe-to-toe with those in charge and tell them what needed to change.

I remember one visit we made to a mental health unit in Greenwich, South London. There were a lot of police officers there that day talking about the role they played and I explained how mugged off I had felt the day I was sectioned.

Hearing it straight from someone who had been through the system really seemed to hit home. I made clear how the police and the authorities needed to treat people they section with more respect.

Norman became a friend. When he went for the leadership of the Liberal Democrats I was delighted to support him. His son Archie was facing his own problems with obsessive compulsive disorder and I was happy to offer support to him.

The difficult chapter in Norman's life underlined to me an important fact I was slowly learning about my own illness – that it didn't just affect me. No, mental health conditions have a massive impact on the lives of those close to the sufferer, too. I'd seen first hand how hard it had been for my kids, my mum and Nina to cope with me when I was at my lowest ebb.

My main aim in the campaign was to try to change opinions, to make clear no-one was immune. The massive numbers of people affected by mental ill health left me really shocked. Experts I met told me that one in four people are likely to have a mental health crisis in any given year. So if you are reading this on the bus or train, the chances are a person sitting near you will be fighting a problem, possibly with no-one in their corner.

I was really shocked to hear how many kids are affected. One charity I worked with told me that at least one in 10 children will experience a serious mental health condition before they leave school.

Time and time again on my travels around the country I'd be greeted with the same response – "It's great to have a man open up about how he feels," people would say.

That made me realise there was clearly a problem with blokes talking about how they felt.

We achieved a hell of a lot in the months after the campaign was launched. The Government promised to spend extra money on improving mental health services and they put loads more cash into projects to help kids in school.

My agent's phone was ringing off the hook as the campaign took off. All of a sudden, people wanted me to attend events to talk about my illness. I accepted many of the invites. Giving a speech about something so personal was tough at first, but it became easier over time. And, at that point, being open about my feelings was helping in my own recovery.

As well as attending events on the campaign I threw myself into a lot of charity work. It gave me tremendous strength at a time I was fighting for my own peace of mind. The work I did with an organisation called the President's Sporting Club helped so much. It is run by a dear friend of mine, called Mike Jackson, who I've worked with for many years now.

The children we support through the charity have to cope with such terrible illnesses – many of them can't walk or talk and don't live very long lives. I found myself crying in the car after I drove back from some events where I had met parents whose children were suffering terribly.

At other events I'd meet squaddies who had lost arms or legs fighting in Iraq or Afghanistan. I saw how people were struggling to cope with all sorts of pressures in life but that they were managing to find a way. Surely I could as well?

Every hand I shook, every picture I posed for, every pair of eyes I looked into, every story I heard, every speech I made, was another step along my road to recovery.

People didn't realise it at the time but, silently, they were helping to heal me. I was using the experiences of others to learn about my own. I do it a lot. I hold and I clinch.

When bad days struck I would jump in the car and drive down the M1 to some of the council estates in South and East London where I used to knock around when I was a kid.

I'd do it late at night – so I wasn't spotted. I'm lucky no-one did because they'd probably have said I was going mad again and carted me back off to hospital!

I'd park up and just watch the world playing out around me. It reminded me how tough life is for lots of people out there on the streets I grew up on.

I used those experiences to put my own life in perspective. I realised how blessed I was. And, as I started to win back peace of mind, something became crystal clear. I may have won back my freedom and helped launch a very public fight for change but, to truly recover, I could see that I had to win a battle far closer to home.

It was time to restore the broken relationship with my family and to try to return to the happier days we had enjoyed in the past.

It wouldn't be easy – but fighting for those I love most was something I'd done in the past. Now I needed to go and do it again.

Chapter 13

BLOOD IS THICKER THAN WATER

I know people see me in many different ways. Some look at me and see the boxer. Others see the bloke off the telly with the silly laugh. Many, I know, see a man who ended up losing his mind.

But for a long time, there were people out there who saw me very differently indeed.

They branded me "nigger trash" or a "sell-out" – and they wanted my mother dead.

I have never spoken about this before. When I released my autobiography, Fighting Back, it was a part of my journey to the world title that I couldn't bear to tell.

The repeated death threats my mother received were a chapter in my story that I wanted to put in a box and forget. But if writing this book has taught me one thing, it is that keeping secrets gets you nowhere. No, it only brings you hassle and heartache down the line.

So I want the people who put Mum and I through such hell to know I will never forget it. When I think about it now it makes me shake with rage. One thing's for sure, they picked on the wrong woman and the wrong son.

From a young age I was incredibly proud of my mum. She arrived from Jamaica in her teens and trained to become a nurse.

By the time I started primary school, she'd qualified as a district nurse and had earned big respect working across the South London streets where I grew up.

It wasn't easy for Mum, a black woman, trying to do the job she did. There was a lot of prejudice around then but she blocked her ears to it and was very caring and worked tirelessly for her patients, and to put food on our table.

Mum was out at all hours travelling around places like Tooting, Mitcham, Clapham and Wandsworth, visiting her patients in their homes.

Some days at school, kids would come and tell me how she was looking after someone in their family and my heart would swell with pride.

Mum's world seemed to revolve around her nursing, us kids and the church. Religion was a big part of my upbringing. Mum knew her Bible back to front and was a preacher at the Pentecostal Church in Fulham.

Every Sunday, when all I wanted to do was play out with my mates, I would be dragged off to church to watch as mum preached to the congregation. I may not have wanted to be there but I quickly found her incredibly inspiring. I was in awe when I saw her getting people up on their feet and singing. She had so much confidence and self-belief and was able to hold the attention of people so easily. Maybe that's where the showman in me comes from. Whenever Mum was preaching, the church would be jumping and it was a wonderful sight. People walked out inspired.

Members of the congregation would regularly phone up or arrive at the front door of our house for advice. What with that and the nursing, it was as if my mum was a counsellor to the whole community.

When I eventually left home and started doing well with my career, Mum never forgot her roots. As I started to earn some serious corn I always made sure she was provided for, but she preferred to carry on living her life as she always had – within the community that she adored and down at the church.

But my success under the bright lights of boxing stadiums like Wembley – and my growing reputation – brought out people from the shadows who were starting to look at my mum in a very different way indeed.

I first became aware of the threats that were coming her way in the late 1980s. It started with hate mail shoved through the letterbox by random racists telling her to watch her back. My mother's crime? Giving birth to a black man who was making a name for himself in the world.

There was more vile abuse about my wedding to Laura – how dare your black son marry a white woman, you should be ashamed, the letters would say. And when I started to pop up on TV adverts and other shows on the box, the letters just became more and more extreme.

We tried to shrug it off at first. My management team told me the best thing to do was to deal with it privately so we stepped up security around her. My brothers or nephews were on hand 24/7 to make sure she was OK. But, as time went by, the letters became more sinister. She even received one with a swastika saying: "Go home and die." Another had a picture of a gun with the words: "Bang. It is that easy to blow your head off."

Then there were frightening phone calls, full of even more threats. The calls made clear that these monsters knew exactly where my mum lived and even her day-to-day routine.

In the end we all realised that Mum's life was truly in danger and we had no choice but to get the police involved. They started investigating and took away all the letters she'd received and worked on trying to trace the people making the calls.

As the police went about their business poor Mum was really suffering. She was having so many sleepless nights that she eventually had to move into a new house round the corner from our family home.

"You will be safer there, Mum," I told her, when I helped her move in that day. But her eyes were filled with sadness. She realised she had no choice but to pack up and leave the home where we'd all grown up and where my dad had seen out his final days. All because of bigots who wouldn't let her live in peace.

Even in her new home Mum was still too scared to go home alone, so one of my brothers always had to escort her. None of us would rest easy until the police had caught the person behind all the threats. It was a sad and confusing time and for a woman who always saw the best in people it was heartbreaking.

I wish those people had come after me instead. They were picking on an old lady. It was such a relief when we got the call from the police to say they had found the person responsible for the worst abuse. But I was shocked at what the detectives had discovered. This man was publishing a race-hate magazine called Stormer and was also a member of the far-right Combat 18 group.

The magazine had printed Mum's address alongside articles calling for violence and urging death for Jewish and black people. It made me feel all the more relieved Mum had got out of our old house. If she hadn't, God knows what might have happened.

Mum bravely went to court to see the monster who had caused her so much grief get sent down for 21 months. As he was taken away the judge said that in 37 years working in the law he had "never encountered such vileness or evil before". I couldn't have put it better myself. I wish they had thrown away the key.

For years I struggled to understand or accept what had happened. As a black kid growing up in the 1970s, I had to put up with a lot of racist abuse. When I went to Oak Hall, I was picked on a lot at first because of the colour of my skin.

I had to go through all the "Uncle Tom" jibes in the run-up to the Lennox Lewis fight. Then Oliver McCall was at it in the build-up to our title fight two years later, saying I'd turned my back on my brothers.

I hated that side of my sport. I never bothered to get involved in the whole black vs white thing because people are individuals whatever colour they are. Live and let live has always been my motto.

But the abuse my poor mum suffered was unforgivable. So I'm glad I don't have the brains or the knowledge to be able to look on the internet and go and hunt down the person who did it. If I did, then God knows what I would do. Put it this way – he'd never do it to anyone else.

There is no doubt what Mum went through pushed me on to become a champion. I wanted to show the bullies, just like I had at Oak Hall, that I would win. I wanted to show them their words couldn't break me and they couldn't break the bond I had with my mother. Nothing could.

But Mum wasn't the only person I won the title for.

The family memory I hold closest to my heart about that life-changing moment I beat Oliver McCall, was the morning after I won the fight. When I returned home that day everyone wanted a piece of me. The TV channels, the papers, the magazines, but they could all wait, along with the open-top bus parade through London. I only wanted to be with my family.

That morning, September 3, 1995, I had never felt so alive as I burst through the front door. I saw Laura making a cup of tea in the kitchen and cuddled her, then I raced upstairs, lifted Franklin from his cot and kissed him on the cheek.

"I did it, son," I whispered in his ear. "Daddy did it. I won."

I heard giggles from next door and as I walked in with Franklin there was Rachel with my title belt. It was buckled loosely around her waist like a hula-hoop.

When I chased her it fell to the floor and I scooped her up and held her next to Franklin.

Nicola was laughing wildly on the bed so I got down on top of the covers and pulled my three kids in close. In the corner of the room I was on the TV. The girls had been watching my fight again. I was standing centre stage as Jimmy Lennon Jr did his business on the microphone in the middle of the ring.

"Shhhhhhhh....this is my favourite bit," screamed Nicola holding a finger to her lips. "OK, everyone shut up now, please."

Cue Jimmy. "We have a unanimous decision, the winner and new...."

Then, as Land of Hope and Glory burst out, the girls were up on their feet dancing and clapping.

I swear Franklin even gave out a little smile. Or maybe it was just wind. But as I looked at my kids I'd never felt so happy in my life. To be able to fulfil my dream and share it with them was the best feeling ever. As I watched them enjoy the moment I thought my heart was going to burst out of my chest.

But in the days and weeks after I came out of St Andrew's in 2012, that same heart that almost burst with happiness and pride, had been close to breaking.

The good feelings had been replaced by anger and hurt and I was scared that the people I needed the most were slipping away.

My eldest daughter, Nicola might not have signed the paperwork to have me sectioned and taken to St Andrew's like she had in 2003, but I knew my family had been involved in the decision to call in the doctors who sent me back to hospital. And it was tough to live with that.

I am a proud man. I was their father and I felt I should have been the one looking after them. Instead the tables had been turned. I'd lost a lot of self-respect and I was unsure how I was supposed to win it back.

I knew if I truly wanted to make a full recovery from the past I had to stop running away from it. I had to face it and find a way forward, but as the Spring of 2013 arrived it was a fight I was pretty much waging on my own because things had cooled between me and Nina.

It was nothing she had done wrong – I couldn't have asked for more support. But I knew the road ahead of me was a long and difficult one so I decided it was best I took time out on my own to try and get myself better. A huge part of it was pride. I didn't like Nina seeing the man I had become: a man who was sometimes unable to get up and down the stairs on his own or to string a sentence together.

What kind of relationship was that? I felt terrible about it. Nina had her own life to lead and I was worried I might be holding her back from living it. Looking back now, maybe it was me shutting myself off again, but my illness put a huge strain on our relationship.

I hoped, once I'd sorted myself out, that Nina and I would be able to pick things up and find happiness together, but my focus had to be on getting better and rebuilding things close to home.

Then in the spring of 2013 came an opportunity to do just that – but, as usual in the life of Frank Bruno, it wasn't simple and it involved giving the world a ringside seat for my problems once again.

During the time I was in St Andrew's, the BBC made an approach to my management team saying they wanted to make a documentary about me. Dave had refused. He was right to. I was in no fit state to do it. The most important thing was getting well, not allowing a camera crew into my house.

But the BBC weren't taking no for an answer. So they carried on with the plan and went to my former agent Laurie Mansfield instead. I'd said no, so they changed the pitch – this time the Beeb wanted to make a programme with Rachel which would look at how my illness affected her, Nicola and Franklin.

When Rachel heard about the offer she desperately wanted to do it. She and I had given recent interviews to Mind, the mental health charity. At the time I'd done those I'd been in good nick but this was totally different. I was still heavily medicated and struggling to move forward from my illness. Looking back, I think that's why they wanted to make the TV show, but when Dave found out he was not happy. He didn't want me to do it and warned me it was not a smart move.

"You need to be resting and getting better, Frank," he told me. "There will be plenty of time to do TV in the future. Tell them to get on their bike."

But I knew Rachel was keen to make the programme and I saw it as a great opportunity to get closer to my kids and to put my side of the story.

"Blood is thicker than water," I said to Dave when I explained my decision. I hoped it might be a chance for us all, as a family, to try and find a way forward and put the past few months behind us.

As it turned out, letting the cameras back into my world proved harder than I could ever have imagined. I always pride myself on looking my best on telly but I was still struggling terribly with my medication at the time the programme started filming. The first day was a disaster – it took all my energy to even get out of bed. I was too knackered to shave or wash and decided the cameras could just take me as they found me. The BBC wanted to film Rachel coming round to see how I was doing.

Rachel looked taken aback when she walked through the front door that day. I hadn't been out for a bit. I was shaking, I was dribbling, I was stumbling over my words.

They filmed us in the kitchen talking about my recovery but I felt so jumpy and on edge it was hard to sit still. I could barely look my own daughter in the eye.

I had a house full of cameramen and producers but all I wanted was to pull the curtains, get back into bed and be on my own again. I felt a total mug after they all left and was relieved the whole thing was over.

It was a weird feeling. I'd never acted that way in front of the camera before. I'd done enough work on TV to know the drill. Lights, camera, action, smile. Right, be Frank Bruno...*laugh, play the fool, be everyone's mate.*

That was the way. But suddenly I'd lost the script I'd been using my entire life. Maybe doing the programme hadn't been such a good idea after all. A couple of weeks later the cameras were back, this time down at Champneys, and thankfully I was feeling a little bit better than I had been.

Rachel and I were able to speak more openly about how I was feeling and what had gone on in the past. "Do you accept you will always have bipolar?" she asked me.

"Yeah, Rach," I told her. "But I don't accept I need to be sectioned all the time."

It was a bit tense but perhaps we both needed to get a few things off our chest.

Shortly before the BBC screened the programme, Rachel and Nicola gave a joint interview to the *Daily Mail* about my illness. I knew they were going to be sitting down with the paper, but when I read it, I found it tough. It was the most open I'd seen them both be about my illness and how it had affected them.

"As the children of someone with a mental illness, it's hard," Rachel told the paper. "Sometimes you have to step up and take the parental role when you don't really want to. It's not nice, but it's something we have to do.

"I was 16 when Dad was first diagnosed, and my coping strategy was to back off from it all because I felt so helpless."

When they asked her about the months leading up to me being sectioned in 2012 she admitted: "I'm sorry to say that I backed away from my father when he was ill again because I didn't know how to cope. That's the thing about mental illness, it affects the whole family.

"Dad's never been a chatty person. He's never been very open about his life with us. His illness was a taboo subject and we never felt we could talk about it with him. It was only when we were in front of the camera that I had the confidence to ask all those questions I was too frightened to ask before.

"My dad is my dad, not Frank Bruno the boxer. It doesn't matter who you are, everyone suffers in exactly the same way, famous or not. We love our dad and we want him to be happy and well, but if he gets ill again, we will face it as a family."

As I read the words I thought back to that day we'd all been in the bedroom laughing and joking after I'd won the title. How had things gone so badly wrong?

Nicola's words were equally tough to read as she recalled the dark days in 2003 when she'd come to see me in Goodmayes Hospital after I was sectioned.

"He was so sedated," she said. "He couldn't even lift his head up. Nothing can prepare you for that. No-one sat us down and told us, 'This is what you can expect'.

"It was a big shock. At the time, I didn't think he'd ever come round from that. For me, it was better seeing him like that than when he was manic. At least for that time he was in hospital we knew where he was and that he was safe.

"I visited him every day, but after the fourth day he wouldn't let me go near him. Someone, I don't know who, had told him it was me who had signed the papers.

"He said, 'I don't want to see her'. It broke my heart, but I still visited every day. I just had to sit with the other patients instead of Dad.

"After he came out [of Goodmayes] he was very solemn, he wasn't the old Dad, but he wasn't ill either. He seemed to have reached some sort of plateau. He didn't refuse to see me, we just didn't have a relationship. If we did speak, it was very short and sweet.

"I think it was the fear factor. It wasn't that he didn't trust me, but he was wary. He thought I'd always be on the look-out to see if he was manic, which wasn't the case at all."

Reading what my daughters said was not easy, but I knew it was so important that I did.

After years of not really wanting to hear how my illness had affected them I could now see it for myself. When the show, *My Dad Frank, Bipolar Disorder and Me* went out on the telly in late 2013 I found it very difficult to watch.

As tough as it was to see myself on TV looking in such a state, the documentary proved to be a real turning point in allowing us all to move forward together as a family. Looking at myself on screen and seeing how far I had fallen was every bit as shattering as any of the punches which landed on my jaw in the ring. And seeing how badly affected the kids had been was tough to take.

The hardest bit for me was where Nicola, Rachel and Franklin spoke openly about how they'd never really felt able to talk to me about my illness. It was a bit of a cry for help. And they were right.

I have always made sure my kids want for nothing. But, at the same time, for most of their lives they have grown up with a famous dad and that comes with challenges. To the punters I was the bloke in the middle of the boxing ring who was trying not to get his head caved in while 30,000 people roared me on. I was the fella on stage at panto getting a standing ovation. I was the guy on the telly who could make people laugh very easily.

Everyone knew Frank Bruno – or they thought they did.

But for the kids, I was always their dad first and foremost and when they saw me struggling, all they wanted to do was reach out and help me in those early months of 2012. For a long time my illness made me unable to see that. Yet after I was released from St Andrew's I was determined to change.

I could see that to truly recover I needed to not just open up to the newspapers, to the TV programmes and to other people suffering with mental ill health. That wasn't enough. I needed to open up to those people closest to me.

For so long I'd lived my day-to-day life paranoid that whatever I did I would be judged.

When you've been sectioned as many times as me you're aware that your behaviour gets scrutinised. But I knew I had to learn that didn't mean it was better to hide away, and as I found the confidence to be more open with my family I realised those fears were misplaced.

My kids only wanted the best for me – and I soon discovered how talking to them about how I was feeling worked. They didn't push me away like I'd expected. It simply brought us closer. Rachel also got a lot of messages and comments after the programme went out from people who were either having problems or had loved ones going through difficult times. She was able to point them in the right direction to get help.

I knew the programme had shown a different side to Frank Bruno and that made it tough in the days after to look people in the eye. I felt ashamed, but it had allowed me to face up to a reality – my illness wasn't just affecting me. It was affecting those nearest to me as well. I needed to fight for them too.

At the time the programme was filmed Rachel was training for the London Marathon and I was there to see her cross the finish line. As she walked over to me it was the first time we had hugged in ages and it felt wonderful. We both knew that I could quite easily have missed this moment – when she'd started her training I was in hospital. But now I was out. We'd both climbed a mountain.

"I'm so proud of you, Rachel," I said scooping her into my arms.

"Not as proud as I am of you, Dad," she told me.

Nicola and Franklin were there too and we all came together and were smiling. I pulled them all in close. In my mind, for a moment, we were back in that bedroom after winning the world title.

As we stood there together, I hoped the end of the race would mark a whole new start for us and we'd be able to leave the past behind and look forward.

But I should have known better than to expect some Hollywood ending. Unthinkably, my illness was about to catch up with me once again and part of me wondered if I truly had the strength to fight back.

The love and support of my family and friends would prove more important than ever.

Chapter 14
BACK ON THE ROPES

Everything had been going so well as I moved into 2014. Too well, maybe. After coming through the toughest 12 months of my life in 2012 I'd really turned things around in 2013. I'd managed to stay out of hospital. I'd managed to build bridges with my nearest and dearest. And I'd managed to spearhead a national campaign to improve mental health care. It seemed to have got the whole country talking and there was even chatter about me receiving another award for the work I was doing. *"Arise, Sir Frank?"* I rather liked the sound of that. Except, there was a big problem: somehow, none of it was bringing me happiness. My campaign for change had put me under pressure before I had fully recovered from and accepted my illness. It had become a double-edged sword and it was silently slicing away at my mind. As the publicity took off, I found it a struggle to walk down the street without being stopped every 10 seconds. *"How are you feeling, Frank?" "You OK now, mate?" "Why did things become so tough?"* Don't get me wrong – the support was incredible and people only wanted to be nice and wish me well. But my illness was all anyone seemed to want to talk about. The diary was chock-a-block with meetings and speeches. One day from early 2014 stands out. I spent the morning at an event speaking about my illness where I was talking to a woman whose daughter had tried to kill herself due to depression. Then, after a quick bite to eat, it was off to a charity fund-raiser where I met a soldier suffering from post-traumatic stress disorder. Finally, in the evening, I was racing around putting on the dickie bow for a posh dinner where I was guest of honour to meet other people who had been through the same illness as me. That night, as I got into the Bentley and drove home, my head was spinning, but that had become a pretty normal day in the life of Frank Bruno. And, you see, that was the problem. I was taking on everyone else's troubles and wasn't spending enough time dealing with my own: I'd put my demons in a box.

And they were getting ready to escape. I was getting up on stage over and over again and telling the punters my issues were behind me, but, gradually, I began to realise they weren't. The idea that my illness was returning left me terrified. I didn't think I could cope with hospital again so, when those dark thoughts came into my head, I did anything I could to stop them. I'd go to the gym. I'd go to bed. I'd play my music as loud as I could. Anything to stop me focusing on the mental blows jabbing away at my mind. I was spending a lot of time on my own which didn't help either. After things cooled between me and Nina, her business had taken off so she needed to be in Scotland and my work kept me close to London.

So we were only seeing each other now and again and I missed the companionship. I was speaking to the kids more than I had in the past but they had their own lives to lead and I didn't see as much of them as I would have liked. Being on my own meant I kept all my problems to myself, and, rather than opening up, as I had after the BBC documentary, I just buried it. I started slipping back into bad habits and daily life became a struggle. There never seemed enough time for all the jobs I had to do. There was, of course – it was simply that my mind had become so chaotic that I was racing around unable to cope. I wasn't eating right. I wasn't sleeping right. I wasn't living right.

The moment I knew things were going really wrong was in March 2014 when I was booked in for a big photoshoot in London. Dave had arranged for me to be pictured with my title belts for the first time in donkey's years. The snapper wanted me to stick on the gloves that day and the boxing shorts. He was saying how fantastic I looked as he was clicking away on his camera. And, for a 53-year-old bloke, I guess I did. "I feel really well," I said to the reporter who was there to write up some words. "Better than I have in a long time." When I picked up the papers the next day the person staring back at me looked like he was on top of the world – but that just brought it home to me that none of it was real. It was all for show and, deep down, I knew I was unravelling and couldn't make it stop. Around this time one thought started to dominate my mind. It would be there first thing in the morning and was still there when I shut my eyes at night. As I drifted off to sleep I'd dream about it. *I was back in the ring and fighting again.* The crowd were roaring and I'd be climbing through the ropes with people patting me on the back. When I came round in the morning I still felt euphoric. For a few hours I'd changed the script. I was Frank Bruno the boxer again – not that bloke who went bonkers. My head would sink back into my pillow as I tried to keep it real. "You're too old, Frank," I'd say out loud. "Stop being so daft." But it was too late. My illness was taking hold and my mind was telling me that the only thing I could do to stop it was to return to boxing. Finally, I confided in the person I trusted most. "I'm not feeling so great, Mum," I said to her one afternoon when I went round her house for a cuppa. "I don't know what's happening to me. And in the last few weeks I've been thinking more and more about..." She stopped me dead. Somehow she knew. "Franklin, *please* don't say it," she begged. "I can't help it, Mum. I've got to change the picture somehow." She fixed me with a stare that took me right back to the day I'd sat her down and told her I was turning professional. Back then, there'd been a look of desperation and of fear. Now it was written all over her face again. "Please don't say this, Franklin," she said. "You have to stay calm and rest. Keep your head high and please promise me you will speak to the doctors." That was the other problem – I was increasingly shutting the doctors out. Again. Being on my own so much made it easier to get away with that. Nina, the kids and Dave would ask me if I was keeping up with the appointments and I'd make out that I was, but, in reality, I often didn't let them in. Some days when the doctors arrived at my door I'd hide behind the sofa in the lounge and make out nobody was home. I knew I was playing a really dangerous game. But I was scared they'd pick up signs my illness was returning and make me go back to hospital. So shutting them out seemed like a risk worth taking. The stakes – my freedom, my dignity – were so high. I wasn't thinking straight or making sensible decisions because my mind was unravelling. And I also found the standard of aftercare shocking. During my work on the campaign I'd seen good and bad services, but I thought the doctors in charge of my home care were the pits. From where I was standing, they lacked respect, compassion and understanding. They'd pull up a couple of times a week at my gaff in a flash BMW or Merc, hand me my medication, fill out a form then disappear. I was still being asked to take loads of tablets as well as being given injections but I didn't think they were doing me any good. All I wanted was to come off the stuff but, over and over again, I was told this was how things were going to be for ever. I started to become very suspicious and paranoid around all the doctors. One guy who rocked up had so much attitude – it felt like he was trying to boss me around. He talked about when he used to live abroad and bragged that he used to carry a gun around then. To me, that felt like an odd thing to say, as if he was laying down a marker, as if he was saying: "Behave, Frank, because I can look after myself." It might sound a bit paranoid but it was how I felt and, in the end, I got really angry and lost control. I didn't like the way he was acting around me, behaving like he was Mr Big Potatoes, so I booted him out. I just didn't want him near me. It was another risky move but I was past caring. There was another doctor who was always lecturing me and saying I should stop telling the newspapers my medication was making me feel worse.

"You should say how much the medicine is *helping* you, Frank," he said, pointing his finger. "You won't do yourself any favours coming out with all this mumbo jumbo." We had a row about it. I thought he was treating me like a doughnut. I said that I understood a lot of people needed the medicine, but, for me, the idea of having an injection every week for the rest of my life was a no-go. I wasn't interested in seeing my days out like a zombie. The doctor wasn't having any of it.

"You have to carry on taking the medication, Frank, that was the agreement when you left hospital and it is vital you do."

I was frustrated that my protests were always falling on deaf ears, but there was no way he, or anyone else, was going to silence me. I'd had enough of that in St Andrew's. After he left, I stood in the lounge with only one thought keeping me company. "You can fight again, Frank," my head was saying. "That will show them. Don't let these people mug you off." I willed myself to stop, I clenched my fists and remembered the look on my mum's face. But it wasn't making any difference to the thoughts in my head. I wanted to live my life on my own terms. But as my illness took hold, that became harder and harder. When I wasn't down the gym I was spending a lot of time on my own at home. The house became a mess. I was playing my music really loud and sometimes at silly hours of the day. There were complaints from the neighbours and a few times the Old Bill came knocking. I was starting to bring heat down on myself again. One afternoon I was so fed up I just jumped in the car and drove straight to Scotland to see Nina. I hadn't even rung ahead. Thankfully, she was pleased to see me, but, just like before, it only brought hassle. My family and friends were ringing all the time to make sure I was OK and that I was going to be coming back to see the doctors. Everyone was worried I was about to do a disappearing act. It put me on edge. I didn't feel I was being allowed to live my life how I wanted to. I was a grown man, why couldn't people just trust me a bit more? In those couple of days I spent up north I was amazed at how well Nina's business was doing. Her salon was making really decent money and it got me thinking – why couldn't I try my hand at a bit of hairdressing? Nina could train me up and I could get my own place. Yeah, I know what you are thinking – turn it in, Frank. But I was for real. I was so serious I even put a message on Twitter saying I was looking to get into the business and asking for some advice. Within a few hours the tweet had gone viral! People were going bananas and some of the comments were really cruel. Lots of the punters were saying I was acting strange again and talking nonsense. It even made the newspapers. FROM BOXER TO BARBER. MAYBE HE WILL CALL THE SALON UPPERCUTS!

They were the headlines the journos came up with. It felt like everyone was taking the mickey. What did people expect me to do? Sit around my house all day on my own rotting away? Slowly I was getting myself more angry and more uptight. My fists were clenched again. And, as time went on, the only way I could see a way through the fog was to go out and use them.

I was 53 years old, and it had been 18 years since my last fight but, come the winter of 2014, my mind was made up: *I had to get back in the ring.* I'd decided the only way I could find my future was by returning to my past.

I was coming out of retirement. My love affair with boxing had never ended. I missed absolutely everything about it. Most of all, I longed for the structure, routine and discipline that the sport had always given me. My illness, I told myself, was taking that away. Only those who have boxed at the very highest level can explain what the sport gives you. When I was training for a fight I would be on the most unbelievable high. I had a team at my side who were focused only on me and making sure I ended up winning and being the best. From the gym to the training camp to the weigh-in to the press conference to fight night – everything was geared up to make sure Frank Bruno was *number one.* I needed that again. I needed something else too. I needed the feeling in those minutes before I stepped into the ring. I'd stand in my dressing room and listen to the crowd in the arena screaming at me to make my entrance. Yeah, it was terrifying. Sometimes the dressing room would shake and, as I stepped outside the door, I'd be thinking: "Why the hell am I doing this?" But that terror and that fear is so addictive. And the adrenaline it created flowed through my veins and powered my fists. When the win came and my arms were lifted into the air the buzz was impossible to describe.

The embrace from my corner, the roar of the crowd, the belt around my waist. *It was a drug.* And by late 2014, as those long winter nights set in, I just had to get my fix again. I began to convince myself that I'd never been able to finish my career on my own terms.

The injury to my eye had forced me to quit. It hadn't been my choice. What if I'd jumped too soon? What if I had one more big fight in me? I had to see.

I'd spend hours some days sitting in my lounge thinking back to those wonderful fight nights. Then, straight away, I'd be up. "You are not going to get it sitting around here at home," I was telling myself. "You need to go out and make it happen." I had to get moving. And my feet were always taking me back to the same spot – the gym. In there, I felt like Superman. In there, I felt closer to the past. In there, I felt I had a future. I was working out for hours on end and I was feeling so high some days that I felt nothing was beyond my reach. When I looked at the other fighters in the Heavyweight Division none of them bothered me. I thought I could take any of them to the cleaners. After all, I was Frank Bruno. No-one could touch me. I'd show people and I'd remind them about the champion I was. Then they would forget everything that had happened in the past few years. I'd be back in control. In fact, I was losing control – of my mind. The manic thoughts were back in charge.

It wasn't the first time I had tried to get back in the ring. After I came out of Goodmayes I wanted to fight and had asked my pal Danny Salmon to call Barry Hearn to see if he would set up a contest.

"Danny," Barry said to him. "Do yourself a favour, put your arm around Frank and say enough is enough. The arse has dropped out of boxing so he'd be lucky to get 50 grand."

But my desire to fight was still there and as 2014 drew to a close I had a crazy plan mapped out in my head. Those who really cared about me and told me to leave off were pushed to one side. When anyone told me to stop it simply made me more determined. "I've been looking into it," I insisted. "I am going to put on a fight in Nigeria and I will make millions." I was hammering my mobile phone trying to get hold of as many people as I could to arrange a fight. I was belling Frank Warren, Eddie Hearn and his old man Barry asking them all if they would help me return to the ring. I was trying to get Alex Morrison, my old mate from Scotland, involved too. It wasn't long before word got out and people were starting to talk about me and my plans to return to the ring. When my close friends found out they thought I was crazy. "For God's sake, pack it in will you, Frank," they were saying. "You'll end up doing yourself some serious damage." But I was having none of it. "If George Foreman can do it, then why can't I?" I demanded. "I can still look after myself." Then, in mid-November 2014, I found myself back in the headlines again. I'd been invited along to the 63rd annual dinner of the Boxing Writers' Club at London's Savoy Hotel. It was the usual posh, black tie dinner – nice grub, a few drinks and lots of speeches when suddenly, to my left, I saw Lloyd Honeyghan and Errol Christie squaring up. I don't know what happened but it looked like words had been exchanged and they were going to have a tear-up. Instinctively, I was up on my toes and stepped in between them to sort it all out. The story was in the papers the next day and everyone was saying how I clearly still had something about me. Yeah, I thought, I had big plans to show just how easily I could still look after myself. When my family got wind of what I was up to they were frantic. They could see how stressed and tired I was and that I was not living my life the right way once again. I could tell their hearts were breaking but I wasn't listening. I was only interested in pushing forward.

"So have we sorted a date for a fight?" I asked Dave one afternoon. "What are you talking about, Frank?" he replied. "For me to get it on," I screamed. Dave was stunned as he listened. He'd heard the rumours doing the rounds that I wanted to put on a Thrilla in Manila style Ali–Frazier comeback in Nigeria but he hadn't believed it. Now he'd heard it for himself. "Frank, this just has to stop," Dave eventually said. But I wasn't interested in stopping. Stopping was the last thing on my mind. I had to keep on moving.

Some nights I'd go to sleep dreaming about being back in the ring with George. When I woke up I remembered George was gone, time had moved on and perhaps I needed too as well. Suddenly, negative thoughts were flooding into my mind quicker than combination punches. *"Get a grip."*

"Stop this stupid talk, Frank."

"You are going to mug yourself off."

It was so confusing. One minute I had it all figured out – the next I didn't know if I was coming or going. Pretty soon, instead of falling asleep at night dreaming of boxing, I was lying awake into the early hours dreading the following day. I'd often get up and head to the gym. Yes, that place again. The place where I didn't have to stop and think about the dark thoughts invading my mind. The place where I looked in the mirror and liked the man I saw staring back. The place where I looked determined, where I had life in my eyes and determination written all over my face. But the faster my feet moved on the treadmill in those weeks towards the end of 2014, the quicker my illness caught up with me. That was the great irony. The gym calmed me down, but it also speeded me up. And as that year drew to a close I knew the countdown was on. When New Year's Eve arrived I was in no mood for partying. Instead, I was sitting in my lounge at home, alone, and the only thing I had keeping me company was fear. *Fear of what was coming down the line.* As the bongs of Big Ben rang out and Auld Lang Syne burst from the TV, I glanced to the left and at my Sports Personality of the Year 1995 trophy on the cabinet. A thick layer of dust had settled on it. When I blew it away I caught a reflection of myself staring back. And I didn't like what I saw. The light had gone from my eyes. In its place was despair. A noise from outside made me glance through the window, up at the fireworks exploding in the sky. I should have been celebrating too, but my party was about to come to an end. As 2015 arrived, my illness was about to land one more massive blow. And I'd be left with a choice: fight or die.

Chapter 15

PLEASE HELP ME

I've already told you about the proudest moment of my career – September 2, 1995: the night I stood in the centre of Wembley Stadium as world champion. The moment I was victorious, the moment my dream came true. Only seeing my kids arrive in the world, and holding them in my arms, had made me feel happier. Then, 20 years later, I stood tall all over again. September 15, 2015, London's Mile End Road: the moment I took back control of my life, the moment Frank Bruno was reborn. But this time they weren't putting a belt round my waist. No, this time, they were putting an injection in my backside. It was the day I went back into a psychiatric hospital. But this time, I wasn't bundled out of the back of an ambulance. I had walked in the front door. And this time, I told them: *"My name is Frank. Please help me."* My heart was breaking as I said those seven words. It was a great day and a terrible day – and it was the day everything changed. It had taken just 72 hours for my world to implode. That's how fast it happened. That's how quickly the darkness descended and I truly knew I was fighting for survival all over again. Despite the promises I made to protect myself after being released from St Andrew's, the bitter truth is I allowed history to repeat itself. Again. After everything I had been through it was the same old story. When I look back now it makes me feel so angry. My illness had been jabbing away at my mind for many months. Those dreams of returning to boxing were tormenting me to the point I couldn't sleep at night. But what made it all kick off this time was a simple request which came my way in mid-August 2015. It was an innocent, well-intentioned suggestion and it came from a pal, the football agent Tony "Gillie" McGill. Gillie's a good guy, we go way back, and he had asked me to take part in the Great North Run to raise money for his son who was very poorly.

There were only a few weeks to prepare, so if I'd been honest with myself and with Gillie I would have known that there was no way I could take part without mugging myself off. So what I should have done, especially after all the problems I had gone through, was obvious. I should have said no. But I said yes. Why? I didn't want to let anyone down, I guess. Once again, I was putting others first and not thinking about myself. There was another problem too. I was still avoiding my doctors' appointments whenever I could. I'd also stopped taking my medication most of the time. I was desperate to come off it altogether. But I was hiding that from the people close to me. So I made my own choice. I know it wasn't smart. It was what had landed me in trouble two years earlier – but I was not making sensible decisions because I was letting my mind run away with itself. I was trying to run before I could walk, and I was being over-confident. That's why no alarm bells were ringing when the topic of the Great North Run came up. I thought I could do anything. But I was wrong, and, my God, I paid one hell of a price. I started to train like a man possessed. Summer was drawing to a close but I was sucking the life out of every ray of sunlight. I'd be up first thing to be down at the gym and then I would be back after lunch. Some mornings, the alarm clock would be set for 3am and I was up and ready to pound the road for gruelling runs. I was 53 but training like I was 23. In my head, it was McCall or Tyson waiting at that starting line and I had to be ready. "Your pride is at stake here," I'd think as I raced off to the gym each day. "Don't end up looking like a total prat." The training only made me more certain that I could box again. "Get this run out of the way and then focus on the comeback," I was telling myself. Those same thoughts which tormented me in the days leading up to my interview with Piers Morgan were taking over again. I was beating myself up from the inside and I had no way of making it stop. History was repeating itself. Despite everything I'd said, all the wise speeches I'd given, all the doctors' appointments I'd sat through, I'd still not learned my lesson. My illness was bossing my world. The combination of coming off the meds and throwing myself into training quickly turned into a toxic one and as the clock ticked down to race day, the tank was so low I was running on fumes. My head was all over the place, I was barely eating and if I was really lucky I was getting two hours' sleep a night. I'd wake up terrified, the same noise always filling my bedroom: the pounding of my heart as it pumped out of my chest. I'd sit up, drenched in sweat, feeling totally exhausted. But rather than lie back down I was up and I was on my feet. I refused to stop moving.

September 11, 2015.... Three days to go until the Great North Run: and the starting point for the 72 hours that would change my life. My diary was rammed because it was the 20th anniversary of my world title win and everybody seemed to want a piece of me. TV channels, radio stations, newspapers and magazines were all lining up for the chance to speak to me. That evening I had two jobs down at the O2 Arena in London. I was booked in for an interview with the Sky Sports boxing team and then I was guest of honour for a dinner at the Gaucho restaurant inside the O2. The punters had all paid a packet to come and see me talk about my career, but, as I got ready at home, I wasn't feeling up for it. I was anxious and on edge. All I was thinking about was the race and how quickly I could get back to the gym. It was hard to think straight and to concentrate, it had become impossible to sit still. Gillie was with me that night and we drove from Bedfordshire to Greenwich in South London for the event. But on the way there I got a puncture so we had to stand at the side of the road in our Sunday best changing a bloody tyre. That sent my anxiety through the roof and by the time I arrived at the venue being around people was the last thing I wanted. I just needed to be on my own but Dave was waiting for me at the door gesturing at me to get a move-on. "Come on, Frank, we're late," he said to me. "We need to get going." Suddenly the red mist went up. "Don't tell me what to do," I growled at him. "These are my people," I said and pointed at the fans arriving. "Now, who wants an autograph?" I shouted. People walking past were laughing. But they weren't laughing with me, they were laughing at me. I was acting strange, all you had to do was look at my eyes to see things weren't right. Then things got a whole lot worse. I went upstairs to a room where the main boxing presenter at Sky Sports, Adam Smith, and his colleague, the former boxer Johnny Nelson, were waiting with a load of cameramen. The point of the interview was for me to talk a bit about the McCall fight. They also wanted to ask me about Anthony Joshua, who was fighting Gary Cornish for the Commonwealth title the following evening at the O2.

I'd known that was the script weeks before, but as soon as Dave mentioned the running order to me I totally flipped. "Oh, I get it," I snapped. "So it's the old fella talking about the new kid on the block, is it? I suppose you lot just want to mug me off like the rest of the world, do ya?" I've worked with Johnny and Adam loads over the years but I could see on their faces how uneasy they were feeling. They knew I was on the brink. Dave did too, especially when I started shouting and demanding to know how much money he was making out of me – money is something I never, ever talk about unless I'm unwell. But I didn't care. As I stood there, I was just thinking everyone could go to hell. The truth was I was actually surrounded by people who cared for me but I couldn't see it. When the cameras started to roll, I thought it was time for me to have my say. So both barrels went off. Everything spilled out. I was ranting and raving about people getting me sectioned and going back over my divorce from Laura. I was shouting about the money that had been stolen from me and I was saying how I was going to be coming back to boxing. Johnny and Adam were staring at each other unsure what to say or do. They looked like a couple of spare parts at a wedding. Eventually Dave burst in. "Right, that's it," he said breathlessly. "This can't carry on. Frank, you can't carry on. This interview's finished. Over." It was the first time Dave had ever had to pull me out of a job. The Sky blokes were looking at each other like someone had died. In a way someone had: the Frank Bruno they knew. If Dave thought things were going to get better downstairs at the dinner he was wrong. When I was led on stage for the Q&A, the main event of the evening, my head was all over the place. I was so exhausted I had to sit on a stool as Dave asked me some questions. He had to keep repeating the words because I was struggling to follow what he was saying. I was finding it hard to stay awake. Dave's face dropped almost down to his knees. There was gasps from the audience. I was breaking down in front of my fans, the people who loved me. The rest of the night passed me by in a blur. I remember the manager of the restaurant asking if there was anything I wanted. I ordered the finest champagne, vintage red wine and cigars. I never drink, apart from the odd pint of Guinness here and there, yet now I was ordering drinks and sitting there like James Bond. The guv'nor of the restaurant had a right old ding-dong with Dave. He was pointing his finger. "You should be ashamed of yourself," the guy said to him. "He's clearly in no fit state to be here, David. He's so unwell." It went on and on. Dave was apologising and telling him how exhausted I had been. There were a few minutes of clarity where I was up on my feet going round the tables shaking hands. I signed a few autographs and I posed for a couple of photos, but I knew I had to get away. As I walked out of the restaurant I was shattered. The Great North Run was fast approaching and I was physically and mentally exhausted. And I hadn't even reached the starting line...

September 12 – one day to go and the morning after the night before at the O2. I woke up feeling terrible. I knew things hadn't gone well in London but there was no time to sit around feeling sorry for myself. It was time to head north for the run. As I pulled off the driveway, I asked Gillie to flick on my phone. I immediately wished I hadn't. When he looked the papers were commenting about how strange I'd been acting at the O2 and suggesting I needed some help. A few had put photos up and I didn't look well. I hadn't seen any pictures of me for a while and the first thing I noticed was that I'd shed a hell of a lot of weight. Yes, I was training hard but I wasn't eating right and it was clear the results of that had taken their toll on my body and my mind. The pain was etched all over my face. I looked like I had aged a few years. The sparkle had gone and my eyes looked dead. Dave rang to say Sky had been on the phone and said Adam, and particularly Johnny, had been very cut up by what happened the night before. It had been a shock for them to see me the way I was. They were urging Dave to get me some help. They'd heard the new talk about my health that was doing the rounds on the circuit, like everyone else. They'd heard that I'd been banging on about a comeback. Now they had seen it for themselves. Thankfully, the footage never saw the light of day. I was glad, it was one thing I didn't have to worry about. If that film had been put out I'd have been all over News at Ten in a heartbeat. I had enough on my plate. The night before the race we were staying at Gillie's place in Sunderland. I barely slept. I was tossing and turning with worry. It wasn't the race that was bothering me so much. No, it was more than that. I knew I was in the midst of a whole new battle with my mind and that it would last longer than 13 miles. I knew my illness was back and that I needed to get some help. But I still had a race to run. I couldn't pull out. I couldn't let anyone down. There wasn't time to worry about myself. As I lay in the dark I was wide awake and exhausted. I stared at the clock and 11pm soon became 1am, which soon became 4am, and suddenly it was time to get up, to warm up and to have a little jog around the block. Race day was September 13 and it was definitely unlucky for me. By the time I arrived at the event I was out on my feet but there were still all those miles to conquer. As I stood at the starting line, staring numbly ahead, I was unsure what direction I was going in. I was surrounded by thousands of runners but I felt so alone. "Frank, Frank, FRANK!"

I turned round and there were the photographers. "Come on, Frank, give us a smile," they shouted. "Cheer up, Frank, if the wind changes you'll stay like that," another snapper called. "Sorry, boss," I said, raising my fist in the air to give the guy the shot he was after. The cameras flashed, hurting my tired eyes, and then I was taking my position at the start. My mind was racing but my body was shot to bits.

But there was no time to feel sorry for myself. Ready.... "Brunooo, Brunooo, Brunoo," the cry went out from the thousands of people who had turned up to watch.. Get Set.... "Come on, Frank. Do this one for 'Arry! Know what I mean!" someone shouted. Go! Bang. The gun was fired and we were off. A sea of people moved forward. I felt as if everyone was racing past me and panic set in. "For Christ's sake, speed up, Frank," my head was telling me. "You must go faster." I did. But it didn't matter. People were still coming past. I felt like I was standing on a bridge over a motorway watching cars race by. I was falling further back with each second. I gulped in some air and willed myself to move faster. Then finally, at last, the speed of my feet seemed to match that of my mind. I could hear the chants. "Brunooo, Brunooo, Brunooo," they shouted. "Thank God," I thought. Yes, the training was paying off. All the hurt, all the pain, all the long days and sleepless nights had been worth it. Ha! I knew they would be. No-one could stop me. I'd finish this race. Then I'd box again. I'd show everyone. I'd... Arghh! I was in agony. A shooting pain down my side and a popping sound from my hip. I was down on my knees desperately sucking in some air. "You OK, Frank?" one of the stewards said to me. "I'm fine, boss," I said. But I wasn't. I was in agony. Up ahead I could see a lady in a wheelchair who was competing for a charity. I gritted my teeth and tried to run, it hurt like hell but I managed to catch her up. I grabbed her wheelchair and started to push. Cheers rang out from the crowd. "Hooray! Good ol' Frank," someone shouted. They thought I was playing the fool again. Back in panto. Back on the stage. But I wasn't. I was clinging on to her wheelchair to stay on my feet. My hip had gone – I heard a bone pop – and it was hurting like hell. My body, like my mind, was breaking down. I should have stopped there and then. I should have walked away, but I had to keep moving. I couldn't give up. The rest of the race is a blur, I just remember feeling a sense of relief when I got over the finishing line, but when I looked up at the clock I was furious. I'd got nowhere near the time I wanted. I thought I'd let myself down and I didn't want to stick around a second longer. Gillie helped me to the car and we drove back to his place. When I got in, Dave rang and he sounded frantic. "Are you OK, Frank?" he said. He'd been getting lots of calls from people at the race and there'd been a load of messages posted on Twitter from punters watching me take part. Everyone seemed to be talking about how poorly I looked. They were commenting on the amount of weight I'd lost, the torment on my face and the glazed look in my eyes. Once again my state of mind was being openly discussed as if I was public property. I sank on to the bed and held my head in my hands. I tried to rest, but it was impossible. Even after running a half-marathon I still couldn't settle, I couldn't allow myself to stop. It had been weeks since I had had a proper night's sleep and panic was now starting to set in. My entire body was closing down and my heart seemed to be beating so fast. The next 24 hours passed by in a blur. I remember getting up very early on the Monday, the day after the race, and deciding I was going to drive to Glasgow to try to see Nina. I had no idea if she was in or if she even wanted to see me, as I didn't even stop to ring her. As I got near to the Gorbals, I stopped at a petrol station and grabbed a crappy bouquet of flowers. When I pulled up at her flats I'd already changed my mind about knocking. I left the roses on her doorstep and walked back to the car. I drove without a break from Glasgow to Bedfordshire. I didn't want to stop, I had to get home. I'd had it with the world. That car journey felt like I was in the middle of some crazy dream. I was holding the steering wheel, I was driving down the motorway, but I wasn't in control. I was looking in on my own life and I could see that unless I did something I was going to crash and burn. Eventually, not far from home, I pulled over at the side of the road into a petrol station and parked up then reached for my mobile. "I'm not feeling so good, Dave," I said. "I'm confused. I'm not sure where I am. I'm not sure I can cope. Can you help me, please?" As I sat there, I knew. I knew I couldn't keep running any longer. I called my children and told them I needed help and that I thought it would be best if I went back into hospital. Yes. I really said those words. *I need help. I need to go into hospital.* It was the moment in my life that I finally accepted I couldn't beat my illness on my own. Then a wave of fear hit me. The thought of going back into hospital left me terrified, but in my heart I knew there was no other way. I only made one demand – I didn't want to go in by ambulance. If I was going to do this, I wanted to walk in and out on my terms. I was finally willing to surrender but I wasn't prepared to lose my dignity. My family spoke to the doctors overseeing my care in Bedfordshire and within 24 hours a bed had been sorted for me at an NHS mental health unit close to the Royal London Hospital in Whitechapel. Going into an NHS hospital was important to me. Just like all those years ago in Goodmayes, I knew checking out wouldn't be an option. I understood that the doctors had to be in charge. As I packed up my bag on September 15 I tried to stay strong. I stood in my hall at home and looked at the picture of me hanging on the wall: there I was in my prime, the title belt over my shoulder, in the ring, a champion. So alive. So focused. So perfect. I glanced in the mirror by the stairs and quickly turned away. When would I be home again? I had no idea. A social worker was sent to pick me up and, as I got into the backseat, I tried to keep my head held high.

As we pulled out of the gate I was scared about what lay up ahead but took comfort from the fact I was not being taken away in an ambulance again.

When we arrived on the Mile End Road I saw the hospital building up ahead. I thought about the hundreds of times I'd driven down that road in my life and never noticed the building in front of me. But, as I walked through the door, I hoped it was the place I would finally find peace of mind. Then, that sound again.

Clink.

Chapter 16

FIGHTING BACK

It wasn't until I stopped moving that I realised just how ill I'd become. When the doctors sat me down and examined me on that first day in the Tower Hamlets Centre for Mental Health they didn't hold back. "Frank, this isn't good. For a start, when was the last time you slept?" the doctor asked. I thought for a moment, unable to answer, until the silence eventually became uncomfortable. In the end, I had to admit: "I'm not too sure, sir." He looked concerned as he checked me over and straight away he made it clear it wasn't just my mind that had been racing. It was my heart too. The weeks of frantic training for the Great North Run had left me a physical wreck. "Frank, listen carefully," the doctor said "At your age, if you carry on putting your body through all this stress and strain then you are going to end up having a stroke, a heart attack or both. You can't carry on like this." Each time I broke down, the doctor explained, I was moving another step closer to the end. That's how serious things had become.

I had my head in my hands. I knew I had to listen. I knew if I didn't make damn sure this was the last time I ended up in hospital I was putting my life in danger. Coming to terms with my illness and coping with it better was now a matter of *life and death*. That's how important it was. But there was more. "There is one other thing I must say here, Frank," the doctor said. "It is brilliant that you made the decision to come in off your own bat. But now you are here, we think you need to be treated for at least a month. If you were to try and leave we would recommend you were sectioned." *That* word again. It was so hard to hear. I'd hoped that after a few days' rest they might let me go home. The reality was I was going to be locked up for weeks. But it wasn't a lost cause, the doctor said. If I played things straight, if I let the hospital help and if I allowed the nurses into my world, things would get better. "You have got to stop fighting the system, Frank," he said. "We want to help you, but you have got to help yourself first." He was right. It was time to accept that everybody: my kids, my family, my friends, the doctor, even the flipping milkman I imagine, only wanted me to get better. Nobody had it in for me. The doctors warned they needed to put me on very high doses of medication. They had seen my notes and were aware how much aggro I had given the staff in St Andrew's and Basildon about the tablets. But this time the doctors went to great lengths to explain how the medication would help me. They said my brain was like a muscle which was badly bruised and I had to allow them to make it strong again. The doctors said my bipolar disorder was on the F-31 part of the condition's spectrum. In layman's terms this meant I was suffering from serious mania which could lead to psychotic episodes if I wasn't careful.

This condition needed to be treated urgently with medicine, they told me. I needed to face up to the fact I would have the illness for the rest of my life and that if it wasn't properly treated I could eventually become suicidal.

I didn't like the idea of going back on medication but the diagnosis had shocked me so much that I knew I had to listen to what I was being told.

So they put me on a cocktail of drugs in the first few days. Very quickly I was given high amounts of sodium valproate which the doctors said would work quicker than lithium to help stabilise my moods.

Or as one nurse told me bluntly: "Frank, we are injecting you with this stuff to stop you from breaking down." It knocked me out for days and I was sleeping for 18, 19 hours a day at first. I wish I could tell you more about those first few days in hospital but I can remember hardly any of it. I have since learned the doctors were putting my brain to sleep and allowing it to repair itself. Dave was one of the first people who came to see me. As I sit here now, I can picture very little about the visit apart from handing him a Rolex watch. I was paranoid someone was going to nick it. No idea why. The rest is a blur. The curtains had been pulled in on my world. So I have asked Dave to fill in the gaps. This is what he remembers.

The last time I had seen Frank was as he left the Gaucho on the Friday night at the O2. Something in my gut told me I wasn't going to see him again for a while. It was clear to everyone close to Frank that his illness had returned and he was struggling. It was heartbreaking to see. He had worked so hard to get better after coming out of St Andrew's. I managed his diary very carefully. The rule was that his health always came first. That is why I was so against the BBC programme Frank did. Nothing else mattered except Frank getting better.

When he did start to feel stronger, being back at work and leading on the Time For Change campaign was a huge tonic. But for many months leading up to the Great North Run we all became worried about Frank again. He had been talking a lot about boxing again and was asking me how we could put on a fight. I tried to get him to stop but he was determined. I explained the chances of him getting his licence back were close to zero, but when Frank gets an idea in his head it can be difficult to get him to change his mind, especially when he is ill. I urged him to slow down, to take things easy and to forget about the run for a start.

As the Great North Run approached I was getting increasingly worried about the amount of training Frank was doing. I wasn't with him every day but I became aware of how many hours he was putting in and it frightened me a bit. It felt like Frank was training for a fight. The night I saw Frank at the O2 was the first time we'd met up for a few weeks. I could see he was in a very bad way again. He looked just like he had in the period leading up to his illness taking hold in 2012. I was worried how Frank would cope going through it once more. So, when he rang me to say he needed help, part of me was glad. I was proud of the decision he made, it was so brave. After all Frank had been through, to walk back into a hospital took such guts.

As I drove to the hospital that morning with my wife, Michelle, we were both frightened about the person who would be waiting for us on the ward. The reality was a hundred times worse. We were taken through what seemed like a maze of locked doors into a little living room area. Then, suddenly, I could hear the sound of feet shuffling on the floor. I looked up and there was Frank, his shoulders drooped, his head down, with tears streaming out of his eyes. I helped him sit down and Michelle and I both gave him a hug. There were lots of tears. Frank said he loved us and we said how much we loved him, too, and how we were going to support him. Frank and I had been through so much. We'd put on so many wonderful shows together and appeared at countless events. Now we were sitting next to each other in a psychiatric hospital unsure of what the future would hold. He must have fallen asleep three or four times during the hour we were there – it was obvious the medication was knocking him out. Two nurses were at his side the whole time. At one point Frank was saying that he was looking forward to getting out and fighting again. My heart broke as I heard him say that. But the staff were quite firm with him. They said: "No, you won't be doing that, will you, Frank? We've discussed that." It was sad hearing him talk about boxing, but I knew it wasn't really Frank talking. It was his illness.

Whenever Frank is unwell, the talk of boxing returns. It's as if a ghost from the past comes alive and he has to try to re-create everything he had. I am not going to try and pretend I understand it as only Frank knows his mind. But I do know how hard he has found walking away from boxing. The sport made him what he is. It was clear Frank had a whole new fight in front of him. The doctors warned Michelle and I that his heart would not be able to go on taking further punishment.

When the nurses said visiting time was over I didn't want to leave. After everything we'd been through together and all the great times we'd shared, to see Frank like that was devastating. As I got up, he gave me a hug and I saw a look in his eyes that hadn't been there when I'd walked in. I could see the determination and the spirit. He had a long way to go but it was obvious Frank was up for the fight. He may have been on his knees that day, but as he stood up and walked out of the door I had never been more proud of him."

Dave was right. I *was* preparing to fight, but it wasn't easy. A few days after his visit I woke up one morning with the most awful thoughts whirling through my brain. The doctors had warned me the drugs could do that, but as my mind went out of control I couldn't stay in bed a second longer. Instead I was up, on my feet and pacing the ward like a wounded animal. I needed to get out, I needed some space, I needed to be anywhere but in hospital. Then, before I knew what was happening or where I was, I was falling, hard and fast towards the deck. It must be a dream, I was telling myself as I lay on the floor. It couldn't really be happening. But then a sharp pain was cutting through my chest and there was blood gushing out of my head and spilling on to the floor. Why wasn't I waking up? Why was the blood still running? And why was the pain in my chest getting worse? Suddenly the doctors and nurses came sprinting in and I quickly realised I wasn't dreaming. This was for real. It took five of them to lift me up and put me on a chair. I'd hurt my ribs so badly that they thought three of them were broken. Thankfully, they weren't, but I looked a total mess as I sat there. I looked like I did the day I was attacked in the market. The cut to my head was so big I needed three stitches to stop the blood. I still have the scar today. The drugs they were giving me had literally knocked me off my feet. It left me terrified but the doctors were fantastic. They reassured me that the side-effects were normal and to be expected. I was prescribed diazepam to control my moods and haloperidol, a drug that is used to help control mania and psychotic thoughts. And I needed all the help I could get.

Life wasn't easy during the first two weeks. The ghosts of those terrifying times I had spent inside Basildon and St Andrew's were constantly haunting my mind. I spent a lot of time in my room. The bed in the corner and the window above it with a view of the world outside, they were all I needed. I withdrew into myself.

Sometimes I'd lie there and try and work out if I could squeeze myself through the window and run. But what would I be running from? My problems. They would just come back. I knew the only way I could wrestle back control of my life was to stay where I was. Outside, Dave was taking care of business. He released a story to the *Daily Mirror* telling them that I was back in hospital but that I had made the decision off my own bat. One of the nurses showed me the story. I looked at the front page and said: "At least they've not called me bonkers." We both laughed. I understood why I was public property again. I had launched a mental health campaign and now I had broken down again. I got it. I could tell why there would be huge interest from the public, but I tried not to let it get me down. I knew there was too much at stake. The hospital was full of patients involved in terrible battles of their own and it broke my heart to witness the trauma and sadness, the sight of people slowly fading away. Just like in Basildon and St Andrew's, many of them were just normal geezers, the sort you wouldn't give a second glance if you saw walking down the high street. But when I looked closer I could see the suffering. The middle-aged man who sat near me in the TV room most days had once raised a family and held down a well-paid job running his own firm. Every morning in the hospital he would put his suit on, just like those days when he headed off to work. Then life turned bad for the fella and he was sectioned. They wouldn't let him wear a tie in hospital – that was too dangerous for him and for the staff. But he insisted on wearing his grey checked suit every day. I didn't laugh at him like some of the other patients did, though. I could see it was his only connection to the successful person he used to be. For now though, that man was gone, he was history. When I looked, I saw the suit was stained and it hung loosely off his body. He liked to tell me how it had fitted really well when he bought it.

His fingertips were stained yellow with nicotine. Most days they'd shake. He wasn't chairing staff meetings or clinching business deals any longer. Now his days were spent sitting staring at the TV screen in front of him, slumped in an armchair while his eyes looked blankly ahead. He wasn't the only one whose world was on pause. The young kid sitting opposite him should have been in the prime of his life – not fighting for it. He'd done well at school, really well. He was a straight-A student tipped to go to university. He would have been the first one in his family to do that, but things went badly wrong at college when he got himself involved with drugs, and fell in with the wrong kind of friends – a bit like some of the guys I knew at Oak Hall.

Eventually he'd fallen out with his family. Time and time again they'd tried to help until, in the end, they had enough and he was out on his ear and living in a grotty bedsit on his own.

He didn't care, though, he didn't need anyone, he said. He'd be fine. Nothing life could throw at him was a problem. At least that's what he thought. Then the voices inside his head started telling him something else. Now he was sitting in the same room as me. I felt so sad for him. When I looked at him, I saw my son Franklin looking back. They were the same age. Some days, when he was really struggling, I pulled my chair over and we'd talk. I'd give him a hug and tell him that he had his fight and I had mine. "We're no different," I said. "You can get through this." They were the words I told him every day. He insisted he would win that fight, but his eyes couldn't hide how scared he was about what the future might hold. To see such human sadness after all I had done to campaign for change left me heartbroken, but the nurses said I hadn't seen the half of it.

"More and more people are coming through the doors, Frank," one told me. "It's sad, but folk are buckling under the stresses of what life is throwing at them. Mental health problems seem to be affecting more and more people. And we haven't got enough beds or money to look after all those who need our help."

Her words hit home. Although I knew I had to look after myself first, I promised to carry on fighting for everyone else when I got out. But while the NHS was clearly under big pressure, I couldn't fault the doctors, they were excellent. The care which had been lacking in St Andrew's and Basildon was there every single day at Tower Hamlets. Maybe all the campaigning, all the shouting and screaming *had* done some good. In those first few days the doctors said it was important I had total rest for a least a fortnight. There were no visits. It was vital, they said, I focused only on my recovery. The thought of not seeing anyone was tough. I desperately wanted to see the kids and my family and friends. But I agreed. I spoke to my children and my mum on the phone instead. It was easier this time than it had been before. The anger and frustration of the past was gone. I was in hospital because I needed to be.

They said they were proud of me. I was fighting for them as much as anyone else. Just like those days in the ring, I felt like I had a team around me again – and I didn't want to let any of them down. Then there was the support I had from the public. I got so many letters, cards and presents sent to me in the hospital it was wonderful. Many were from people I'd met during my work on the campaign and it gave me such a massive boost. Releasing the story about my relapse helped me win back a little bit of respect. People could see I had made the decision to go back to hospital and I was determined to beat my illness. As I allowed myself to rest things started to get better. Day by day, I was feeling stronger. Each morning when I woke up the feelings of fear and despair were lifting. I could sense something coming alive. My recovery felt a world away from what I had been through in the past. In the terrifying days after coming out of Basildon and St Andrew's I was not only trying to win back control of my mind, I was on a mission to claw back self-respect.

This time I had done that the moment I walked through the hospital doors and asked for help. It was the moment I had looked my illness squarely in the eyes and said: "I am not frightened of you any more." Then I realised what the feeling was coming back to life inside me – it was courage. It was fire in my belly. It was the fire that I had shown when I laid out Joe Christie, it was the fire I had shown when I came back after that defeat by Bonecrusher Smith and it was the fire I had shown to out-point McCall. The doctors were pleased with my progress but they warned me not to rush things. Those 28 days in hospital came and went pretty quickly and I still didn't feel ready to go home. In the past, I'd have been ranting and raving and demanding a tribunal to get the hell out. This time, I knew I had to take my time so I took small steps towards the exit.

I wasn't marking off the days like I had been in the past. Instead I was taking the opportunity to rest and recover. In the end, I was inside the hospital for nearly six weeks. That's how long I needed to give myself. I've had shorter training camps for fights over the years. But I knew this was a fight like no other and I wanted to be in the best shape possible to defeat it. I learned to accept that my bipolar was like no opponent I'd ever faced in the ring. I told myself it was time to face up to the fact I would have my illness for life. I realised it didn't matter how many punches I landed on it, that it would always exist. Like a cancer, my illness could return, so I had to make sure I was ready. During that time, I had a lot of discussion with my family and friends about how I wanted things to be when I packed my bags and went home. I was determined that this time things would be very different. I couldn't remain trapped on this merry-go-round. I had to find a way to get off. I preferred living on my own and being in my own bubble, but that had been causing me problems. I could see that.

Dave said he was going to look at getting someone to help run my daily life to lighten the strain. Whenever he'd suggested that idea in the past I'd always told him to forget it. I didn't want strangers knowing my business. I was paranoid that they'd just try and nick all my money like before and pull a fast one. And I didn't like the idea of being bossed around, but the more I thought about it, the more I realised it was a good idea. I discussed my ideas a lot with the doctors and nurses. There were counselling sessions and meetings with social workers too in the last couple of weeks.

They were delighted by the progress I was making and with the words coming out of my mouth. I was not running away from my illness any longer. I was ready to face it and fight it. And by the time the day came for me to go everybody accepted I was ready. When I'd left Basildon and St Andrew's, I knew none of the doctors had been happy about the decision of the tribunal. This time, I was walking out the front door with my head held high and the support of the doctors and nurses. For six weeks I'd accepted help and felt so much better for it. I agreed that I would carry on taking on the medication and allow the doctors to visit me at home. When I stepped out of the hospital the light hurt my eyes at first. For so long, there had been darkness but now that was firmly in the past. Franklin was waiting for me by his car and smiling.

"Come on, Dad," he said. "Let's get you home." I raced over and gave him a hug. As I walked away from that hospital I didn't look back. I was moving forward and I wasn't going to allow history to repeat itself ever again. But in order to do that I had to let go of my past. It was time to throw in the towel.

Chapter 17

THROWING IN THE TOWEL

I settled down on the sofa in the TV studio and reached across the table to take a sip of water. Beads of sweat had formed on my brow and I could feel the anger bubbling away inside of me. It had been there for days, and now I was ready to let it out. I took a deep breath as Phillip Schofield and Holly Willoughby arrived in the studio and we all shook hands. I heard the theme music playing and the director said we were about to go live to five million people. The interview on ITV's *This Morning* on February 1, 2016, was supposed to be about my recovery. Since I'd left hospital, things had been going well. I was attending appointments with the doctors and allowing them to come and see me at home. And, finally, I had accepted some help by allowing someone to run my life for me, which had taken a lot of the pressure off me.

But, in the days leading up to the TV interview, comments I'd read in the newspapers which had reportedly come from boxing promoter Eddie Hearn had made me furious. Young Eddie is a good kid, I've known his dad Barry for many, many years and have a huge amount of respect for everything the pair of them have done. Eddie is a big deal these days and rightly so. He should be proud of what he has achieved.

But he'd apparently given an interview where he said his man Anthony Joshua would knock me out in two rounds. I was shaking with anger when I read it. I felt totally humiliated. Had everything I achieved, every-thing I'd won in the ring counted for nothing? Eddie seemed to be shooting his mouth off at a time when Anthony hadn't even fought for a world title. I couldn't understand why they were singling me out. Where was the respect? Why was he trying to turn me into some sort of a national joke? I'd lost sleep over it and in the run-up to the interview I was getting more and more wound up. So when the cameras turned to me in that studio a switch just flicked in my head and I hit back. *3-2-1....Action.* "Phillip, listen," I said urgently. "I've got to tell you, I'm coming back to boxing."

If I'd had a Jelly Baby in my hand I could have lobbed it in Phillip's open mouth as he sat there looking at me. He was in shock. At the age of 53 – and 20 years after my last fight, I'd dropped a bombshell on live TV. "I'm coming back into boxing," I repeated, as Phillip spluttered back to life. "Why, Frank?" he asked. I wasn't in the mood for this. "I've got no choice," I countered. "I train every day. Then I get Eddie Hearn, a so-called promoter, saying Anthony Joshua would knock me out. I'm not even dead. That's why I've got to get back into boxing, to get this out of my system." By the time I left the studio the whole country seemed to be talking about my interview. Thousands of fans on Twitter were begging me to think again. Even the author Irvine Welsh took a few minutes away from writing his latest novel to pile in. "PLEASE PLEASE PLEASE FRANK, DON'T DO THIS," he wrote. But I didn't care. I'd gone. On the drive home from the TV studio I turned on the radio and heard people ringing in to talk about the interview. "What would you say to Frank if he was listening?," the DJ asked. "Don't do it, Frank," said a woman caller. "You'll end up dead." I pulled over, stopped in a lay-by and leaned back in my chair. There were a dozen missed calls and a couple of texts. One was from Dave. "What the hell was all that about?" he said. "Call me now."

I closed my eyes and switched off the engine. I was in danger of letting things spiral out of control. Again. So, there and then, in that lay-by I made myself a promise. "This has to end, Frank," I muttered. "It has to end now." When I look back at that interview now I cringe. It was awful. A total car crash. I was talking rubbish, reacting and hitting out. It turned out Eddie had been pretty badly misquoted and now there are no hard feelings at all between us. But, not for the first time, my actions had led to me being at the centre of a media storm and people were starting to ask questions about my state of mind. *Did Frank need some help? Is he really winning this fight?* I could hardly blame them. When was I going to learn? It had been a terrible, rambling interview where I'd lost control. It reminded me how careful I needed to be about the way I conducted myself. And a couple of days later I was left in no doubt what my kids thought about my idea of returning to boxing when Rachel and Nicola gave an interview to the *Daily Mail*. It was hard to read. "When you're ill, you reminisce about the past," Rachel told them. "I understand he's never going to lose that urge to box, having had that career for so long he's never stopped training, but it's just not happening. He may say he's making a comeback, but he's not." Nicola had been left equally upset by my appearance on the show. "I don't think anyone would be silly enough to try to arrange a comeback fight," she told the paper. "But if they did, I could never watch it. I can watch videos of Dad's old fights and they still stir up some nice memories, but I think this talk of a comeback is just one of his lightning ideas." They were right. I had to face up to the reality that my boxing career was over. It was the only way I could move on. So my agent and I prepared a statement for the papers. Those words, released on February 6, 2016, and five days after the *This Morning* interview, were the full stop on my career. I'd finally faced it. My boxing career was over. But it was also about so much more than that. I'd overcome one of the final obstacles that was threatening to stop me from winning control of my mind. *I'd accepted my fighting days were over.* Just like I had done that day when I walked into hospital and asked for help, I had faced down a demon and knocked it out. I fully accept now I will never, ever fight again. The game is up. At my age it is simply impossible. Not long after I announced my retirement, I appeared on a Channel Five documentary called *Me... & My Mental Illness*. Tony Blair's former spin doctor Alastair Campbell was in it too, as were about a dozen people suffering with bipolar. The programme, where the producers wanted everybody to talk about how their illness affected them, was the first step on my journey towards learning more about my condition. I was keen to do it because I wanted to lay the ghost to rest of that BBC documentary I had appeared in with Rachel – where I had looked so unwell.

One thing I took out of the programme was that I had been able to complete my boxing career without any regrets. Well, there is one: I do dearly wish Harry could have been ringside to see me win the world title. He'd retired the year before, so it was Ian Darke I spoke to first in the ring after that belt was put around my waist. No disrespect to Ian, but when I imagined winning the world title, I'd always seen Harry there at my side. When we did eventually see each other after the McCall fight we had a big hug. We'd been through so much together. So it broke my heart when he died seven years ago. I miss him terribly. When I close my eyes, I can still hear his voice. That precise, intelligent commentary, painting a picture of the battle as it unfolded before the viewer's eyes. When I released my last book he was still around and he sent me a nice message. I know if he was here now, he'd be reading this, willing me on, encouraging me to keep well and to stay focused on my recovery. Harry's family quite rightly wanted their own private funeral after he died. But there was a big memorial service and, as you'd expect, it was standing room only. Sadly, I was unable to be there because I was overseas, but I was very honoured that they asked me to put together a few words in tribute. It felt strange sitting down and writing them. We always seemed to come out with great lines together. Now, suddenly, I was on my own. The show was over and somehow I had to do justice to my dear old mate 'Arry. Apparently a few people chuckled when Des Lynam read them out. "We didn't set out to be a double act," I wrote. "But with my intelligence and Harry's good looks it was inevitable we would go far." We will never see his like again and I feel so lucky to have had him at my side for so long in my career. There aren't many people who have had such a big influence on my career. Another, however, is my idol Muhammad Ali. Sadly, like Harry, we've lost Ali in the time that has passed since I released my life story. Like the rest of the world, I was broken-hearted on June 3, 2016, when news broke that he had died. Ali, quite simply, was the reason I wanted to be a boxer. As a kid growing up, I looked at this amazing man and this amazing fighter in complete awe. I saw his story as a pathway to a brighter future. I wanted to fight like him. George taught me the old Ali trick of pushing down on an opponent's neck when I was in doing my work at close quarters. But I learned there was no way you could copy Ali. He was unique and truly the greatest. It wasn't just Ali's fighting in the ring I found so mesmerising. When he spoke in interviews I would get goose pimples. I remember thinking as a kid how Ali was proof you could land a punch on the world with your words as well as your fists. One of my most treasured possessions is a letter he sent to me. *"Dear Frank," it says. "When I watch you fight I am relieved that you didn't come along in my time. You might have given me a whole lot of trouble. I know that you are a good man and you have a nice personality. "And you're not bad looking either. If we were matched for a title bout it would be awful hard to make myself angry enough to fight you. So, Frank, I'm glad we never fought and I'm glad we'll never have to fight because I like you too much."* Then Ali signed off with a poem – written just for me. *"I'm no fool, I've been to school, And you're too cool, You're not dumb enough to stay on the stool and let me rule."* They are words I will cherish for ever, not only because they were sent by The Greatest but because Ali had noticed I was a good man outside the ring. To me, that was as important as him recognising my skills as a fighter. I was lucky enough to meet him a couple of times when I was preparing for fights in the US. He'd come down to the gym and give me advice. To come face to face with the man I'd grown up idolising was a dream come true.

But I could see his illness was taking hold and it was a tragedy to witness the way he deteriorated in his final years. He was a shadow of the man he'd been in his prime. Those who want to put boxing down and talk up the dangers use Ali as an advert for what the sport can do to a man. But those people forget the Parkinson's disease Ali had suffered can strike down anyone.

Having come through tough times myself, I know one thing for sure – Ali would not have wanted to suffer, and in the end I think his death was a blessing for him and his family. Finally he was free of pain. But the legacy he left will live on. They'll never be anyone greater.

Like Ali, my illness has led to talk about a possible link to boxing. Over the years, I've been asked many times about whether I believe my days in the ring led to my mental health problems.

When I was first sectioned in 2003 all the newspapers seemed to be talking about were the reasons behind my illness.

Could the years of blows to my head have led to me developing mental ill health?

Lots of doctors were piling in. They were insisting there was a definite link between brain injuries and depression and other conditions like dementia, Alzheimer's and Parkinson's disease.

I understand why people make the connection, particularly with all the talk over the years about the so-called condition, "boxer's brain". Only recently I was out driving with my old pal Cass Pennant, when the talk turned to some of my toughest fights. I replayed those big blows to the head I took against Bonecrusher Smith. I thought back to that brutal stoppage against Tim Witherspoon. I pictured the punch that shattered my dream against Lennox Lewis. And, of course, I reflected on the two defeats against Mike Tyson. They're pretty difficult to forget.

"We weren't put on earth to take such beatings, Frank," Cass said to me. He's been in enough scraps himself in his time to know!

I've thought about it a lot. And I've followed the tragic stories about the England 1966 World Cup winning team, whose repeated heading of those heavy old leather footballs is thought to have led to some of them getting dementia. But I don't believe my boxing career has led to me developing bipolar.

No, I have a very different theory. I can say with certainty that the punches over the years did me far less damage than the lifestyle changes which came after I walked away from boxing. The divorce from Laura, the loneliness, the battle to find something, anything, to replace that boxing drug: they truly were the hardest punches I have taken in life. They took me to the edge of a cliff and, sadly, I fell hard. But after I announced my retirement I began to feel stronger and stronger. I was walking away from the past and towards a brighter future. I knew my defences were up and I was ready for whatever punches my illness would throw at me. I'd come so far. I'd been able to ask for help. I'd finally accepted my boxing career was over. So now was the time to start winning the biggest battle of all. Winning back peace of mind. And keeping control of it.

Chapter 18

NATIONAL TREASURE

The noise was so loud I thought my eardrums were going to burst. "Brunooo, Brunooo, Brunooo." The last time I heard my name ring out like that was when I was standing on the starting line at the Great North Run on the brink of a breakdown. Now, as I sat at a table in the centre of a posh dining room, my feelings couldn't have been more different. As I got to my feet at the Grosvenor Hotel in London's Park Lane I was buzzing. I danced across the stage and threw a couple of boxing combinations, left then right, and the 500-odd guests were up on their feet clapping, cheering and singing my name. For a few moments I felt like I was back in the ring, back at Wembley and back to my best. It was February 6, 2016. Only a few days had passed since I had appeared on *This Morning* but I was on top of the world again. From low to high: but this time it wasn't my illness that was taking me there. It was life. I was about to accept a lifetime achievement gong at the second ever British Ethnic Diversity Sports Awards. It was my first major public appearance since leaving hospital. I walked up to the microphone and, as I looked out at the sea of faces, one stood out, the young super-middleweight fighter James DeGale. My mind flashed back to the terrible Sky interview I had given at the O2 a couple of months earlier. I'd come so far since then and I was determined not to let myself down. Young boxers like James were the future, I understood that now. My success was in the past. But the past belonged to me: that's why I was standing where I was now, about to make a speech. The room fell silent. I took a deep breath. I hadn't planned to say too much but then my heart took over.

"To get a lifetime award while only in your 50s is a little worrying, especially with

my youthful looks and young man's body. But seriously, when I think back to when I was a child the moment I saw Muhammad Ali fighting I only had one dream. I wanted to hear the ring MC saying 'Frank Bruno, champion of the world'. Well, in 1995 it happened and that is my legacy. As a boxer I was a fighter, and for those with mental ill health I will try and continue fighting. Thank you and goodnight."

As I stepped away from the microphone and headed for my seat, the room exploded into a noisy standing ovation. Everyone was on their feet, including James, patting me on the back. I knew they weren't just applauding my speech. It was their way of showing they knew I'd come through the toughest fight of my life. I couldn't speak as I sat down at my table. I had to grit my teeth to hold it all together. The emotion was building up. All the pain, heartache and torment of the previous weeks came to the surface. I knew I had to look forward and forget about the past. The shiny trophy I had in my hands was a huge honour, but the prize I needed to win was my sanity. I had to get back control of my mind. That was the only way I could enjoy the rest of my life. It didn't all quite go according to plan at the Grosvenor, though. It wouldn't be Frank Bruno without a bit of a drama, would it? When dinner was served my head was still in the clouds. In my mind, I was still up on the stage accepting my award so I was not properly paying attention to the lovely grub the waitress had put in front of me. And when I put the "asparagus" in my mouth and swallowed it, I wasn't expecting what came next. Suddenly my head was on fire, tears were running from my eyes and sweat started to pour from my face. I looked across at Dave's plate and saw the massive green chilli sitting untouched. So that was the "asparagus". "Are you OK, Frank?" he asked... "Not really, Dave," I croaked. The fact I was loosening my bow tie and necking water like it was going out of fashion was a bit of a clue. Everyone at the table was looking at me now and they all had the same expression – one of absolute horror. "Frank's having another bloody breakdown," I heard one posh lady say. The waitress walking behind me nearly dropped her tray of drinks. They all seemed to be holding their breath. Then Dave's laughter boomed out. And when they realised what had happened, God, did they look sheepish.

Thankfully, some nice ice-cold yoghurt sorted out my chilli burns. And when the steam eventually stopped coming out of my ears I really enjoyed the rest of the evening! Being back out among my fans and my friends was the tonic I needed. It had only been a few weeks since I'd left hospital and I had been keeping a pretty low profile. I was being true to my word and not overdoing things. As I had promised the doctors, I was resting and trying my best with the medication. It wasn't easy – but more on that in a moment. The kids were round a lot and they took it in turns to stay over for a few nights which was nice because having people around me felt good. And I had also made another big change in my life – I'd finally allowed someone in to help take the pressure off me.

I first met Carmen at the end of 2013, when my mental health campaign was in full swing, and she wrote out of the blue to Dave to ask if I would be willing to come and meet some of the pupils at a school in Northampton where she worked. Dave gets requests like that all the time. But he liked her letter.

She said she was looking for somebody inspirational and that her pupils had behavioural, emotional and other difficulties. Carmen thought meeting me might help in some way. When Dave mentioned it I was only too pleased to go along because my own experiences at Oak Hall had taught me how important it was to get a good start in life.

Carmen was in charge of the visit that day and when I turned up we just clicked straight away. She was bossing me around a bit and I wasn't used to people doing that. Most places I went, especially when I was giving a speech, there would be people going out of their way to do stuff for me and roll out the red carpet. But Carmen was keeping it real and I just liked her style.

I called Carmen a week later because the young people really touched my heart and made me so welcome. I told her I'd like to go back to the school and it became an ongoing thing. I would go and visit and take the kids on the pads and do a bit counselling with them.

Carmen eventually went on to work for Women's Aid and offered me the chance to help out some youngsters who needed support.

I did as much as I could and we quickly became friends. In the run-up to the Great North Run in 2015 we lost touch a bit because I was so focused on the training.

But Carmen was one of the first people to call Dave when she saw the story in the *Daily Mirror* saying I had gone back into hospital that year. She wanted to pass on her best wishes and, as they got talking, Dave mentioned to her that we needed to bring in someone to help run my life.

So on the Monday after I came out of hospital, Carmen came over to my house for a coffee and we talked it through. The next evening we went for dinner. My boy Franklin came and she brought her son along, too. As we were eating pudding, she just said: "Look, Frank, if you want me to do it then you need to let me know by next Monday morning." It was typical Carmen, straight to the point, no messing. She had a good job but was prepared to jack in her post to come and work for me as my personal assistant. I wasn't sure about having someone around me every day because I liked my own space. But I could also see accepting help was a good thing. It would take pressure off me and stop me getting stressed. So we agreed to give it a go. I didn't expect it to last long, but I was totally wrong. I knew within days Carmen would not be going anywhere. She was a godsend. She just got everything sorted. She helped manage the work diary so I knew exactly where I needed to be and when each day. And she built in rest days so I didn't overdo it.

In the past I'd been dashing around, burning myself out, but she quickly put a system in place that gave me order and routine. Discipline had returned to my world. The confusion vanished. And my old disappearing acts with my doctors weren't an option any more – Carmen was very strict about that. We'd go to every appointment and answer every knock on the door. She made me understand why I needed to see the doctors.

"If you have nothing to hide, what are you worried about, Frank?," I remember her saying to me one morning. "I will be at your side and we will just go with the flow. If you don't see the doctors, if you don't let them into your world, there is only going to be more and more concern."

Having someone alongside me when I had questions to ask or problems to discuss made things easier. Carmen was able to monitor the side-effects from my drugs and could see for herself how badly I was struggling at times.

That was such a relief. Often, I suspected the doctors didn't believe me when I told them how the tablets affected me.

Suddenly, just like during the years I was boxing, I felt as if someone was in my corner again. There was routine, order and things felt calm. I wasn't having to do everything for myself. And rather than feel guilty about that, I felt empowered. The little things – *doing the washing, buying the shopping, paying the bills, making sure I was at jobs on time, driving to events* – were being taken care of.

Pretty soon I didn't even have to ask if things were being sorted out. Carmen knew what needed doing and just got on with it.

My chaotic life of the past which had often seen me spending lots of money on food and other things I didn't really need, and raised so much concern, was history.

I finally felt I had some support, and no-one was happier about that than my dear old mum. She'd been worried sick during the weeks I was in hospital. When I spoke to her on the phone, she told me again and again how I needed to accept some help. "At last," she joked when I told her. "Whoever the woman is, she deserves a medal. Now don't be giving her any gyp, Franklin, or you will have me to answer to." There was no chance of that though. I wasn't stupid. I knew accepting some support had made things easier. I was able to speak openly with Carmen about my condition. For the first time in my life I was properly facing up to my illness. Rather than shying away from my condition I started to read a lot more about it. I wasn't afraid of it any more. I spent a lot of time watching YouTube videos and listening to others talk about their illness. And it helped me to accept I wasn't alone.

I'd always been fully prepared when the bell rang in my fights. Now I had to treat my illness exactly the same. Carmen and I talked about the symptoms that people who have bipolar often display and discussed which ones applied to me. *Wild swings in mood?* Yes. *Energy levels off the scale some days? Yes. Talking excessively now and then?* Yes. *Occasionally blowing loads of cash for no real reason?* Yes. *Struggling to sleep for nights on end when I was manic?* Yes. But *why?* Had I been born this way, or was there a reason? Were there triggers, as the doctors called them, for my illness? Or was I clinically bipolar and dependent on drugs for ever? These were the questions

I needed to find answers to. Everything I discovered left me convinced I wasn't born with this illness. No, I believe my condition has been caused by issues in my life that I needed to deal with in a better way. There have been many triggers. The biggest ones, without a doubt, were my divorce and my retirement from boxing. The money which had been stolen and all the distrust and paranoia that came with it had also driven me to the edge. Living on my own had been such a hard blow, too. For years, I had people around me and then, suddenly, I was having to do everything for myself and I wasn't coping. So I turned to something familiar, the gym. But that had become a place of both peace and turmoil. Yes, it kept me calm and on the level, but when I overdid things, like I had in the run-up to the Piers interview and the Great North Run, I was making myself manic and exhausting my body in the hope it would slow down my mind. I learned to see how big a part stress and trauma play in my condition. Controlling all that was the key to keeping it at bay. Carmen was always able to quickly spot when I was getting myself stressed out or run down and if my mind was racing. When those moments came we'd talk and try to come up with ways to deal with things.

She was one of the first people to call me after my *This Morning* interview. At the time she was on holiday, but when she saw it online she was straight on the phone.

"What were you playing at?" she asked me.

"I don't know, I just lost it a bit," I explained. "It was a mistake. I can see that."

I always felt I could be honest with Carmen and she wouldn't judge me. We then chatted for an hour about what we could learn from the interview and how we'd make sure it wouldn't happen in the future.

Learning to understand my condition was only part of the problem, though. To keep it at bay I needed to go much further.

One of the things that helped was turning to counselling again. But this time I came at things from another angle. Pouring my heart out to a stranger had never really helped me but I knew I had always been a good listener.

So, instead, my management team arranged for me to do a few sessions with a trained counsellor and learn how to support others. I wasn't sure people would take me seriously as Dr Frank! I'd played that role years before on an Irish TV chat show and I brought the house down. But the more I thought about the idea, the more it grew on me. Eventually I enrolled on a counselling course. Going back to school felt a bit daunting at first because I was never the most academic of kids. But as well as taking part in counselling sessions, I underwent training in how to support young people struggling with their own mental health problems. It taught me a lot of very useful tips about how to manage my own stress and anxiety far better. I learned meditation, breathing techniques and how to mentally walk myself through a possible situation, visualising how I want to react, to help me to manage my stress levels. The gym came up. I learned that exercise is key in keeping stress levels low but overdoing it can have the opposite impact. I started to become a lot more open with my family about how I was feeling. For too long we'd all been walking on eggshells. Now, for the first time, if I felt things were getting on top of me again I started to tell them.

In the space of a few months I'd come up with a little formula for dealing with my illness better and, in the end, I decided to write it down.

To cope I had to:

-*Realise I had my condition for life*

-*Accept help*

-*Be more open*

-*Not be afraid to say when I felt down*

-*Not overdo it down the gym*

And, most importantly:

-*Live my life how I want – not how others want.*

I was really proud of the changes I was making. For years I'd been ashamed to look in the mirror because I didn't like the person who was staring back at me. At times I didn't even recognise him.

Now that was all changing. Each morning it felt as if the light was returning to my eyes. My recovery was a million miles from where it had been in the past and I felt a completely different person to five years earlier.

Week by week, I was making positive changes that were all combining to ensure my illness was under control.

If I was getting ill again I knew I could speak to Carmen or to Dave and to the kids. I stopped worrying so much about people judging me. For years and years, I felt I couldn't trust anyone. But now those feelings were gone and it was really empowering.

I learned that sleep is a vital part of keeping my bipolar under control, too. My days were often still very busy with work, but Carmen insisted on allowing enough time to rest and sleep and make sure I was never over-doing things.

When I was training for my fights, rest time was almost as important as sparring sessions. So that's how I started to see it with my bipolar, too.

I also became far more disciplined about the amount of time I was spending down the gym. Two full rest days a week were built into my diary.

I learned to surround myself with good people again, too. I got back in touch with some old pals, I was seeing a lot more of the kids and, of course, Carmen was always around to keep me company. The only problem was getting a word in edgeways sometimes!

Carmen was also able to support me in one of the most important parts of my journey to recovery – coming off the meds.

In the weeks and months after I was discharged from hospital in London I followed doctor's orders and made sure I was taking my medicine.

But by the end of February 2016 I was really struggling to cope with the medicine. The doctors were insisting I have monthly depot injections – but my body simply couldn't handle the side-effects.

I'd find it hard to sit still, my legs and arms were constantly shaking and my mind always seemed to be racing.

I remember clearly the moment things came to a head.

"Carmen," I pleaded one morning as we sat in the kitchen of my home. "You've got to help me. I can't carry on like this. These injections are turning my mind to mush.

"I can't function properly, I am fidgety, exhausted... I am not saying I need to come off the meds totally but these ones can't be right. How does anyone expect me to recover when I can't think straight? I feel like I am dying from the inside."

Carmen instantly knew the importance of this moment and the struggles I was having behind closed doors. I'd accepted my illness but this was the cry for help to get off the meds. They were stopping me from taking the next step back towards being the man I wanted to be.

Working closely with the doctors we were able to change the medication – switching from injections back to sodium valproate tablets and, week by week, I was feeling so much better.

My mind became calmer, I stopped shaking and I felt my brain coming back to life. After months of living in darkness there was light.

Carmen was always very firm with me, though.

"If you ever feel any of your symptoms returning, Frank, you must talk to me," she'd insist.

I always promised I would. But as the summer of 2016 came around I was feeling so much better. And I had no intention of letting myself fall again.

Promises, medication, doctors, counselling, books and hospital stays... It all sounds quite complicated, doesn't it? But there was one other very simple change I made in my life after coming out of hospital. Two letters, one word – I learned to say NO. For years and years, I'd lacked the confidence to turn people away and to be kinder to myself, but my recovery had given me the strength to say no to doing things I didn't want to do. Even to one of the most persuasive blokes on the planet.

I remember getting a phone call one afternoon from Dave in June 2016 as I relaxed in the garden.

He sounded even more chirpy than usual so I knew a deal must be brewing. And I was right. "Frank, my old son," he said to me. "You were asking me about what work was coming in. I've just had Channel 4 on the phone. Good news. Very good news, in fact. Right, are you ready for this: they want you to do The Jump." "Jump?" I asked him. "Nah, you're all right, Dave, I have never fancied parachutes."

"No, no, Frank," he said. "It's skiing. Well, skiing and jumping about a bit." "Jumping about a bit?" I said worried about his vagueness. "Look, give me five minutes. I'll call you back." I put down my phone, went over to my computer and typed The Jump into Google. I'd like to say the colour drained from my cheeks but you'd know I was taking the Michael. I could see The Jump was a skiing show where many of the contestants end up breaking bones. I phoned him back. "Dave – I will die," I said. "You won't Frank, you'll be fine," he said. "They are offering serious dough here, mate, serious dough. Have a little think about it." "Dave, listen to what I am saying here, boss. I. Will. Break. My. Neck. Why don't you do it?" But there was no stopping him. "OK," he says. "What about the Jungle?" "What jungle?" I asked him. "I'm A Celebrity, Frank. You know, Ant and Dec, bushtucker trials, girls in skimpy bikinis, creepy crawlies. They're very keen to have you on that, too." I was having none of it. "Dave, I don't want to go in somewhere they are going to ask me to eat crocodile testicles and put spiders all over me. And rats. Rats are not my best friend, as you know, David. And I don't want to be washing my smalls in the lake with Kim and Aggie. Plus I hate heights."

"All right," he said, but he still wasn't giving in. "You are a good mover. Maybe I can offer you to Strictly. How's your tango?"

"Better than yours, Dave, but I'd rather have a Diet Coke. Maybe we will do that show next year!" Poor Dave. He was only trying to earn me a few bob. But saying no was no longer a problem. And Dave would never have pushed me into a show I wasn't up for. Maybe I will do one of those programmes one day. I've had offers to do all the reality TV ones over the years: Strictly, Big Brother, even the bloody ice dancing one. I think I'd be quite good at Strictly, actually. But come on, can you imagine me doing a Torvill and Dean in Lycra? They'd have to rename it Nutcracker On Ice! Still, it was very nice to be asked, but I had other plans as the year drew to a close. I had decided to buy myself a little present to celebrate how well I was doing. Years ago it would have been a new Bentley. But I had my eye on something else, something a little different, something by the sea. Yep, that caravan on the Isle of Sheppey. Sorry, I mean mobile home. The moment I set foot inside it for the first time I felt at peace. It was somewhere I could escape to, relax and be myself. I know people thought it was all a bit weird – a millionaire former world champion chilling out in a caravan by the Kent coast, but there was nowhere else I wanted to be. And, besides, the world was about to see our country's new boxing hero had come from pretty similar surroundings. Sadly, Tyson Fury's story was going to end up just like mine.

Chapter 19

BOXING'S SILENT BLOWS

I was punching the air and jumping for joy when the final bell rang. As I celebrated the scenes unfolding on the TV screen in front of me my caravan was shaking from side to side. God knows what the neighbours thought.

I knew Tyson Fury had done it. Against all the odds he had gone and done it.

In my eyes he had boxed the perfect fight against Wladimir Klitschko on November 28, 2015. The Gypsy King had come good.

And when I looked at him, standing in the centre with the world title belts, I saw a bit of myself looking back. Just like I had on that night at Wembley, Tyson Fury had come up from the bottom to reach the top.

Nobody had given him a hope in hell of becoming a champion. He was a gypsy fella after all, and they all said the people who lived in caravans didn't come good. So when they lifted Tyson's arm in the air, he'd shown them – he'd rammed the words back down their throats. Good on him.

It should have been the start of something very special for Tyson and the beginning of a fairytale, but what unfolded next was a nightmare. It broke my heart to see how quickly things then fell apart for him.

It wasn't long after winning the title that Tyson was putting up all kinds of crazy stuff on Twitter. You could see he was out of control and that his illness was taking over. In front of our eyes, the world heavyweight champion was falling apart.

As I write this, Tyson hasn't boxed since that incredible night when he won the titles. When he pulled out of his rematch with Wladimir Klitschko the papers went bananas.

Why wouldn't he fight, they demanded?

And when Peter Fury, his uncle and his trainer, said he was struggling to get out of bed some mornings the story only took off. It was obvious Tyson just needed some time out to deal with his depression and get better.

But despite him being brave enough to publicly own his illness, a lot of people were laughing behind his back. All the haters on Twitter went into meltdown. How could this big, brave gypsy champion not be able to stand on his own two feet?

My heart sank when I saw those messages. It showed how stuck in the past boxing is. Despite all the work I was doing, it felt as if we were going back 100 years.

Tyson deserves more respect. I think being world champion just became a bit too much for him to handle. The saddest thing is that people have forgotten what a warrior Tyson is. He is a seriously under-rated boxer and I hope he'll prove that one day.

I appeared in a Sky Sports Ringside Special with him a few years ago where we were sat around a table with Lennox Lewis and Anthony Joshua. It was before Tyson became a champion, but you only had to look into his eyes to see he feared absolutely no-one and believed he could defeat any man. He had that hunger, that edge, that something extra that all champions need.

During the show, Lennox and I were having a bit of needle about all the Uncle Tom jibes nonsense which had gone on in the run-up to our fight. For a few moments I thought I might have to get out the gloves!

In the end we both calmed down and made our peace, but Tyson was loving it. He enjoys the needle that goes with boxing. He's got confidence and he believes he can beat anyone and I know he will include AJ in that.

It might not be long before we get to see that fight and what a contest that would be. I really hope it happens.

Tyson is such a huge talent and there is still a lot he can achieve. When you look at fighters who come up through the travelling community, like Tyson did, they start in the ring at a very young age.

Many of them find it really hard to have a long career because of early burnout, but Tyson is still only 30 so his best years should be ahead of him. He dragged himself up from the bottom before and I reckon he will do it again.

Tyson isn't alone in facing problems with mental illness. My mate Ricky Hatton has also had his fair share of torment. Ricky has the heart of a lion and I just loved watching him fight. He was so exciting, so explosive, so brave. I can't remember another boxer who always had such tremendous support behind him, cheering him on to become a champion.

Like me, Ricky found it really tough when his career came to an end. He threw himself into training his own fighters, but it wasn't enough. It couldn't replace what had gone before.

Ricky needed to find happiness in other places and for him it was out and about on the town with his mates. He's a very sociable guy and would be down the pub, in the nightclubs and doing the boozy holidays in Tenerife.

That was Ricky's way of coping without the buzz of boxing. I was exactly the same when I retired, out in clubs doing DJ sets and shoving things down my neck and up my nose I'd never have dreamed of wanting to do when I was fighting. My discipline had gone.

It was a world away from the lifestyle I led when I was boxing and one I now avoid. I prefer a quiet life at home or in the caravan now: it is how I keep my illness in check.

In the end Ricky's lifestyle caught up with him a bit. I have huge respect for the way he has spoken so honestly about his problems. It was terrifying to hear him talking about wanting to jack it all in and end his life. I didn't realise things had got that bad for him.

Thank God he was able to pull himself back from the brink.

A few months ago we spent some time together at his gym in Manchester. Ricky was on great form, the smile was back on his face and it was fantastic to see how he has turned things around.

We got in the ring and did some work on the pads. It was two old fighters trying to be kids again really, but it felt great. Afterwards we spoke about how he was doing, I told him how I was getting on and we talked about how we both plan to stay on the straight and narrow.

It was nice to be able to talk to someone who has gone through the same problems as I have. I know Ricky is a friend I can rely on. He seems to be back in control and I hope things stay that way. He knows if he ever needs anything from me he can call.

Of course, Ricky and Tyson are the cases everyone talks about, but the sad thing is there are so many other boxers who have struggled over the years.

Since I released *Fighting Back* there have been countless other horror stories. Do yourself a favour when you get five minutes. Stick the name Kenny Rattray into the internet and watch the video that pops up.

I've never met Kenny, who is a boxing coach, but I can tell he is one of the sport's good guys. Last year, one of the fighters he trained, a talented young kid called Mike Towell, died after he was knocked out in a fight with Dale Evans in Glasgow. I remember watching the bout at home on the telly.

Mike's death was an absolute tragedy and it sent poor Kenny right over the edge. It would for most trainers. Kenny started to drink too much and he ended up getting very badly depressed.

For a long time he could not see a way out. But then he decided he was going to fight back. He went on the attack with his illness. He filmed a video telling others, not just boxers, to never be afraid to ask for a little bit of help if you need it.

Many have not been as lucky as Kenny. It hurts to think about Dean Powell, who killed himself not long after I came out of St Andrew's. I first met Dean about 30 years ago and he was a special guy.

When I was a young boxer he was a big name around the scene in the gyms of East London and was regarded as one of the best cornermen in the business. He worked a lot with George and it was clear from day one how Dean was thirsty to soak up as much knowledge of boxing as he could.

He was a proper gentleman and ended up becoming a bit of a match-maker in the sport, doing his bits and pieces as a promoter. Dean knew the fight game inside out and was so enthusiastic. We used to crack jokes and have a laugh.

But what none of us realised was that he was battling depression in private. When I read Dean had thrown himself in front of a train I was stunned – he was the last person I thought would end up doing something like that.

It's hard for me to think about what Dean did without thinking about George too. Sometimes I picture them both together in my mind, standing in the gym. Both full of life. Now both are gone after ending their lives.

George was as hard as they came and had started his career as a bare-knuckle fighter in the slums of North London in the 1930s. But after losing his wife Joan to cancer and then his son Simon two years later, again to cancer, he just wasn't able to cope and he hanged himself.

Fifteen years have passed now since his suicide but I still think about George most days and how he must have been feeling when he ended his life. I wish there was something I could have done to stop him.

It's hard to believe I have lost both Dean and George, two special men and two special friends. But sadly, boxing has more than its share of people with big problems they can't overcome. My heart goes out to them all, and to their families who've had their own struggles.

A lot of people have asked me if I ever considered ending my life when things got bad, when I was really low.

No way! My recovery has made me see that I have too much to live for, too much to hold on to, too much I want to see and do in life. I've got a family I love and the thought of doing that to them just makes me feel sick to the stomach. I know when this illness takes hold it can be difficult to feel like there's any hope. When I was heavily medicated I felt hopeless, but I was one of the lucky ones – I was able to come back.

I worry terribly about the number of boxers who find themselves having problems. I don't think anyone should be surprised that so many end up suffering with depression when they walk away from the sport.

After all, boxing is a roller-coaster. You climb on board and you're racing along, having the time of your life, until bang, you're out – and then it's oblivion. High to low, up and down, sometimes in less than 30 seconds.

And all that is waiting to greet you when you get home is devastation, emptiness and fear – fear of what happens next.

It's no wonder many of those who buy a ticket to ride that roller-coaster get off with their heads spinning. More often than not, all the people you had around you fade away and you are suddenly on your own.

In many ways the sport I love so much is walking away too – walking away from its responsibilities.

It pains me to say it, because boxing gave me everything I have in life, but the big noises in the suits running it really need to wake up now. We must do more to help boxers who end up having problems with mental ill health.

It's not just the retired guys like myself and Ricky. No, it's the young lads who don't make it in boxing and find the world they had mapped out for themselves has suddenly been turned on its head by a defeat.

For too long now, the sport has just turned a blind eye and hoped these problems will go away. But they won't.

Barry McGuigan came closest to bringing about real change. He launched the Professional Boxing Association in 1993 which tried to tackle the problems boxers face outside the ring. Within 10 years it was disbanded because there wasn't enough money around to keep it going.

I can't get my head around that. Boxing is still making a hell of a lot of dough and some of that money should be spent on trying to make sure the mental health of boxers is looked after far better.

When you are fighting, you have regular brain scans and health checks to make sure the physical injuries of the sport are carefully monitored. But what about the silent blows from boxing? The ones nobody else knows about but the man on the end of them.

I'd love to see a home or a centre set up where boxers who are struggling could go to get help. We see it a lot in other sports, but boxing doesn't have a one-stop shop for fighters whose lives spiral out of control.

Boxing needs to step out of the shadows because, compared to other sports, it is stuck in the dark ages. In cricket, Marcus Trescothick, Michael Yardy and Jonathan Trott have all suffered with mental illness during their careers. Their openness has led to really good work from the Professional Cricketers' Association.

They now work with the England and Wales Cricket Board to keep a closer eye on players. They have even published a book looking at mental health and the support available.

When the Wales manager Gary Speed hanged himself, the Professional Footballers Association sent its members guidelines on depression. The PFA also has a 24-hour helpline backed up by trained counsellors.

Several of these organisations have also signed up to the Mental Health Charter for Sport and Recreation, which, like my campaign does, aims to tackle the stigma surrounding mental illness.

But what about boxing? It doesn't make happy reading, I am afraid. There isn't really a place for boxers in the UK to turn to.

And the sport's main governing bodies – the IBF, WBA, WBO and WBC – have so far failed to address mental health issues.

England Boxing, which oversees the amateur side of the sport, has signed up to the Mental Health Charter. But the British Boxing Board of Control, which regulates professional boxing in the UK, hasn't.

That can't be right because the stakes on this are so high. I should know. Boxing is a drug which gets into your bloodstream and you quickly become addicted.

My recovery has shown me how hard it is to kick it. Saying goodbye to boxing was so hard.

In fact, there was only one goodbye in my life which was harder to face. And that came last year.

Chapter 20
LOSING MUM

I was staring up at the departures board in Dubai Airport, waiting to board a flight for a speech I had to make at an event, when I noticed the missed call on my mobile. "Dad, it's Nicola," said the message on my voicemail. "Can you call me back urgently? It's about Granny." After I listened to the message, I just stood in the centre of that airport and closed my eyes... I was recalling a chaotic scene. I'd just won the world heavy-weight title and was bursting through the front door of my mother's house. George was with me, along with a load of my mates. The Frank Bruno entourage had arrived big style, armed with my belt, all set to show off. "Mum, Mum?" I shouted, as we all swaggered through the house. I could smell the stew cooking in the kitchen: rice and peas, my favourite combination, was on the stove so I grabbed a spoon from the cutlery drawer and prepared to help myself. "FRANKLIN," boomed a voice from behind the door. "What do you think you are doing?" Then... WHACK – that wooden spoon was plucked from my hand and came down on the back of my neck. The memory tears me up even now. I might have been the new world champion, but to my mum I was still the same Franklin. I was still her little boy. I wanted to stay in that memory, to make it last for ever. But... somehow, standing in that departure lounge, I knew I was about to hear the words which would turn my world on its head. There were thousands of people around me, charging about, dragging cases, smiling, on their way...

And I'd never felt so alone. *My mum, my inspiration, my world, was gone.* This chapter has been the hardest by far to write.

When mum died on October 31, 2016, I lost my best friend and the person who helped me more than anyone else through my illness. She was such a towering figure in my life – an inspirational role model. Now, when I'm having a bad day, she isn't there to support me and that is still hard to live with. In the days after she passed away, I was scared that I'd slip again and that my illness would overcome me. The heartache of losing a parent is enough to push a lot of people over the edge, however old they are. And, after all I have been through, I worried I wouldn't have the strength to cope. As the youngest of all those brothers and sisters, I always had a special bond with Mum and my father's death brought us even closer. I know that my career choice caused her so much worry and stress. Before I had my first professional fight mum took me to church and had my gloves blessed and we both said a prayer together. Every little helps, I thought. But Mum simply couldn't bear to come to my fights. She was only ringside twice: the night I lost to Tim Witherspoon in 1986 and then three years later when she was there to see my defeat at the hands of that man Tyson. Well, I say ringside. Both times she apparently spent most of her time in the toilets saying a prayer for me. I guess the Lord was off work those nights! In the build-up to fights, when I was at my training camp for weeks on end, I would speak a lot to Mum on the phone. She always gave good advice and when I eventually won the world title nobody was prouder than her. Even then, though, she warned me not to get too carried away. She urged me to remember who I was. I was still her Franklin. When I announced my retirement from boxing nobody was happier than Mum. She later told me how she had said a big thank you to God that I had got through my career relatively unscathed. I said a thank you to God too – that she'd come to no harm either after all the threats that had come her way. I felt blessed we had both got through it. But relieved as she was, Mum still sensed I had a big challenge ahead.

"Your life has been boxing for so long, Franklin," she told me. "You must find something else now to replace it." When the first symptoms of my bipolar started to show, it was my mum who I turned to first. I'd go and see her or talk to her on the phone and I carried on doing that after I came out of hospital in 2015. I knew I could tell her anything and it wouldn't go any further. I know some people with mental health problems find it hardest to tell their parents but I never felt that with Mum. I didn't feel ashamed. I knew whatever happened to me she would be there to help me rebuild. It broke my heart to see her in the final few months of her life. By the end she was very ill. She had diabetes like my dad and her legs had swollen up, which made it hard for her to get about. Cancer also got to her in the end, like it had my brother. The last time I saw her was in Tooting Hospital shortly before I flew overseas to work and she was struggling to look after herself. We held hands on the ward and she said how well I looked and how proud she was of me. Even then, when she knew the end was near, she was thinking of me. Carmen was with me that day and Mum told her how grateful she was to her, too. "I am just glad you are finally accepting a bit of help, Frank," she said. "You look so well now. Don't ever let go of this help, and never be too proud to ask for it. I love you, Son." As I walked out the hospital, I did worry that I might not see Mum again, but when the news arrived that she'd gone, it still left me deeply shocked. In a heartbeat she'd been taken away.

But I was determined to stay strong. That's what she would be telling me to do. I willed myself to not let her death destroy all the work I had done to get better. Mum had been strong for me all her life. Now I had to be strong for her.

Her funeral was incredible. So many people packed into the New Testament Assembly Church in Tooting that a lot of the mourners were forced to stand outside.

One poor guy managed to crash into the car carrying mum's coffin to the church. God knows what he thought when he looked out of the window and saw it was a hearse – and then saw me walking towards him. Mum would've had a little laugh. She would've seen the funny side. Then she would have forgiven him. Kindness ran through her soul. As I sat at the front of the church I was transported back to the days, as a kid, where Mum would stand and whip that congregation into a frenzy. Lots of people who were at the funeral had been there all those years ago when mum was a preacher. To see them again and to hear their stories gave me goosebumps. One of them took my hand as she left the church. "Your mother was terribly proud of you, Franklin," she said. "Not only for what you achieved in life, but for the man you have now become." Those words will stay with me forever. Eventually, after all the people had gone and everyone had said their farewells, I was on my own. I stood alone at Mum's grave and made her a promise: to stay well, to stay safe and, most importantly, to stay standing tall.

Chapter 21
STANDING TALL

The doctor looked up from his paperwork and put down his pen. "Frank," he said. "You are looking great and I can see from your records you are attending all your appointments. But, something still troubles me."

"What's that?" I replied, feeling uneasy.

"How can I be sure you won't end up in the same place you were five years ago?"

"No way," I replied firmly, feeling relieved. "I am a completely different person now to then."

I sat back in my chair. I was in front of my consultant for what I thought was just another routine appointment. But, as our meeting rumbled on, I noticed he had a lot more questions than usual.

Where was all this heading?

The doctor leaned forward

"Right OK, Frank, but *how* are you different to the person say, 14 years ago, when you were first sectioned in 2003?"

"There's no comparison," I said. "Look, they had to take me kicking and screaming into Goodmayes Hospital. When I came out I wasn't interested in facing up to my illness. All I wanted to do was get back on with living my life, but I was not living it in the right way. I can see that now."

"So when did you really start to accept you had an illness, Frank?" he asked.

"Honestly?" I replied. "About 18 months to two years ago. It was only when I made the decision to go into hospital off my own bat in 2015 that I started to face up to how serious things were.

"And when the doctors explained how badly my body was struggling with all the strain I was putting on my mind, I knew I had to do something and I needed to make some changes..."

"So what have you changed, Frank?" my doctor asked.

"Everything!" I told him. "For a start, I'm not on my own so much. I see my family a lot more than I used to and I have good friends around me. Dave, my agent, makes sure my health always comes first and I know I can rely on him 100 per cent. I've got a wonderful personal assistant called Carmen who organises my days around my diary for me. We factor in rest time and make sure things move a little slower than they used to. Blimey, sometimes I worry that if I sleep any more I'd be dead! I've learned it's OK to slow down and I've learned it's OK to talk to the people closest to me about my illness. I'm not afraid to ask for help any more. I know that by asking for help I am not going to be put into hospital, in fact it's the opposite: it is more likely I will stay out. There will always be challenges. Towards the end of last year I had a little wobble and wondered if I needed to go back on my meds. I sat down with Carmen and we chatted it through. In the end, it was fine."

"Good," he said. "Any other changes?"

"There's just so much going on in my life, doc," I said. "I'm still doing a lot of after-dinner work. It's great to travel around, speaking about my career. I know I'll never box again but that doesn't mean I can't enjoy talking about my career and sharing all the highs and lows."

"And how are you finding not being able to box now, Frank?" "I'll always miss it," I admitted. "It was a part of my world for so long that I can't just expect all the things I loved about it to die away. But I understand now that boxing is part of my past and the future has to be about something else. Staying well. "

The doctor put down his pen, looked me squarely in the eyes and smiled.

"Well, Frank," he said. "I won't need to see you again."

I thought I was hearing things at first.

"Er, could you say that again please, sir," I asked.

"I'm signing you off, Frank," he said. "I reckon you can cope just fine. I think you are managing your illness very well without medication. But, listen, if you need me you know where I am. I think you are ready now though, Frank."

I sat there in shock, just looking at him.

"Well – say something!" the doctor laughed. "Blimey, Frank, you've been talking about this for long enough and begging me to discharge you from these appointments. Now it's happening. You can go. Oh and Frank…"

"Yes, doctor?" I asked, standing up and heading for the exit.

"Bloody well done!"

I couldn't find the words. As I walked out of that doctor's room on February 9, 2017, it felt like I was floating. I'd regained control of my life. I was standing tall.

As I write this, it has been 182 days since that appointment.

Yeah, I count the days.

That's how I deal with my illness now. Day by day. Step by step. Moving forward. Never forgetting what happened in the past, but learning from it. And making sure I secure a brighter future. I've now been medication-free for 18 months and my head has never felt clearer.

When I finish this chapter I've got to grab my suitcase. It's the same one I was holding when I arrived at the door of Basildon Hospital. And it's the one I had at the end of my bed for five weeks while I tried to win the toughest fight of my life in St Andrew's.

Tonight I will be packing it with clothes ready for a flight in the morning. I'm off to make a speech about my career and the new mission in my life – the Frank Bruno Foundation.

Then I'm going to take a couple of days off and go and sit in the sun. I might even get a tan! I can't wait. It doesn't matter now if people don't hear from me for a day or two.

It's no biggie. My family and friends won't be on the phone panicking because they know I am in control of my illness better than I ever have been in my life.

And that is proving to be the best thing about my recovery – getting my life back.

Only those who have gone through a mental health condition will know what I mean by that. Over the past five years, when I was in the grip of my illness, the world closed down around me. I spent so much time sleeping. The medication shut down my brain and I went into myself. Now I am desperate to make up for all the time I lost and I plan to live my life to the full.

As I sit here now, I am still medication-free and only need to see the doctors if I want to. I know that people are always on the lookout to make sure I don't fall down again. When you've been sectioned three times people will always be wary.

And I am a famous person, so I get it. But, as I hope this book has shown you, people don't always know the full story.

Let me give you an example. A few months ago, I was shopping down at a market in Leighton Buzzard. I'd parked the Bentley up on a hill and wandered off to buy some meat for my dinner, but when I got back all hell was breaking loose. My Bentley had rolled down the hill and into a market stall!

It was a right old mess. Everyone was pointing at me and staring. I knew what they were thinking. And I overheard what some of them were saying.

"Poor old Frank. Isn't it a shame?" one woman said to her mate. "He can't help it, he's not all there."

My little mishap even made the papers! But that's all it was. An accident. I rarely park on hills and I hadn't put the handbrake on properly. I paid for the damage to the guy's stall but it still made headlines and the whispering started again. That's the way it is for me.

It was the same when I bought the caravan – people were mugging me off and questioning my state of mind.

But rather than let it get me down any longer I just try to roll with life's punches. Life will always smash you across the chops, often when you least expect it.

I recently had to get through the first Mother's Day since I lost my mum. It was tough. I wanted to be on my own. I headed to the gym and when I came home I went through a load of old photos. It helped to pull me through. In the past I might have gone to pieces, but I didn't and I take huge strength from that. When I think of Mum now I take comfort in the fact she is in a better place and free of pain.

I am too. The sun can't shine every day. Now I can see that simply being able to get up in the morning is the start to a perfect day.

When I go out I know some people can't help judging me. It does bother me sometimes – I am human. I do cry. I have good days and I have bad days. I worry sometimes that if people see me having a bad day then they will think I'm having another mental breakdown. That's why the thought of the illness coming back is so terrifying. But I'm not going to allow myself to fall again.

I have a different suit for every day of the week, I have a nice car, a nice house, money in the bank. But I now have something money can't buy – I have peace of mind.

I've learned that managing my stress levels is really important in keeping my bipolar under control. The key for me has been staying fit, focused, relaxed and away from stress. It's all about learning how to look after yourself, and practising good self-care.

I have spent a lot of time investing in my happiness and being kinder to myself over the last few months. As I told the doctor, I'm not afraid to rest any more and, as I've already explained, I'm not afraid to say no.

Don't get me wrong, I'm not about to announce my retirement like my old mate Prince Philip. Someone still needs to come out with the daft soundbites. And I am rather good at them.

I keep myself busy. But now, when I am working, I feel blessed that I get to go up and down the country, meeting people and putting a smile on their faces. The last few months have been among the most rewarding of my life. I am enjoying myself in a way I didn't think possible in those early days after my retirement.

My focus, most recently, has been on getting my foundation up and running. With Carmen's help, I've appointed a governing board and we meet regularly to discuss the work we want to focus on.

My aim is simple, but ambitious. I want to help as many people as I can who have been going through, or facing mental ill health, to wrestle back control of their lives.

The goal in the short term is to create a centre where people can be supported. We are trying to set up a system where GPs can refer patients to the foundation for support. I want to offer exercise, non-contact boxing, counselling, mindfulness and meditation – alternative treatments for people who would like to try something other than medication to get through difficult times.

In the long term, I'd like to have centres up and down the country so the foundation can reach the maximum number of people.

We had a brilliant fundraising dinner a few weeks ago at Champneys. Tickets sold out within hours. The DJ Johnny Vaughan hosted it and Ricky Hatton and I both spoke about what we've been through in and outside the ring.

And so many family members and friends were there to support what I am trying to do. The evening raised a lot of money that will go towards assisting those people who need help.

I'm also really proud to say that I have now gained my boxing trainer's licence. I had an interview with the British Boxing Board of Control earlier this year and, thankfully, it all went like clockwork.

So now I can get in the ring and train young fighters. I have accepted that my boxing days are over – but I know I have a hell of a lot to offer the sport. I am still fanatical about boxing and would love to help build stars of the future and put something back into the world that gave me so much.

I am still travelling the country, making speeches and attending dinners. That's my bread and butter and I love it – meeting my fans and talking about the days in the ring. This year I travelled to the Far East which was a wonderful experience. To know I have fans across the world still interested in hearing what I have to say is very humbling.

Earlier this year I had a reunion with some of my old teachers from Oak Hall. The school closed years ago but Carmen tracked them down. Writing this book made me realise how important Oak Hall was in my life so I wanted to thank the teachers there and to see how they were all doing.

It was great to see them all again – we spoke a lot about my new foundation and the plans I have to help kids like the ones they supported for so many years.

My work to raise awareness around the need to improve mental health services is going from strength to strength. Recently, the campaign I work on with the *Sunday Mirror* celebrated breaking through the 100,000 barrier

– that's how many people have signed a Time To Change pledge saying we need to end the stigma and start talking about mental ill health.

I also turned out to support my old pal Norman Lamb in his recent general election campaign.

He's not in the Government any more but he still has a lot of clout and continues to fight to improve services. I was delighted when he won back his seat in Norfolk. We even made the TV news!

Closer to home, I've decided to make one big change. As a write this, my house in Bedfordshire is on the market. I've had some great times there but it's time for a fresh start. I'm not sure yet where I'll settle – but as long as it's nice and comfortable, I'll be happy.

If the last few years have taught me anything, it's to be grateful for living my life the way I want it. Now I have my freedom back I do not plan to throw it away. I wake up each morning feeling like I used to when I set off on my journey as a young boxer. And that's because I'm happy with the world around me again. I'm confident and comfortable in my own skin.

Eating well, sleeping properly and not working too hard has helped keep my illness at bay. *My illness... bipolar.*

Time has given me the space to think about the B-word. I'm not sure I agree with the doctors and experts who warn I will have bipolar for the rest of my life.

What I do accept without question is that I have a mental health condition which needs to be very carefully managed until the end of my days. It will always be there in the shadows, but my aim is to deal with it better than I did in the past.

That is easier now I have Carmen to organise my life and take the heat off me. Dave, who has been with me all the way through my illness, is one of my best friends. He's more than an agent. Sometimes, you've got to allow people to come into your life and give you the support you need. Ever since I did that I've coped far better.

Just like when I was in the ring, I have a solid team watching my back.

The strong bond I have with my family has been vital, too. Everyone has had their say about what went on in those terrifying months in 2012. I've explained that if I'd had a bit more support after I retired from boxing, things may have turned out differently. I don't believe it was right that I was sectioned so many times.

But I was and I have to accept it. I can't rewrite history. If I could, I'd wipe those five defeats from my record and bring back all the special people I lost like my mum, Michael, George and Harry.

I have to focus on the future now because the past will only pull me back.

The kids have told their side of things. And I know, without doubt, that everything they ever do for me is out of love. There is no dad out there more proud of his children than I am.

My relationship with the kids is brilliant. We spent last Christmas together at my place and had a wonderful time. Rachel had a few tears as she left.

"I just feel so happy we have you back, Dad," she said to me.

I gave her a massive hug. I didn't want to let her go. I feel I can be a lot more open these days. No, I don't tell my kids everything – what father does? But I am able to ask them not to worry so much about me. I don't need to be mollycoddled because they know I can cope a lot better with what life throws at me than before.

I am able to tell them if I am having a bad day and we talk things through.

Fortunately, right now, those days rarely come. I still spend most of my time on my own. I prefer it that way but I haven't given up on the idea of meeting someone. There might be a little bit of life in the old Black & Decker just yet!

When I look back on my relationship with Nina, I regret the timing of when we met. It was always going to be hard to make things work during a period when there was so much hassle and heartache in my world.

But Nina and I shared great times together. She was a brilliant support through the really dark days and we parted on good terms.

My recovery has made me see two things. One, is that it is time to move on. No, I won't ever forget the hell of the past and being locked up. That experience drives the campaigning I do. But what happened was yesterday, so I am only looking to the future.

Two, I have to accept that what happened is not down to anyone else.

It's about me. I am the only one who can make sure I stay in control. And I feel like I finally am.

Others are not so lucky. We still need to do so much more to help all the people out there suffering from a mental health condition.

Maybe that's you? If not, perhaps you know someone who is.

Recently I was at a Craig David concert at the O2 in London. A woman came up and hugged me. Her daughter is suffering from bipolar disorder and she said she had followed my story in the newspapers really closely. It had given her a lot of inspiration and we had a proper chat about how her girl was doing. Sadly, like many stories I hear, she wasn't getting the right treatment.

I passionately believe the way we care for the mentally ill needs to be totally turned on its head. Those suffering with depression and bipolar disorder too often find themselves stripped of their confidence and self-esteem.

I certainly was when they carted me off to hospital. Tablets and medication can become a crutch. A sticking plaster if you like. They can help clear the fog for a little while. I know every case is different and I'd never encourage anyone to ignore medical advice, but once that fog has lifted we should encourage people to walk towards the light on their own two feet.

I read in the papers not long ago a report saying a million people were taking anti-depressants which they didn't need. A million! How can that be right?

I encourage people I meet to try to talk about how they feel and look at the way they are living: the food they eat, the amount they drink, the lifestyle they lead and the amount of exercise they take.

Yes, I know I am a sportsman, but I am convinced I was able to exercise my demons away. And I think others can, too.

I know what I am saying will raise more than a few eyebrows but I plan to carry on saying it.

Long-term medication might be the answer for some. I have met lots of people along my journey who tell me they have a chemical imbalance in their brain. They choose to take medication as it really helps to keep their illness at bay. I have so much respect for them for that. It didn't work for me. It does for them. So fair play.

But there's another group I have met – the people who tell me they wish they could come *off* drugs but who don't feel they are given enough support to do that. It is very easy to give someone a tablet or inject them with drugs, then tick a box and move on to the next patient.

Too many people are trapped in the system and don't have the confidence to say to the doctors: "Please stop, I want to try something different."

I did and it worked.

And my advice is to try and do what's right for you: because if you can't be good for yourself, you can't be good for anybody else.

I think doctors need to listen to patients a bit more and avoid telling people they need to be on tablets for the rest of their lives.

We need more positive thinking, to give those fighting an illness something to focus on and aim for.

And the Government isn't doing anywhere near enough to help. David Cameron liked to talk the talk on mental health, promising to spend loads of money, making things better. In the run-up to the general election, Theresa May was saying the same.

She promised to rip up the Mental Health Act and pump £1 billion into the system to make things better.

Who knows if that will ever happen? But change can't come soon enough. More than 63,000 people were sectioned in 2015/16 – compared to just over 43,000 a decade earlier.

The shortage of hospital beds for the most seriously ill is scandalous. But the number of people with mental health conditions is going up and up. Patients, including kids, are regularly being sent hundreds of miles away from their home to find help.

Parents are being torn from their children. It's not right. I still get so many letters from people telling me about the appalling standards of care received by themselves or loved ones.

For me, those in power should be treating mental ill health as seriously as they do drink and drug addiction. I know from my own work and from the people I meet that services are nowhere near good enough.

I would love to sit down with the Prime Minister to say that politicians should be spending more time in mental health hospitals to see how services are struggling.

If they did, they would come face to face with patients, like I did, who are trapped and suffering needlessly. Credit to Norman Lamb, he did it. We need more like him.

A few months ago Channel Four's investigation programme Dispatches showed *Under Lock and Key* revealing life inside St Andrew's through the eyes of the patients and their loved ones.

It was filmed the same year I was in there. I found it difficult to watch. I'd tried to delete those terrifying weeks from my mind as I focused on my recovery, but the pictures on the TV screen brought back to life the hell I went through.

Patients were pulling their hair out and scraping skin off their hands. The staff used a technique involving face-down restraint in all the wards.

Some of the relatives of children being treated were fighting to get them out. Four patients taking a drug used to treat schizophrenia died in the space of seven months on one ward.

Yet last year, they opened a brand new £45 million wing at the hospital – making it the biggest in Europe. I'm not sure throwing money at shiny new hospitals where patients live under lock and key is the answer.

It's time more politicians followed the TV cameras behind those locked doors. If they did, I think they would get a nasty shock.

There is still so much improvement needed and still so much I need to fight for. That's why I have launched the Frank Bruno Foundation to try to help those not getting enough support. Adults and young people who've had mental ill health and who may be facing social or emotional difficulties. The aim is to take a "healthy body leads to a healthy mind" approach to their problems using lots of different techniques. Making this Foundation work is now my main ambition. All my life I have been striving and aiming high. So I am not going to stop now.

As I write this, Aaron Lennon, the Everton footballer, is trying to win his own battle after he was discharged from a mental health hospital where he was taken to when he was sectioned. I am praying that he will overcome his demons.

Mental health has nothing to do with how much you earn or the flash cars on the driveway or pretty girls on your arm. It doesn't matter if you are taking home £100,000 a week or a fiver.

Everyone thinks because footballers get paid loads of money they shouldn't have any worries or concerns. Maybe the pressure of playing the game at the top makes footballers even more likely to suffer from problems. Has anyone ever thought of that?

I've discovered boxing at the highest level is a very lonely place. I reckon many sports are the same. Glory, success and money in the bank are never worth more than peace of mind.

One good thing is that other celebrities are beginning to open up about how they feel now.

I was really moved when I watched Rio Ferdinand's BBC documentary *Being Mum and Dad*. To see him talking about how tough it had been after his wife Rebecca died in 2015 was heartbreaking.

Rio did a really courageous thing. He showed how men shouldn't be afraid to talk about their feelings. That British stiff upper lip stuff is cobblers.

I take my hat off to Prince Harry, too. It was incredibly brave of him to come out and talk about the problems he suffered after the death of his mother, Princess Diana.

Harry was able to sort out his issues with a little bit of counselling and by getting in the ring to do some boxing. So talking and keeping fit were the keys to His Royal Highness's recovery. Sound familiar? *I know what you mean, 'Arry.* I really do.

Now the third in line to the throne has given my ideas the royal seal of approval, I'd love to get him in for a sparring session. It's a little dream. It would be lovely. But if it doesn't happen it's no big deal.

My dreams these days are pretty simple. I had my dream when I was eight and I achieved it. Now I dream of keeping well, remaining happy, carrying on training and making sure I stay on the right side of the tracks.

I've got no regrets. Boxing has been wonderful to me and I hope I have managed to put something back.

Everything I have been through in life has been worth suffering to be able to say I stood in the middle of a boxing ring as the WBC Heavyweight Champion of the World.

I've had the most incredible life so far. I've met Queens, Princes, Princesses, Presidents, Prime Ministers and scores of celebrities. But I've got just as much joy meeting dustmen, builders, cleaners and tramps.

It's made me see I am no different to anybody else. I've got the same feelings. I have the same fears. I will never forget where I came from. The tough streets I grew up on prepared me for the life I have led.

I kept in touch with a lot of the guys from Oak Hall. One guy who I clicked with more than most was a guy called Steven Parker. He was a really sweet guy, a bit of a rogue and a bit of a hustler.

It's fair to say our lives went in different directions after Oak Hall. But he touched my heart and we kept in contact. Steve really struggled in the years after leaving school and spent a lot of time behind bars. I went with his mum to see him in Wandsworth Prison a couple of times.

It was hard to see what Steve was going through and, as much as he tried to control his demons, he never could. As I stood at his funeral, I was thinking how I had a life worth fighting for.

I don't want to die and end up being known as the bloke who kept getting sectioned. I will never let my illness beat me. I am going nowhere.

I have learned to accept that no matter how tough life gets, there's always tomorrow and there's always the chance to start again.

If I lost my home, I'd get a tent and sleep in the park. If I lost my car, I'd get a bike. If I lost all my money I'd be down at the Jobcentre asking them to find me something to do so I could earn some corn.

I have been fighting all my life so I am not going to stop now.

There have been so many blows along the way. Being packed off to Oak Hall. Losing my dad. Those painful defeats in the ring. The agony of divorce. The loneliness of life after retirement. Losing George. Being locked up against my will. That betrayal by someone close. Accepting that my illness was knocking me down again.

It's no wonder I was on the floor so many times. But boxing is like life. You get knocked down and you just have to get back up.

I had to fall before I could rise. But today I am standing tall.

This was not a story I should have been telling. What you have read over these pages was never meant to happen. But I am so glad I am still here to share it.

So, thanks for reading but, if it's OK, I am going to stop now and get on with living my life.

Because it's high time people just let me be Frank.

EPILOGUE

I was dancing around the kitchen at home with my headphones in and my iPod up full blast. So I didn't even hear the knock.

But when the track ended, the bang of a fist on the front door boomed through my house like a sledgehammer smashing concrete. And the voice behind the door was screaming at me to come outside. "Frank, Frank, FRRRRAAANNNKKKK!!!!" Blimey, what a noise. "Thank you, but I'm not interested in double glazing," I shouted as I went to answer it. "Don't give me double bloody glazing, Frank Bruno," Carmen said, as she stood on the doorstep tapping her watch. "You need to get your arse in gear, mister. "All right, Miss Stroppy," I said. "Keep your hair on." "We need to get a wiggle on or we'll be late. Now come on, your carriage awaits..." I looked behind Carmen and there, sitting on the driveway under a perfect summer sky, was my Bentley, freshly polished to perfection with a beautiful white ribbon tied on the bonnet. I stood in the hallway and allowed myself a smile. Five years earlier, in the very same spot, I'd been looking out at all the police cars parked up. Then they put me in the ambulance and my world descended into darkness. Now I was putting my suit in the boot and about to go and walk my daughter, Rachel, down the aisle at her wedding. As I went to the Bentley I caught sight of myself staring back in the wing mirror and I liked the man I could see. Life was back in my eyes. As I drove out the gates, I'd never felt so free. The world outside my window, which for so long had passed me by in a fog, was clear now. I felt so alive. When I arrived at the hotel and I saw Rachel I thought my heart was going to burst out my chest with pride. There she was: my little girl. The little girl I held in my arms as a baby in hospital, the little girl for whom I became World Champion, the little girl who tightly gripped my hand as I lay in bed in a mental health unit. Now I was clutching Rachel's hand and leading her to the car waiting to take us to Brentwood Cathedral. We'd rebuilt our lives – and it was time to give her away. The past was history now. It was time to let go of the daughter I feared I might lose for ever when my illness left me questioning everything in the world around me. As we made our way to the service we travelled along the same roads the ambulance passed through that day I was locked up in Goodmayes. Now there was no nurse at my side. And there was no hospital bed waiting up ahead.

As we pulled up, there was a chance for a last few words. "You will always be my little girl, Rach," I told her. "I will always love you. Always have. Always will. I love all you kids, you know that don't you?"

"Yes Dad," Rachel said. "We love you too." As we waited at the door to the Cathedral I closed my eyes for a moment. As I did, I thought about how I'd overcome so much to be standing where I was.

My eyes opened as Wagner's Bridal Chorus burst into life. Then, Rachel and I stepped, together, as one. All eyes were rightly on my beautiful daughter as we walked past the rows of family and friends and made our way to the altar. Up ahead I could see her husband-to-be Bobby. He would take good care of her. I knew that. But it was still tough to let go of Rachel's hand. The moment had come to do it, though. I shook Bobby's hand and I stepped back. As I sat down I heard the cathedral door shut behind me, sending an echo through the building.

For so long that noise – the slam and clink – had brought me nothing but misery. But I wasn't locked up any more. I was free. I looked to my left at Nicola and Franklin and we shared a look. Then Rachel glanced over her shoulder at us all.

As Rachel and Bobby said their vows I thought about Mum and how I had sat in the pews watching her at the front of the church when I was a kid. Oh, how I wished she could be with me – Michael, too. But I knew they were both with us today. As Rachel and Bobby made their way out of the church my little girl flashed that smile – the same one she had on the afternoon I brought the title home.

Rachel was about to set off on the start of an exciting new journey. And so was I. But first the photographer wanted a picture. She wanted Rachel and I together. Then she wanted Franklin and Nicola alongside us, too. There, under a glorious blue sky, we stood – the Brunos, *together*.

The photographer didn't need to tell me to say cheese.

Nobody was wiping the grin from my face. I was winning. I was on top. I was back.

And I'd never felt so happy in my life...

SECONDS OUT

TALE OF THE TAPE

Born: Hammersmith General Hospital, November 16, 1961. Christened Franklin Roy Bruno.

Schools: Swaffield Primary, Wandsworth, and Oak Hall, Sussex.

Married: Laura Bruno in February 1990. Divorced in 2001 after 11 years of marriage. Now open to offers. Makes a mean rice and peas and likes to keep fit and healthy.

Children: Nicola, Rachel, Franklin and Freya.

Boxing: Started boxing aged nine after joining Wandsworth Boys Club. Boxed as an amateur for the Philip Game Amateur Boxing Club from 1977-1980 winning 20 out of 21 fights. Represented Young England and, at 18, became youngest ever ABA Heavyweight Champion. Turned pro in 1982.

Fight Record: 45 contests, 40 victories. 38 KOs − 17 by clean knockout. European Champion 1985-1986. Won World WBC Championship on September 3, 1995, beating Oliver McCall at Wembley.

Honours: Awarded the MBE in the 1990 New Year's Honours list.

Campaigns: Named a Government ambassador for mental health in 2013. Launched a major campaign for change with the *Sunday Mirror* in the same year.

Launched my own foundation, The Frank Bruno Foundation, in 2017. Full details here: **www.thefrankbrunofoundation.co.uk**

A NEW KID ON THE BLOCK

Wow. Just wow. Where to start?

I feel so privileged to have been standing among the 90,000 people who saw Anthony Joshua become world champion.

His victory over Wladimir Klitschko on 29 April, 2017, will rightly go down as one of the greatest ever performances by a British boxer.

It was a seriously good night's work from Anthony. He showed a lot of patience and concentration and the way he finished the fight was unbelievable.

He answered a lot of questions that people were asking about him and I think he will now go on to reign for a very long time.

Anthony has shown from day one, as an amateur, that he is a very dedicated fighter.

I like how he doesn't get involved with all the trash talk that leads to boxing often getting such a bad press. He prefers to let his boxing speak for itself and you have to respect him for that.

Anthony's a good example for youngsters, too. I like the fact he has stayed true to his roots, living with his mum in a council house and not letting any hype get into his head.

As Anthony has said himself, he could easily have ended up going down the wrong path when he was growing up, but boxing gave him something to focus on and provided him with an amazing life.

Remind you of anyone? Yeah, lots of people have made the point that our stories are very similar. And the fact Anthony was crowned at Wembley wasn't lost on me either.

It was quite emotional being there with my son Franklin watching the fight. I was back in the place where my nightmare unfolded against Tim Witherspoon and where my dreams came true against Oliver McCall.

Incredibly, a lot of people I met at the AJ fight had been at both of those bouts. It was wonderful to meet them and listen to their memories of the fights. Speaking to them reminded me no-one can ever take away my title: I'm a former world heavyweight champion. Like I said to the BBC's Garry Richardson the next day, that's not the kind of thing you can buy down Primark!

But guys like Anthony are the future now and it is going to be really exciting to see how his career develops from here.

That's no disrespect to Wladimir. He showed tremendous heart in the fight and, on another night, he could've easily walked off with the belt. He announced his retirement a few months later and he can bow out with his head held high.

I expect Anthony to go back to the workshop, polish up a few things and come back even stronger. He's a very honest fighter. He admits himself he is raw and still learning, but he is only going to get better.

The fight which really makes me lick my lips is AJ against Tyson Fury. Tyson's apparently back in the gym now trying to get his weight down and focus himself on a comeback. A fight between the two of them would be brilliant.

Although I'd tip Anthony to have the edge, Tyson is a seriously underrated fighter and has a lot more experience. He will believe he can take Anthony out and become one of the great fighters in this era in the process. He will feel that his pride is on the line.

But if Anthony keeps on winning there are no limits to what he can go on and do. People have been saying he could become the first billion-pound boxer. A lot of people get sniffy when stuff like that is said. I say to Anthony – good luck to you.

Boxing is a tough, tough business so he should aim to make as much money as he can.

Anthony has something about him, an edge, that makes him stand out and it's obvious why all the sponsors are lining up to work with him.

I expect him to go and fight in many different countries like in China and Japan, perhaps even parts of Africa, where there is massive potential for the sport.

Anthony's victory really feels like it has turned around boxing in this country. The day after he won everyone I bumped into seemed to be talking about the fight.

It came just a few weeks after I was ringside to watch Tony Bellew beat David Haye.

That was a great contest, too. David Haye proved he had the balls of a donkey to keep fighting with such a bad injury, but Bellew won against all the odds and proved boxing can still throw up the odd surprise.

I was listening to Tony a couple of days later on the radio talking about maybe packing it all in because he needed to think about his kids. It's tempting to go out on a high, but I wonder if Tony will feel the same if a big purse is waved in front of his eyes for a rematch? The temptation will be so strong. He won't want to look back with regrets.

The two fights reminded me of the golden days of the mid-1990s when I was fighting.

Back then all the divisions were kicking. At middleweight you had Nigel Benn, Michael Watson, Steve Collins, Chris Eubank, Gerald McClellan. They were all world-class fighters who could hold their own in any era.

And in my division there were so many people you'd be trying to avoid. The heavyweight field was full of monsters like Mike Tyson, Riddick Bowe, Lennox Lewis, Tommy Morrison – it just went on and on.

The only thing that saddens me a bit is that now, unlike then, boxing is not as accessible. When I was fighting, it was on ITV or the BBC and everyone got to see the fights. Now, with Sky's pay-per-view Box Office, it costs a packet and a lot of punters are being priced out.

I hope it doesn't stop kids from wanting to get involved with the sport because it is a really good way for young people to keep fit.

My son Franklin has boxed and a lot of people ask me how I feel about him stepping in the ring. It was bitter-sweet when I watched him win his first contest.

You've gotta have balls to step into a boxing ring, so I'm glad he did it. But I was relieved he copied his old man by getting his opponent out of there double quick.

Franklin still goes down the gym, he trains and he does a bit of sparring. I am pleased he does, because boxing teaches you so much: manners, discipline, survival. It gives you confidence. I think all kids should have to do a bit of boxing training.

Franklin doesn't box competitively any more and part of me is pleased about that. I don't think my heart could take it. But, if he changes his mind, I'll be there to support him 100 per cent.

I will be his biggest supporter – and critic!

FRANK'S TOP 10 BOXERS OF ALL TIME

Time and time again when I turn up at events I am asked who my top 10 boxers are.

I've got to say my list often changes because it is hard to whittle down the numbers.

It wasn't too tricky to pick the best – there will only ever be one Muhammad Ali. He was, is and always will be The Greatest.

But below him I've listed the other nine who get my vote: don't ask me in what order because that would be impossible! And I'd never have finished this book.

People may be surprised I've included my old enemy Mike Tyson in there. They shouldn't be. Despite the difficult ending to Mike's career, for a long time he was the best fighter on the planet by a hell of a distance. He was a seriously tough cookie. And the two defeats I suffered to him will live long in my memory!

So here goes – my top ten. And maybe, in 10 years' time, I will be adding AJ to it!

MUHAMMAD ALI
Fights 61; Wins 56 (37 KO); Losses 5.
First fight October 29, 1960 – last fight December 11, 1981.
Known as "The Greatest", Ali is one of the most celebrated heavyweight boxers in history. Born Cassius Clay on January 17, 1942, in Louisville, Kentucky, he was a controversial figure in and out of the ring. Aged 18, he won gold at the 1960 Olympics in Rome and went on to lift the heavyweight title in 1964, 1974 and 1978, taking part in some of the

most memorable bouts ever seen.

His unorthodox style, quick feet and lightning-fast reflexes won him legions of admirers as he took on all challengers. His fame transcended boxing thanks to his quick wit and charm. He died on June 3, 2016, aged 74.

SUGAR RAY ROBINSON

Fights 200; Wins 173 (108 KO); Losses 19; Draws 6; No contests 2.
First fight October 4, 1940 – last fight November 10, 1965.

Considered one of the greatest boxers of all time, Sugar Ray Robinson was born in 1921. He turned pro in 1940 and won his first 40 fights. Over his 25-year career he won the world welterweight and middle-weight crowns and was dubbed "pound for pound, the best". By 1958, he had become the first boxer to win a divisional world championship five times. Robinson died in Culver City, California, in 1989. Robinson lit up the 1940s and 1950s with his dazzling skill, power and courage. Many boxing experts say Robinson was the greatest boxer there has ever been.

SUGAR RAY LEONARD

Fights 40; Wins 36 (25 KO); Losses 3; Draws 1.
First fight February 5, 1977 – last fight March 1, 1997.

Sugar Ray Leonard was born on May 17, 1956, in Rocky Mount, North Carolina. He won the gold medal in light-welterweight boxing at the 1976 Olympic Games, and went pro the following year. His 1987 defeat of Marvelous Marvin Hagler for the World Boxing Council's Middleweight Championship is considered one of the greatest profes-sional boxing matches of all time. Leonard retired in 1997, and was inducted into the Boxing Hall of Fame. In the 1980s he was part of a group of boxers known as "The Fabulous Four", which also included Roberto Durán, Thomas Hearns and Marvin Hagler. Leonard was the first boxer to earn more than $100 million and was named Boxer of the Decade in the 1980s.

ROCKY MARCIANO

Fights 49; Wins 49 (43 KO).

First fight March 17, 1947 – final fight September 21, 1955.

Rocky Marciano was born on September 1, 1923, in Brockton, Massachusetts. He started fighting as a professional boxer in 1948, winning a fight against Harry Bilazarian. In 1952, he beat Jersey Joe Walcott for the World Heavyweight Championship. He retired in 1956 and died in a plane crash on August 31, 1969, near Newton, Iowa. During his undefeated career he defended the title six times and was known for his relentless fighting style, stamina and iron chin. His win percentage of 87% remains one of the highest in heavyweight boxing history.

MIKE TYSON

Fights 58; Wins 50 (44 KO); Losses 6; No contests 2.

First fight March 6, 1985 – last fight June 11, 2005.

Born in Brooklyn, New York, on June 30, 1966, "Iron" Mike Tyson became the youngest Heavyweight Boxing Champion of the World in 1986, aged 20. He lost the title in 1990 and later served less than three years in prison over rape charges. He subsequently earned further notoriety by biting Evander Holyfield's ear during a rematch in 1997. Tyson has gone on to appear in several films, including a documentary and Broadway show on his life. Tyson was known for his ferocious fighting style which intimidated opponents. Despite his behaviour outside the ring he is still regarded as one of the best heavyweights of all time, earning him another nickname, The Baddest Man on the Planet.

JOE LOUIS

Fights 69; Wins 66 (52 KO); Losses 3.

First fight July 7, 1934 – final fight October 26, 1951.

Born in Alabama in 1914, Joe Louis became boxing's Heavyweight Champion with his defeat of James J. Braddock in 1937. Nicknamed "the Brown Bomber", his knockout of Germany's Max Schmeling in 1938 made him a national hero, and he established a record by retaining the championship for 13 years. After boxing, Louis endured financial problems while working as a referee and a celebrity casino greeter. He died in 1981. In 2005, the influential International Boxing Research Organisation ranked him as the best heavyweight of all time. His cultural impact was also felt outside the ring where he is regarded as the first African-American to achieve the status of nationwide hero.

JACK JOHNSON

Fights 101; Wins 73 (40 KO); Losses 13; Draws 10; No contests 5.
First fight November 1, 1898 – final fight November 27, 1945.

Jack Johnson was born in Galveston, Texas, in 1878. In 1908 he became the first African-American to win the World Heavyweight crown when he knocked out the reigning champ, Tommy Burns. The fast-living Johnson held on to the title until 1915. He died in a car accident in Raleigh, North Carolina, in 1946. Nicknamed the Galveston Giant, he was one of the most dominant champions of his time, and remains a big figure in heavyweight boxing history. His 1910 fight against James J. Jeffries was dubbed the "fight of the century" and triggered race riots across the US.

LARRY HOLMES

Fights 75; Wins 69 (44 KO); Losses 6.
First fight March 21, 1973 – final fight July 27, 2002.

Larry Holmes was born on November 3, 1949, in Cuthbert, Georgia. In the mid-1970s he was a sparring partner for both heavyweight champions, Muhammad Ali and Joe Frazier. From 1973 to 1978 Holmes won 28 consecutive bouts. In 1978 he won the World Boxing Council Heavyweight Championship. Nicknamed the "Easton Assassin" because he grew up in Easton, Pennsylvania, his left jab is rated among the best in boxing history. Five fighters beat Ali – but he is the only one to have stopped him on October 2, 1980, in a fight that was dubbed The Last Hurrah.

FLOYD MAYWEATHER JR.
Fights 50; Wins 50 (27 KO).
First fight October 11, 1996 – last fight August 26, 2017.
American boxer Floyd "Money" Mayweather Jr has won champion-
ships across five weight divisions. Born on February 24, 1977, in Grand
Rapids, Michigan, he won three national Golden Gloves and an
Olympic bronze medal before turning professional in 1996. Mayweather
claimed his first championship as a super featherweight in 1998, later
accumulating titles in four other weight classes while retaining an
undefeated record. In 2016 he was ranked as the greatest boxer, pound
for pound, in the last 25 years. All the talk in 2017 has been about
Mayweather vs McGregor. And Floyd showed, in the end, how he is a
true champion by easily winning that fight to bring the curtain down on
a remarkable career. His total earnings are estimated at $700 million.

Fights 47; Wins 39 (28 KO); Losses 6; Draws 2.
First fight December 1, 1979 – last fight June 24, 2008.
Azumah Nelson, born 19 September, 1958, is a Ghanaian former
professional boxer. Known as "the Professor" he is widely considered the
greatest African boxer of all time. He held the WBC Featherweight title
once and the WBC Super Featherweight title twice. He was known for
his powerful jabs and earned his nickname for the lessons he'd teach
opponents in the ring. He is now a national hero in his home country
and in 2004 became the first African to be inducted into the
International Boxing Hall of Fame.

AFTERWORD

By some of Frank's friends and colleagues

RICKY HATTON, FORMER LIGHT WELTERWEIGHT AND
WELTERWEIGHT WORLD CHAMPION

THIS has been hard for me to write. Very hard.

To see what Big Frank has gone through in the five years since 2012 just breaks my heart. If someone had put me in a hospital and locked the door I would have probably tried to smash it down. Then I would have legged it.

But Frank has battled his illness like a champion. He didn't run away. He stood and he fought it. And in the end he won.

That was not a surprise to me, after all it is the only way he knows. He is a warrior.

I was proud that only a few weeks after Frank came out of hospital in 2015 he decided to pop into my gym in Manchester.

The night before Frank turned up I was like a kid at Christmas. I could hardly sleep, I was so excited about the thought of spending some time with him in the ring.

Growing up he was my hero. Big Frank and Nigel Benn: they were gods to me and I idolised the pair of them.

When he arrived at the gym, I worried about how Frank would be. But he looked as good as he did during those fights in the 1990s which I used to sit and watch with my dad. It was great to be able to introduce him to my son Campbell.

"This is a proper man," I said to my boy. "Watch and learn."

We got in the ring and I put the pads on.

To feel the power Frank still has in his punches was incredible. No wonder he talked about a comeback.

We took a picture and put it on Twitter. Christ, it nearly broke the bloody Internet. It was nice to see people still cared.

"Maybe we could both come back," I joked to him that day.

But, seriously, Frank knows those days are over. It is not easy to say that. It wasn't easy for me – saying goodbye to it all. When it all stops and the fans go home you are alone.

Frank found that tough to cope with and, God, I found it tough, too. When you are fighting, when you are standing in that ring with thousands of people screaming at you to knock your opponent out, you can take on the world.

But this problem called depression, you don't want to take on.

For boxers it is particularly hard. We are tough men, after all. We have been in battles. Often, we have come up from the street.

Then, all of a sudden, there's a voice in your head telling you that you don't even want to be in the world, let alone take it on. That's how bad things got for me.

Respect to Frank – he says ending his life has never ever crossed his mind. I wish I could say the same.

My depression started after I lost to Floyd Mayweather. It was terrible. I had suffered from depression for quite some time and a lot of things were going wrong. I got beat by Mayweather and I was down. Then I fought Lazcano at the City of Manchester stadium and I was back up. I fell out with my trainer, Billy Graham, who was my best mate, so then I was down. Then I beat Paulie Malignaggi, which was probably one of my best wins, and I was up. But then I fell out with my parents and I was down again. My mind was going up and down so much I didn't know whether I was coming or going half the time.

And, for a short while, I didn't care whether I lived or died. I thought about killing myself several times. I used to go down the pub, come back, take a knife out and sit there in the dark crying my eyes out.

The pub, that was the problem for me. Drink was my demon. Then drugs. There were times I thought: "Sod this, I will just drink myself to death."

I felt like I had let everyone down.

Compared to me, Frank has lived his life like an angel since retiring. My lifestyle hasn't helped. I've always ballooned in weight: hence the "Ricky Fatton" nickname the papers gave me.

I've always liked to drink but you can't drink when you've got depression. You feel all right for about an hour and then the more you do it, you just get worse.

The more you drink, the more depressed you get, the more you start worrying and you start looking towards other options such as drugs. I didn't care what I was doing.

My family and my friends had to see me go through it and they were helpless seeing me crumble. But that is in the past.

When Millie, my second child was born, I held her in my arms and said to myself: "Come on, Ricky, get yourself together now."

That was a turning point. A moment I needed to make me see I had to get a grip and change. To fight. I have not looked back since.

I feel I am in control now. But yeah, depression is always waiting around the corner. I am always on my guard, like Frank.

I am so happy to see the way he has recovered and put his life back together, but he is spot on when he says we need to do more to help boxers.

I train a lot of young fighters and sadly many of them won't make it. They might go on to have jobs, they might go and stack shelves down Tesco, work on a building site or they may even have to sign on the dole.

The lucky ones, the ones that make it, will have the money, the cars, the flash house, the girl on the arm, but boxing does not last for long and when it stops we have to make sure the support is there to help fighters who can't cope.

I think Frank's new foundation sounds like a great idea. Anything we can do to help must be a good thing.

I saw him a few weeks ago when he was back at my gym and we talked a lot about the foundation he is launching. We spoke a bit about how we were both doing. And we chatted about how hard it had been for Frank when he lost George all those years ago.

It is so important not to be afraid to talk about how you feel. If two fellas like Frank and I can talk about their feelings, then anyone can!

I don't care now when people ask me about my depression. You have got to be open and honest and, like Frank says, you should not feel ashamed about asking for a bit of help.

He knows I will always be here for him. But I know Frank can and will beat this on his own.

TIM WITHERSPOON, WHO DEFEATED FRANK IN 1986 TO RETAIN THE WORLD TITLE

More than 40,000 people were screaming for me to show my face. All they wanted to see was their man knock me out.

As I sat in my dressing room at Wembley Arena I closed my eyes to try to block out the noise. Then came the knock on the door and the nod from my corner that it was time to go. Outside, 20 bodyguards were waiting.

If you believed what people were saying ahead of the fight and writing in the British newspapers, you'd be forgiven for thinking I was walking to an execution. On my way to the gallows, 10 men either side of me.

Me, dubbed by the British press an "overweight American", who was apparently no match for this new great hope of British boxing, Frank Bruno.

What people didn't realise was that I had been working like a warrior for the fight at the training camp I'd set up in Basildon, Essex. I'd been chopping a lot of wood and I'd been running like I'd never run before.

And everywhere I went I was picking up the sense that Frank's countrymen didn't believe in him. The day before the fight 40 Jamaican guys came down from Brixton and said that they wanted me to kick his arse.

They were ranting and coming out with all this rubbish that Frank wasn't doing enough for black people.

I was like: "Woah, what's going on here? Why don't his people believe in him?'"

But I had no doubt in my ability. I believed.

And, as I got to my feet in that dressing room and said a prayer I knew there was no place in the world I would rather be.

I felt good. I'd always wanted to come and defend my title in someone's back yard and be victorious. I didn't want to go home for people to tell me I'd punked out. That gave me the energy I needed. I knew it was my time.

The fight was a dream.

Frank hit hard. He popped my hip in the fight, that hurt like hell but I had to keep moving forward. He blew himself out in the early rounds and although his punches were landing I knew I could take them.

And I knew that if I was patient I could stop him. I knew he was vulnerable to my power. My moment came towards the end of the 11th round when I caught him with an overhand right.

I knew it was over. When it landed his eyes told me that. Three shots later and Frank's corner threw in the towel.

I'd proved them all wrong. I'd come to London and broken Frank's heart. The British public would have to wait a little bit longer for a world champion.

I was taking the belt home and it felt amazing – better than I had imagined it would. It was my finest moment.

Twelve hours later, when I woke up in my hotel room, I was still reliving those closing seconds of the fight when the phone rang.

"Tim, it's Frank," said this booming voice at the end of the line. "I look like ET this morning, boss. You deserved it, man. You are a great champion."

I was stunned. It was the only time a boxer I had defeated phoned me after a fight to congratulate me. My eyes watered.

I realised at that moment there was something very special about Frank Bruno. That's why, when he eventually won the world title 11 years after our fight, I was so delighted for him. He deserved to achieve his dreams.

But don't let anyone kid you that Frank earned his success because he is a nice guy or because he is a gentleman.

Frank was a brilliant fighter and in my opinion he was seriously under-rated.

I have read all about the problems Frank has suffered since retiring from boxing, and I feel really sad for him. Retiring from the sport doesn't come easy to some.

All the wars we are involved in leave you with battle scars – not just on your body but inside your head too. That's why it is so important to have really good people around you to make sure you stay healthy.

I was one of the lucky ones. When I stopped fighting, I found things pretty easy. I got involved in training, I was able to work with my son Tim Jr and I do a lot of events like Frank does where I get to meet so many incredible people. I have been fortunate enough to be able to pass some of the things I learned on to young kids.

Maybe Frank didn't have the right people around him for a while. He got divorced, his life went down a dark path and he got sick.

I have seen Frank many times over the past few years and there were occasions I could see he was struggling and he didn't seem himself. You could tell he was in a battle.

But last July when I was with Frank at a dinner in Wolverhampton to mark the 30th anniversary of our fight at Wembley he was truly back to his best.

It was brilliant to spend some time with him. He was well, looking good, calm and in control. It was brilliant to see how he has managed to rebuild things.

That kindness he had showed when he phoned my room all those years before was still there. After meeting my daughter Shania, he handed me some money to put in her bank account.

We were both really touched. When I think about it, Frank's illness mirrors what happened that night we fought in 1986.

He got beat. He faced up to his challenge like a man. And he came through and battled back. Then, in the end, he ended up victorious. He's a true champion.

PIERS MORGAN, TV PRESENTER

Fame can be a lethal drug. And when you achieve the level of fame Frank has experienced it can be intoxicating and difficult to manage.

Frank and I go way back. I first interviewed him as a 19-year-old local newspaper reporter in South London. His mum put up a picture of us together on her fridge and my mum put one on hers, too.

So I have always had a soft spot for Big Frank. I was a huge fan of his: first as a boxer and then as the character he was outside the ring.

I was very sad to see the problems he developed after he retired from boxing. That was one of the main reasons I was so keen to get him into the hot seat on Life Stories.

What interested me most about Frank's journey was how he, like a lot of sportsmen, struggled to cope when fame started to recede. In Frank's case he was on his own a lot, he wasn't with his family so much and he was working out intensely at the gym.

It was a pretty lonely existence and it was really tough.

Frank, and stars like Gazza and George Best, are put on such a pedestal by the British public. They are so adored, so loved. They are such huge news. But then, all of a sudden, it just stops.

These guys, our national heroes, who sometimes performed in front of 80,000 people and were idolised, suddenly find themselves on their own. And it's damn hard.

In the build-up to my interview with Frank I did my homework and was asking around to see how he was doing.

So when we sat down for Life Stories, I suspected Frank would be one of two things. I would either be interviewing someone who didn't really want to be doing it or, as it turned out, with someone who was ready to open up about his remarkable life.

When Frank walked in that day he seemed to react so positively to the atmosphere of the room. The audience included people who were too young to even remember him as a boxer.

But as the interview got going, Frank, who had been nervous at the start, really started to relax. He began to enjoy himself and I could see I was sitting across from a guy who had learned a lot of self-awareness about his problems.

I didn't think to myself: "OK, as soon as Frank walks out of here it is all going to be fine." Far from it. But Frank enjoyed the show and it reminded him just how popular and beloved he was. That's why I was so sad and shocked a few weeks later to be told Frank had gone back into hospital. My first thought was it might have been something to do with the interview, but, as Frank has made clear in his own words in this book, it wasn't that.

I think it comes down to the fact he was simply having a downward turn. And he is going to continue having them from time to time. There is a depressive streak to him and an addictive streak to him.

Celebrities can be very good at hiding these things. I've seen it a lot. I am good friends with Freddie Flintoff and I thought I knew him really well. But I didn't know about the depression he was suffering. Whenever I saw Freddie, there was always the big laugh, the big personality, the super-confident guy who could hold the room.

Yet behind closed doors, Freddie was bordering on a manic depressive.

Think about those three names I've mentioned. Gazza, Frank, Freddie. Three of our biggest sporting heroes – and all of them have suffered from quite similar problems.

That's why I think that fame is often the most dangerous drug of all. When that level of fame is taken away and these stars are not able to perform in the arena that made them so widely loved they find it very, very tough.

Maybe that's why training is so important to Frank. It gives him a focus. But he doesn't have that fight at the end of the training to release everything and that must be difficult.

Fame and success can be exhilarating, but the time in your life when you experience it can be crucial.

I talked to Simon Cowell about how he is able to handle it so well. And in his case, it's because he wasn't on TV until he was in his 40s. If you are propelled into TV fame in your 40s it is far easier to handle than when you are a 19-year-old football wonderkid.

When I was first doing America's Got Talent in front of 25 million viewers it brought such a huge adrenaline rush. Afterwards, if you are not careful, you can have a big crash.

And I don't care who you are – that sort of fame can be dangerous.

I have experienced enough of it to know how difficult it is to manage at times.

When I was a judge on Britain's Got Talent in 2010, when Susan Boyle was on the show, my fame was at its peak. I remember being chased by hundreds of schoolkids across playing fields when I went to watch my sons play football or cricket. It was very uncomfortable to be literally mobbed in the street. I was relieved when it eventually calmed down. I didn't want to spend my time being chased around by people. Not least because I was 45 years old and I was just trying to enjoy watching my kids playing football! But if I had been 20 or 21, I would probably have loved it.

It is great to see Frank doing so well now. I believe he is going about things the right way. I think in Frank's case medication was a short-term way of dealing with a bigger problem.

And his biggest problem is dealing with what his life is after boxing and after being a sporting hero.

Frank needs to remember he has an amazing personality. He's the kind of guy who would be hugely loved and popular if he'd never put on a pair of boxing gloves.

I saw him recently at Arsenal FC and I was struck again by what a brilliant guy he is.

That belly laugh was there, he was quite thoughtful, insightful and back to his best.

If Frank is well and in a good place then there are a lot of things that can bring him fulfilment. It might be TV work, charity work or just living a happy, peaceful life.

I urge Frank to play to his strengths now, which isn't hitting people with his fists, but being Frank Bruno – the great personality.

My advice is: just be Frank. If he does, then this national treasure will be fine.

ALASTAIR CAMPBELL, FORMER SPOKESMAN FOR
TONY BLAIR AND MENTAL HEALTH CAMPAIGNER
When you look at Frank, he is incredibly fit, incredibly strong and has so much incredible success behind him.

So the less informed might look at him and think: "God, just what the hell has he got to be depressed about?"

But Frank has shown mental ill health can and does affect anybody. In many ways, his story has already helped spark so much discussion.

We all remember the terrible "Bonkers Bruno" headline in The Sun when Frank was first sectioned in 2003.

The Sun quickly realised it was a bad, ignorant decision and they changed it to "Sad Bruno in Mental Health Home" for later editions.

There is never one thing alone that sparks change, but that second headline was the moment when everyone realised, actually, there already was change.

The reaction was clear, it was instant and it was obvious for the newspaper to understand why their words were wrong. I think it was a really significant moment in terms of the way we now talk and write about mental health.

It has been a privilege to work with Frank over the years to help raise awareness. We both starred in Me… & My Mental Illness on Channel 5 in 2016 and we have worked on the Time To Change campaign together, too.

Frank and I have very different views on medication. It is hard because no person can know another's condition intimately.

As I write this, I am currently taking medication for my condition. I have been on the same one for the past two years and I have not had a really bad episode when I have been on it.

Like Frank, I was personally very resistant to medication at first but I have swung round quite a bit because it does seem to have helped me a lot. But there was a lot of trial and error along the way and if you have a bad experience it can be difficult.

I have huge sympathy for what Frank says about his experiences with hospitalisation. The authorities have a really difficult job with balancing the needs of an individual and ensuring a person is kept safe. It is never an easy decision to make. But of course it is vital when someone is sectioned that the care is correct and that the help is there.

Seeing Frank being so open in the way he talks about his illness will hopefully encourage other men to now do the same. That's so important. We still have a big problem with men talking about their feelings. Women are much more open.

It is not that long ago that people were really shocked to see a man cry. Slowly, that is changing but there are still too many men who feel it is a sign of terrible weakness to admit they need help, when in fact, it is the opposite. Being open is the first step towards recovery.

For me, the most important part of that journey to recovery is having love, friendship and family.

Like Frank, exercise is important to me too, as is staying busy. I feel that if I don't have something to focus on then I am at risk of falling down again.

Being open helps me a lot. Being able to say "I don't feel very well" and talking about it and campaigning helps enormously.

I have a very simple aim with the campaigning I am involved in – to get to a position where people feel they can be as open about their mental health as they are about their physical health.

I know from personal experience how that openness can help the patient, but more importantly it can help us as a society.

Frank's fight is another great way of showing people how you can come through mental ill health and bring genuine hope to others.

NORMAN LAMB MP, GOVERNMENT MINISTER FOR CARE AT THE TIME FRANK WAS SECTIONED IN 2012

OK, I will admit it. I was starstruck at the prospect of Frank Bruno, former world heavyweight champion, no less, coming to see me in the Department of Health.

I knew that it would impress our sons, one of whom, Archie, is a boxing fanatic. And my Private Office, the civil servants who support the minister, were exactly the same. There was competition over which one of them would take notes at our meeting!

Frank had asked to come to see me to discuss his experience of mental ill health and of the way he was treated.

Our meeting has stuck with me ever since. Frank spoke powerfully of what happened when he was sectioned. He talked of the acute embarrassment of seeing several marked police cars turning up outside his house and how he feared that neighbours would assume that some dreadful crime had been committed.

After all, Frank was ill, not a criminal. I confess that, probably like most people, I hadn't fully considered the effect of a police presence.

But what he was saying made sense. It all reinforces the stigma that those with mental ill health suffer.

So when we published the Crisis Care Concordat – the first ever attempt to define standards of crisis care in mental health – we specifically included a clear statement that marked police cars should not be used to transport people experiencing mental ill health to hospital.

We also spoke about the way Frank was treated in institutions in the weeks that followed his sectioning. Too often disrespectful. Too often treated as a second-class citizen.

It is important to acknowledge that there is great care and treatment in many places.

But there are too many exceptions to that. People waiting far too long for treatment, sometimes poor attitudes from staff, excessive use of medication, people regularly controlled by the use of physical restraint and so on.

I have enormous admiration for Frank. We have come a long way in terms of public and media attitudes to mental ill health in the last decade. A long way since that appalling headline in The Sun, "Bonkers Bruno". That progress has been driven by brave individuals speaking out about their own mental health problems.

And Frank has led the way. Every time someone with the stature of Frank Bruno speaks out, it makes it easier for the next person to do so. A sporting icon like Frank cuts through and reaches people that others could never reach.

This has led to a growing cascade of people in the public eye talking openly about their own mental ill health. I know, from our own family experience, that pioneers like Frank confronting the conspiracy of silence that surrounded mental ill health, makes it easier for a teenager, perhaps struggling with anxiety or depression, to seek help.

He helped inspire our son, Archie, to talk publicly about his experience of obsessive compulsive disorder.

So thank you, Frank. You have made a difference to people's lives.

After that first meeting we had several more encounters during my time as Minister. Always, Frank demonstrated a willingness to give up his time, without charge, to promote mental health and wellbeing. I remember our joint visit to a mental health unit in Greenwich, South London. Staff and people using services there were bowled over. They weren't that interested in a Government Minister turning up – but they loved Frank and his easy charm and impeccable politeness.

On a personal level, we seemed to build up a strong rapport. I was immensely grateful when he readily agreed to contribute to a video promoting the work I was doing as Minister advocating for those with mental ill health. And what better person could I get to support my bid for the leadership of the Liberal Democrats than Frank Bruno? I'm sorry I let him down by falling short on that venture!

Frank and others have done a lot to change the way in which society deals with mental ill health. There aren't too many people who make an impact on their fellow human beings in two areas of public life. But Frank has managed it.

An iconic sportsman and a pioneer in changing attitudes and culture in respect of mental health...

Respect!

FOOTNOTES

This documentation of Frank Bruno's life with bi-polar disorder is his own personal journey and his own unique experience. Neither the authors nor the publisher are recommending that this experience is used to alter, modify or remove anyone's agreed treatment for this or any other disorder.

Everyone's experience is individual to them.

If you do need any help or advice on any of the issues raised in this book, please contact:

The Frank Bruno Foundation
thefrankbrunofoundation.co.uk
0800 368 8196

Time To Change
time-to-change.org.uk

CALM
Thecalmzone.net
0800 58 58 58

Big White Wall
Bigwhitewall.com

Bipolar UK
Bipolaruk.org
0333 323 3880

MIND
Mind.org.uk

Samaritans
Samaritans.org
Call: 116 123

THE FRANK BRUNO FOUNDATION

The Frank Bruno Foundation is a direct result of Frank wanting to give something back to the community. Frank has faced challenges both in and out of the ring and has always done so with determination, dignity, humour and humility.

The Foundation is set up to work towards relieving the needs of those diagnosed with mental health conditions.

Frank is a Trustee and is actively involved with the running of the Foundation alongside the other Board Members.

The Foundation hopes to help people through the provision of structured non-contact boxing sessions and wellbeing programmes designed to assist with the development of self-confidence, feelings of self-worth and self-respect.

Those involved with the Foundation will be given access to both specialist and non-specialist facilities and have the potential for access to grants. The Foundation is still in its infancy so funding is urgently required to be able to provide these services.

Getting involved in helping to raise funds is easy.

Visit the website **www.thefrankbrunofoundation.co.uk** for more information on the work of the Foundation, how you can get involved with the Foundation and how you can be part of helping to raise funds.

 #knockoutstigma

The Frank Bruno Foundation is a Registered Charity in England and Wales, Number 1171012

Also by Mirror Books

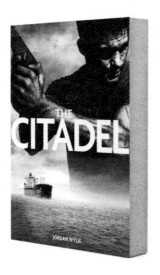

The Citadel
Jordan Wylie with Alan Clark

An inspirational true story of danger, adventure and triumph over adversity.

Jordan Wylie, a young man from a tough area of Blackpool where kids like him often go off the rails, opted for life in the army. He saw service in Iraq and learned to cope with the horrors he'd witnessed, then suffered an injury that blocked any chance of climbing up the military ladder.

But an old army colleague suggested he join a security team on a tanker in Yemen. Ex-servicemen were offered dazzling salaries and 'James Bond' lifestyles between jobs protecting super-tankers. However, the price they paid was a life of claustrophobia and isolation along with the ever-present possibility of death skimming towards them across the vast, lonely blue sea. In Citadel, Jordan writes the first account of these dangerous years from someone 'at the front'. A young soldier from the backstreets of Blackpool, determined to make the most of his life, but unsure of the way forward. He found his answers in the perilous waters of 'Pirate Alley'.

Mirror Books

Also by Mirror Books

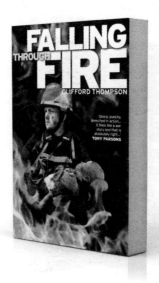

Falling Through Fire
Clifford Thompson

The true story of a London firefighter, now journalist, and his involvement in domestic and high-profile disasters across 25 years.

One incident, early in his career, had a profound effect on him that he carries to this day.

In a frank and honest way he recounts his personal experience of the 1988 Clapham train crash, the 1993 bombing of New York's World Trade Centre and the aftermath of the King's Cross fire.

Clifford describes the trauma that firefighters deal with on a daily basis – and reveals that despite facing many horrific situations and experiencing major disasters, he cannot escape the haunting memory of a three-year-old boy dying in his arms after a house fire just days before Christmas.

Also by Mirror Books

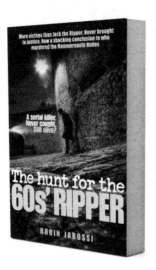

More victims than Jack the Ripper. Never brought to justice. Now a shocking conclusion to who murdered the Hammersmith Nudes

A serial killer. Never caught. Still alive?

The hunt for the 60s' RIPPER

ROBIN JAROSSI

The Hunt for the 60s' Ripper
Robin Jarossi

While 60s London was being hailed as the world's most fashionably vibrant capital, a darker, more terrifying reality was unfolding on the streets. During the early hours a serial killer was stalking prostitutes then dumping their naked bodies. When London was famed for its music, groundbreaking movies and Carnaby Street vibe, the reality included a huge street prostitution scene, a violent world that filled the magistrate's courts.

Seven, possibly eight, women fell victim – making this killer more prolific than Jack the Ripper, 77 years previously. His grim spree sparked the biggest police manhunt in history. But why did such a massive hunt fail? And why has such a traumatic case been largely forgotten today?

With shocking conclusions, one detective makes an astonishing new claim. Including secret police papers, crime reconstructions, links to figures from the vicious world of the Kray twins and the Profumo Affair, this case exposes the depraved underbelly of British society in the Swinging Sixties. An evocative and thought-provoking reinvestigation into perhaps the most shocking unsolved mass murder in modern British history.

Mirror Books